BURN
AFTER
READING

THE ESPIONAGE HISTORY
OF WORLD WAR II

By

Ladislas Farago

BLUEJACKET BOOKS

Naval Institute Press
Annapolis, Maryland

Naval Institute Press
291 Wood Road
Annapolis, MD 21402

First Bluejacket Books printing, 2003

Library of Congress Cataloging-in-Publication Data
Farago, Ladislas.
  Burn after reading : the espionage history of World War II / by Ladislas Farago.
    p. cm. — (Bluejacket books)
  Originally published: New York: Walker, 1961.
  Includes bibliographical references and index.
  ISBN 1-59114-262-8 (alk. paper)
  1. World War, 1939–1945—Secret service. 2. World War, 1939–1945—Military intelligence. 3. Spies—History—20th century. I. Title. II. Series.
D810.S7F3 2003
940.54'85—dc21
                          2003048837

Printed in the United States of America on acid-free paper ∞
10 09 08 07 06 05 04 03   9 8 7 6 5 4 3 2 1

TO

JOHN MICHAEL ARTHUR FARAGO

". . . your name burning past you like a pure lamp."

G. A. Borgese, from
Dream of a Decent Death

Contents

Preface

Espionage has played a conspicuous and often memorable part in every war of history, but it was not until the Second World War that it became a kind of Fourth Estate of war. The nature and scope of this bitter conflict produced special armies that fought clandestinely behind the lines and on their own fronts. The true magnitude of this furtive contest can be seen, for example, from the casualties of Greece. Of the seventy-three thousand Greeks killed in World War II, twenty-three thousand died in conventional warfare—fifty thousand were killed in various surreptitious enterprises. In Norway, where the blunt phase of the war lasted only a few days, the underground war continued for five years, waged by an army of forty-seven thousand stealthy combatants. The Yugoslavs, fighting their hugger-mugger war in the black mountains, suffered greater losses than any of the Allies—one million, seven hundred six thousand men and women killed in hit-and-run actions.

I trust it is clear that I am using the word "espionage" in a generic sense. While this book is the history of espionage during World War II, it also covers the whole curriculum of clandestine operations, the several forms of intelligence, espionage and sabotage, subversion and counter-espionage, the whole secret contest conducted apart from the formal and conventional operations of modern war.

Espionage was practiced by both sides, but only on the Allied side was it such a vast enterprise. This is understandable; in the occupied countries of Europe and Asia it was the only opportunity for the oppressed to defy and harm the oppressor. It was this spontaneous rebellion born in the soul of men and borne by their indomitable will to freedom that endowed the dubious business with an aura of decency and that justified its larcenies and homicides.

It was but a side show of the greater war, yet it was a war itself in all but name. The defunct Duce may not be a proper character witness on any other score, but on the essence of war he was an eloquent authority, refreshingly free of hypocrisy. Mussolini once said that war alone brings human energy up to its highest tension and puts the stamp of nobility upon the peoples who have the courage to confront it. Nowhere was the war more noble and courageous than in the resistance of millions to tyranny.

It was largely this redeeming feature of the secret phase of World War II that induced me to write this book. A student of history can play no favorites. To the historian of espionage, a German spy performing his sordid functions for his country and cause is as proper an individual for study as an American agent spying for his country and cause. Yet in World War II there was a difference, and even the most pedantically objective historian is bound to recognize the distinction. I was inspired in this by General Sir Colin McVean Gubbins, chief of Britain's Special Operations Executive, who wrote: "What resistance entailed through the long years of dreadful night in the occupied territories was a day-to-day battle with the Gestapo, the Quislings and the Japanese secret police, one long continuous struggle, with torture and unbelievable suffering and death waiting round every corner at every moment. Yet there were countless thousands who undertook the task, to whom all that mattered was their own eternal spiritual indestructibility. They dedicated themselves to a cause they knew to be higher than self."

Even so I have certain reservations. One who was as closely preoccupied as I was for years with such a romantic and emotionally supercharged activity inevitably develops a point of view, and I confess I did develop a certain bias. For one thing, I came to regard some of the business with a mild contempt, in the spirit of Virgil who warned that vice is nourished by secrecy. Much of the business is rather childish, a relapse of grown men into boyish antics, a nebulous pastime to which no adult who cherishes his full dignity and integrity should devote uncritical attention. For another thing, I could not wholly sanction the inherent deceit of the game. What usually began as temporary skulduggery frequently led to corruption that the *ad hoc* practitioners of the game carried like an ugly scar for the rest of their lives.

This is evident today in the Cold War when espionage is rampant and is, indeed, its major implement. The dismal way in which the Cold War is fought, even by great nations of traditional decency, is the direct outgrowth of this wartime experience; it is the acceptance of something designed as a temporary expedient as an enduring instrument of national power.

I did not try to eradicate completely this bias from the pages of this book. I refused to take the business of espionage too solemnly, as some writers do; they place too much emphasis on the heroics of the game and too little on its theatrics. I trust the reader will bear with me if I became not carried too far by the sheer melodrama of the subject and did not solemnize the exploits of all spies, but rather tried to view them with a sense of proportion.

In view of the huge scope of this clandestine struggle, any narrative trying to describe it must be incomplete and inadequate. I am sure this narrative is no exception. In order to give a rounded picture, I had to deal with both the topic and the events selectively. I regret that limitations of space prevented me from dealing fully with all the resistance movements and especially the guerrilla war in the Philippines. I deliberately omitted incidents already very well known, such as the mute adventure of "the man who never was" and the case of Tyler Kent. Several well publicized adventures, like the penetration of Scapa Flow by a U-boat allegedly guided to its target by a

spy, were omitted because they never really happened. I am
sure that students of the subject will find many more omissions
and also, inevitably, errors. While I apologize for any errors
that may occur, I can only point to the obvious difficulty of
getting everything straight in a business that is so crooked.

This is the proper place to express my gratitude to my
friend and colleague, Jay Nelson Tuck, for his invaluable and
heroic help in editing what was a formless mass of manuscript
into an organized and cohesive book. If ever an acknowledgment of this kind was deserved, this is it. His work on my manuscript went well beyond the usual editorial task. If there is some
merit to this book and cohesion in its presentation, it is to a
large extent his astonishing achievement.

While this book deliberately refrains from drawing any
conclusions, its facts—projected against the giant screen of current history—may still supply certain pragmatic lessons. The
emphasis is on the facts. They are, as Churchill put it, so much
better than dreams.

LADISLAS FARAGO

New York, 1961

BURN AFTER READING

1

"Operation Canned Meat"

On the sultry night of August 10, 1939, hardly a passerby disturbed the nocturnal calm of Berlin's venerable Kaiser Wilhelm Strasse until, shortly before midnight, rapid, heavy-booted steps sent echoes rattling down the famous street. The guard in front of the Air Ministry's big gray edifice saw a tall man pass him by in great hurry, breathing heavily as he went. Since the stranger was wearing the uniform of an SS officer, the young airman saluted him with outstretched carbine and remained stiffly at attention until the man turned into Prinz Albrecht Strasse where the Gestapo—Reinhard Heydrich's secret police— had general headquarters.

In the lobby the man was greeted with a rush of jumping feet, clicking heels and *Heil Hitlers*. Swinging his right arm loosely in a relaxed version of the Nazi salute, he acknowledged the greetings and climbed the steps, going straight to the big office at the head of the staircase where Heydrich ruled supreme.

This late disturber of the Wilhelm Strasse's deceptive quiet was a Gestapo goon, Alfred Helmuth Naujocks by name. A brainless tool in the hands of a master craftsman, this apoplectic bully resembled Somerset Maugham's "hairless Mexican" even to the point of scenting himself. He was a tall, heavy-set, big-boned, smooth-skinned man with a coarse, florid scarface, blonde hair and big pink freckles on his enormous hands. Naujocks was a star in Heydrich's fraternity of assassins, whose mere shadow struck terror in the soul of Germany. He belonged to a new caste of secret agents whose activities behind the scenes infused the ancient war of espionage with the spirit of gangsterism.

It was ten minutes past midnight when Naujocks entered Heydrich's big, plainly furnished office. Heydrich beckoned him to a chair, got up, circled his subordinate and handed him the mission of his life.

"I need not remind you," he began, "that what I'm about to tell you is a top secret matter of state and must, therefore, be handled with the utmost discretion." Naujocks nodded and Heydrich continued: "The Fuehrer has decided to settle the Danzig question once and for all and smash Poland. Both X-day and Y-hour are set. All is prepared—*except a pretext for war.*

"What the Fuehrer needs, we will supply, you and I, my dear Naujocks! We are going to create the cause for this war!

"We will begin the Polish campaign without a formal declaration of war, with a counterattack, telling the world that it was the Poles who fired the first shot. But telling it isn't enough. Practical proof is needed, hard clues Goebbels can *show* to the foreign press."

Heydrich paused melodramatically before coming to the point: "We will simulate a series of frontier incidents and make it appear that the attacking forces were Poles."

He walked to a map on the wall and pointed to marked spots in Eastern Germany. "The incidents are to take place in this general area," he said, "around Gleiwitz in Upper Silesia, and here at Pitschen, near Kreuzburg, at Hochlinden near Ratibor, and in Gleiwitz itself. We'll put a couple of hundred of our men into Polish uniforms and let them shoot up places, burn farmhouses and run amuck for a few hours."

His bony index finger came to rest on a particular spot on the map. "Here at Gleiwitz," he said, "we have a radio station. It will be your job to stage an incident there. Party Comrade Mueller is in personal charge of these operations. He has all the necessary details. You'll find him either at Gleiwitz or in Oppeln. Report to him when you get there. Good luck!"

Naujocks opened his mouth for the first time. "Thank you, *Herr Obergruppenfuehrer,*" he said, "for your confidence. Heil

Hitler!" He stood up, clicked his heels and backed out of the room.

"Mueller" was Heinrich Mueller, chief of the Gestapo under Heydrich. Naujocks found him in Oppeln, stage-managing the impending operations. When Naujocks arrived, Mueller called a conference of his seconds-in-command, and gave each man his instructions. A thug named Mehlhorn was to direct the Pitschen branch of this bloody masquerade party with a hundred Nazis clad in the uniform of Polish regulars. Another, Langhans by name, was to storm the customs house at Hochlinden. To Naujocks, Mueller explained the attack on the Gleiwitz radio station.

"You will pick six trustworthy SD men and dress them in Polish uniforms. At zero hour, you'll attack the radio station and seize it. You need not hold it long, five or ten minutes at the most, just long enough to enable a man who'll accompany you to broadcast an anti-German speech in Polish."

He went on: "I have here in Oppeln, in the Gestapo jail, a dozen inmates of concentration camps. We'll use them to make these incidents look goddam real. We'll put them in Polish uniforms and leave them dead on the ground as if they had been killed during the attack. They'll be given lethal injections and we'll also provide them with gunshot wounds. After the incidents, we'll show them to members of the foreign press Goebbels is going to bring from Berlin."

Mueller told Naujocks he would let him have one of these dead "Poles," complete with the lethal injection and gunshot wounds.

"By the way," he said, "we refer to these fake Pollacks by the code name of 'Canned Meat.' " They laughed. "Operation Canned Meat" was off to a promising start.

On August 25, Naujocks rehearsed the attack with his men, but without the dead Pole. Then he sat tight. At eleven a.m. on August 31, Naujocks was summoned to the phone. It was Heydrich, calling him from Berlin.

"Naujocks," he said, "the die is cast. *It* will start at five tomorrow morning. Your operation is to take place at 20 o'clock—tonight. You better call Mueller right away and ask him to send you one of his 'canned meats.' "

At 11:10 a.m. Naujocks phoned Mueller in Oppeln and asked for the fake Pole. At 7:00 p.m. he sent his men to their posts near the radio station and at 7:30, a car arrived with the "Pole." He had had his injection and the gunshot wounds, and his face was smeared with blood, but the man was still breathing. At 7:50, Naujocks had the human prop carried to the main entrance of the station and arranged him on the ground.

It was now 8:00 p.m. Naujocks looked at his wrist watch and almost casually gave the order to attack. A moment later, his six "Poles" seized the station and the phony "Polish" agitator stepped up to the live microphone. He shouted that the time had come for war between Germany and Poland and called on all patriotic Poles to kill Germans. The delivery was punctuated by a few staccato shots before the open mike, as Naujocks' men fired into the air and into the "canned meat" on the ground, providing random sound effects.

At 8:07 p.m. the show was over. Naujocks and his "Poles" climbed into their cars and disappeared. They had given Hitler his excuse for war. Left behind on the ground was a man, now indubitably dead. He was the first casualty of the Second World War—truly its Unknown Soldier.

At 5:00 a.m. on September 1, 1939, the Wehrmacht crossed into Poland, all along the frontier, commencing a three-pronged drive. In that same split second, bombers of the *Luftwaffe* appeared over Gdynia, Cracow and Katowice.

At 5:11 a.m., Hitler issued a proclamation to the *Wehrmacht*, justifying the attack. "The series of border violations," he said, "which are unbearable to a great power, prove that the Poles no longer are willing to respect the German frontier. In order to put an end to this frantic activity, no other means is left to me now than to meet force with force."

At 8:00 a.m., exactly twelve hours after the incident at Gleiwitz, the *Wehrmacht* was already deep inside Poland. The

"Pole" on the steps of the radio station was no longer alone in death. At 9:10 a.m., an army ambulance drove into Gleiwitz, returning the first three German casualties. Two were wounded. The third man was dead on arrival.

The world was at war again.

For Poland, the war was to last just twenty-seven days. Never before had a major military power been subdued so rapidly and with such finality. How was it possible, military experts asked, for a nation of thirty-two million people to melt away before the German attack? Nobody in his right mind expected the hapless Poles to succeed single-handed in driving back the Nazis, but some did expect that the Polish resistance would be longer and more costly for the Germans.

Within twenty-four hours after Hitler launched his Blitzkrieg, seventy-five per cent of the Polish planes were destroyed— most of them in their hangars. The Nazis forestalled aid from Britain and France by destroying every Polish airfield equipped to receive military craft. In the first few days of the campaign the Germans smashed Polish communication lines and railroad bridges behind the Polish lines. Army transports operating on secret schedules were located by the *Luftwaffe* planes and bombed at their terminals. Mobilization centers and staging stations, presumably known only to the upper echelons of the Polish High Command, were found by German planes and smashed. Munitions dumps and oil stores, to the last isolated gasoline depot, were blasted. Nothing of military significance escaped.

Among the mysteries, the case of Leczyca was the most enigmatic. Leczyca was a town of only ten thousand people in the district of Lodz, off the beaten path of armies, devoid, it seemed, of anything of interest to an invader. It had a garrison of only one hundred and fifty soldiers and even they had been hastily sent to the front, leaving the town without a single soldier. And yet, squadron after squadron appeared over the small city, until Leczyca had the unhappy distinction of being the most intensely bombed area for its size in the world.

Staff officers asked themselves why the Nazis were dropping tons of bombs on such a singularly wasteful objective. Sixteen air raids failed to solve the puzzle. The seventeenth told the tale. While it was in progress, the countryside suddenly quaked and roared with a cataclysmic explosion. The city was destroyed; hardly a window was left intact within a radius of fifty miles.

The Germans had touched off one of the largest *secret* munitions dumps in Poland. Its very existence was known only to a few of the highest Polish officers. How did the Germans know about it?

The answer was given by inference a few days after the conclusion of the campaign. A group of foreign newspapermen was taken on a conducted tour to the ruins of Warsaw, and Colonel von Wedel, their guide from the High Command's press section, was asked to explain the secret of this amazing success. The colonel answered with unusual candor: "Victory was due to our superior arms *and to our superior intelligence service.*"

Intelligence and espionage have figured prominently in all of history's great wars, but never before had the debt the warlords owed to their spies been so publicly acknowledged.

The tragedy of Leczyca was an illustration of what von Wedel meant. For several years before the war, a German spy had been stationed in Leczyca to keep an eye on the city's great secret. On the day of reckoning, Leczyca was among the first targets of the *Luftwaffe*. The dump was skillfully concealed. Despite the beam of the local agent's radio on which the planes flew to their target, it escaped sixteen raids. But so certain were the Germans of their information that they returned for the fatal seventeenth time.

The same accuracy prevailed elsewhere. Military trains, for example, do not operate on timetable schedules, and their destinations are known only to a few. Yet the bombing of Polish rail communications was carried out with uncanny exactness. On September 5, for instance, an army transport left Warsaw's

Central Station en route to the front. Its secret routing called for its arrival at Praga station, on the other side of the river, fifteen minutes later. A few minutes before the train was due at Praga, German planes appeared from nowhere and bombed the station out of existence. The transport was marooned, blocking the progress of following trains. A single spy, planted within the stationmaster's office in Warsaw, operating a clandestine transmitter, had alerted the Germans and thus prevented thousands of troops from reaching the front.

Obviously, someone was turning a new page in the annals of war. There was more to Germany's military might than met the eye. The secret mission of *Gruppenfuehrer* Naujocks that ushered in the greatest war in history somehow became the bizarre symbol of a new kind of war.

This fresh conflict had a mysterious, intriguing new dimension. Deep in its bowels fought a brand new army, organized well in advance to fight in a brand new war.

It was an army of spies.

To be sure, throughout all recorded history spies have played an important part in both diplomacy and warfare, but never before like this.

As World War II was about to break, an American historian of the secret service drew up an estimate of the world's espionage population and found that there was hardly a white spot left on the map. The globe was covered with intelligence officers, secret agents, femmes fatales, confidential informants, troublemakers, and police spies.

This was a remarkable increase, if only because espionage is by no means an activity whose growth should normally keep pace with the growth of mankind and the progress of civilization. The halcyon days of espionage were supposed to be over. In fact, they were just beginning.

2

The Fox in His Lair

On August 31, 1939, the *Wehrmacht,* deployed for the campaign in Poland, sizzled with excitement and tension. But in a plain, tastelessly furnished office in Berlin, a small, sallow man with snow-white hair sat back and relaxed. To Wilhelm Canaris, the actual outbreak of war was an anticlimax. He had worked long and hard to pave the way for it; now battles that the *Wehrmacht* still had to win or lose were far behind him. He and his men had fought their own underground war with enormous determination and rare skill. Though they had lost some skirmishes, they had won most of the battles. Now they felt confident they would win the war.

Who was this man, this great captain and brain of the vast underground army? Certainly the most important spymaster of World War II, Canaris was also one of its most controversial characters. "Seldom," wrote a former high official of the German secret service, "has a figure of historical importance been judged with so many contrasting verdicts as the small, silent, eccentric figure, Admiral Wilhelm Canaris, the chief of the German Military Intelligence Services."

His enemies regard Canaris as the sinister originator of the Hitler regime's vilest crimes. His friends eulogize him as the spiritual leader of the pathetic anti-Nazi movement, a man who died a martyr for his courage and convictions. And there are those who brand him a traitor whose betrayal of the *Wehrmacht* in its darkest hour was directly responsible for Germany's defeat.

A lot of nonsense has been written about Canaris. He has

been portrayed as Germany's greatest mystery man of all time—the sly link between the intrigues and cabals of the two world wars. He was said to have been one of the lovers of Mata Hari and has been called "the admiral who never wore a uniform," though he spent the greater part of his adult life in that of the German Navy. He has been described as a humanitarian and moralist, but also as a lifelong intriguer.

In fact, the greater part of Canaris' life was humdrum. He was born at Aplerbeck near Dortmund, in the heart of the Ruhr, on January 1, 1887, the youngest of three children of a prosperous mining engineer. It may be symbolic that in his youth he received the nickname *"Kiecker,"* which in English would mean either "Peeper" or "Snooper." Young Wilhelm joined the navy and, during the First World War, dabbled in intelligence work, though it was not yet his specialty. He commanded a U-boat in World War I, and after the war the old battleship *Schlesien*. Then came the last sinecure, a gentle hint that his navy had no more use for him. In the early thirties, he was given a shore assignment as commandant of Swinemuende, an insignificant naval station on the Baltic, where he had a couple of coastal guns and nothing but seagulls to shoot.

Then, suddenly and inexplicably, on January 1, 1935, he succeeded Captain Konrad Patzig as the head of the Abwehr, the military intelligence service. Canaris was forty-eight, but he seemed far older. He was small, soft boned and slender, had a quiet voice and leisurely gestures, his shallow skin furrowed by wrinkles, his hair snow-white. His subordinates called him *der Alte*—"the Old Man."

Canaris was continually pulled to and fro between the amorality of his job and his innate moralism, between a mystic belief in chance and a meticulous dedication to purpose. He was a good man and a weak one, an opportunist and a compromiser, forever vacillating between firmness and procrastination. His character was mirrored in everything he did, even in his pursuit of his favorite sport, sailing. "He always keeps close to the wind," a friend once said, "and sails forever with sloppy sails."

He was sensitive to a degree which, as someone remarked, was "incompatible with his choice of the career of an officer and which caused him to regard force and any expression of force with horror." Perhaps because he was himself so unsoldierly in appearance, he looked with aversion upon dashing officers. The mere sight of a decoration on a soldier's chest provoked him to sardonic outbursts and sufficed to bar the man from his entourage. He preferred to wear civilian clothes and he surrounded himself with officers who were as non-military as possible.

His inner sanctum on the top floor of the *Abwehr* building, called by insiders *Fuchsbau* or "Fox Lair," reflected the hodge-podge of this strange man's character. Its furnishings had no style or taste. On his desk stood a little piece of bric-a-brac which Canaris had chosen as the symbol of the *Abwehr*: the familiar little statue of three monkeys who hear, see and speak no evil. One wall was covered with a big map of the world. On the other walls hung three pictures: an autographed photograph of Generalissimo Franco (reflecting his consuming love of Spain, his adopted country, whose civil war in 1937 he helped to ignite); a Japanese painting of the devil; and a picture of his favorite dachshund, Seppl.

This strange man had neither friends nor confidants, but he was inordinately fond of dogs. His concern for his canine companions once threw his adversaries into confusion. Traveling with an assumed name on a fake passport, Canaris visited Spain in 1936 to plot the coming rebellion. The Republican police spotted him and tapped his telephone, for Canaris occasionally committed the apparent indiscretion of calling Berlin long-distance.

The Spanish monitor heard him talking about an ailing dog, and receiving from someone in Berlin a detailed report on the pet's bowel movement. The police were positive this was a clever code and cryptoanalysts burned the midnight oil trying to decipher it. They couldn't. Canaris really was talking about a sick dachshund.

Canaris personified the secret service at its worst. He was a politician, therein violating the very first rule of the secret service by using the information his agency procured as a weapon for his own plots. He came into the *Abwehr* a convinced Nazi, then drifted away from Hitler and wound up in a conspiracy against him. He is now frequently described as one of the top leaders of the anti-Nazi plot, but his real contribution consisted of omissions rather than commissions. He let the Nazis plant their spies within the *Abwehr* and permitted the anti-Nazis to plot behind his back. And he tried, with a good deal of success, to use both groups for his own ends.

In the end the Nazis hanged him on a specially constructed gallows with thin piano wire to deepen and prolong the agony of his death. Hanging may be, as Wotton remarked, the worst use a man can be put to, but it seems reasonable that he deserved his savage death.

But on September 1, 1939, he was still years from this mildly elevated terminal point of his career. In fact, he was at the pinnacle of his power and fame—because, strangely enough for a man of mystery, Canaris was internationally famous. The *Abwehr* was Hitler's greatest prop and Canaris was one of his most valuable accomplices.

In a semi-official history of the *Abwehr*, Paul Leverkuehn, a Hamburg lawyer who served as an intelligence officer throughout the war, wrote of Canaris: "He was more than the titular head of the *Abwehr*. It was very largely his creation, and when he was removed it began rapidly to disintegrate. In fact it would not be a great exaggeration to say that the *Abwehr* was Canaris, and Canaris was the *Abwehr*."

On the eve of war Canaris had a permanent staff of eighteen thousand men and women, with additional thousands in the field serving as confidential informants.

Canaris himself stood alone at the apex of this hierarchy. Under him were five major sections. There was the Central Section, headed by that courageous and determined anti-Nazi, Colonel Hans Oster, the executive officer of this labyrinthine web. The Foreign Section, under Captain Buerkner, maintained liaison with foreign powers. Section II, under Colonel von Lahousen, was responsible for sabotage and other underhanded secret operations. Section III was charged with *Abwehr* in the true sense of the term—security, counter-espionage, and counter-sabotage.

Secret intelligence (including espionage) was the responsibility of Section I, also called *Geheimer Meldedienst,* or Secret Information Service. It was organized in three "subsections" (one each for the army, navy and air force) and five groups. Among these, Group I-G developed ingeniously concealed weapons, extraordinary methods of microphotography, invulnerable secret inks; it forged passports and manufactured all the sinister paraphernalia indispensable to the efficient functioning of a secret service. Group I-I was in charge of wireless communications, including the design of clandestine radio equipment for agents in the field (the so-called Afus) and the organization of secret (black) radio networks.

Section I had a relatively small staff at headquarters in Berlin, in a five-story stucco building on the Tirpitzufer. In the field, it maintained an enormous network of so-called V-men (the "V" standing for *"Vertrauen,"* or confidential, in this context). Many were permanent resident agents; still more worked on a temporary, hit-and-run basis. The majority of the V-men were volunteers whose chief motive in aiding the Nazis was their sympathy for Hitler's New Order. A handful were mercenary spies, but they were not paid well, on the sound theory that the best intelligence cannot be bought.

But no matter how firmly entrenched Canaris seemed at the apex of this hierarchy, he knew that his lonely place was perilous. He would have been indeed a negligent spymaster had he not known of a danger that threatened both himself and the *Abwehr*: Reinhard Heydrich, the young boss of the Gestapo whose *Sicherheitsdienot* (security service) was a vulgar imitation of Canaris' *Abwehr.*

The *Abwehr's* chief function was to defend Germany from

foreign opponents by aggressive espionage and defensive counter-espionage. Heydrich's SD, designed to defend the Reich from the "inner foe," was supposed to perform largely police intelligence functions. But this demarcation could not be maintained. Beneath a veneer of collaboration, and even personal friendship, Canaris and Heydrich battled for control.

Heydrich was determined to dismantle the *Abwehr* until it was confined to military intelligence. Although this plan was based primarily on professional ambition, he also had a personal reason for disliking Canaris. Heydrich was Canaris' junior by seventeen years, but both men were products of the German navy. There was one difference: Canaris had risen to the rank of rear admiral and left the navy with honors and dignity; Heydrich made the grade of a junior lieutenant, then foundered and was kicked out.

Though he was now in a position of enormous power, Heydrich's hurt pride still made him self-conscious with Canaris, in whom he saw the navy personified.

For his part, Canaris went to considerable lengths to carry out his instructions and make Heydrich happy. He encouraged Heydrich to visit him at his home, persuaded him to become his neighbor in a Berlin suburb, and cultivated an apparently warm social relationship. But he was thoroughly contemptuous of the young Nazi, and Canaris had a trump card, as secret services usually do. He had evidence in the little safe he kept in his private office in the *Fuchsbau* that this fanatical, Jew-baiting Nazi blood-hound, Heydrich himself, was partly Jewish in origin.

The Nazi espionage service pitted against the *Abwehr* was a catch-all organization, called *Reichs Sicherheits Haupt-Amt,* or RSHA for short, the Main Department of Reichs Security.

Headed by Heinrich Himmler, it was organized in major branches whose functions and duties ranged from the selection and training of personnel to weird medical experiments using inmates of concentration camps as human guinea pigs. Its Sections IV and V performed police functions. Section IV was the dreaded Gestapo, headed by Heinrich Mueller, set up to combat opposition to the regime, to persecute the churches and the Jews and also to carry out the usual police supervision of all ports of egress and ingress. Section V was the *Kriminalpolizei*, or Kripo of Arthur Nebbe, the Reich's orthodox criminal police.

Intelligence and espionage were concentrated in the SD Sections III (Inland) and VI (Foreign), over which Reinhard Heydrich ruled supreme. The Nazis' aggressive espionage was a job reserved for his Section VI, the notorious *Amt Sechs,* where he was aided by a shrewd, opportunistic intellectual named Walther Schellenberg, a pinch-faced little busybody whose cold efficiency and penchant for methodical intrigue well supplemented Heydrich's broader approach to the activity.

Section VI was developed step by step, until it became the Nazi counterpart of the *Wehrmacht's* cloistered *Abwehr,* a secret service in all but name, complete to functional and regional sub-sections patterned after the *Abwehr's* structure. Though considerably smaller than the *Abwehr,* Heydrich's agency actually duplicated its functions, frequently arrogating to itself prerogatives which should have been exclusive to the Canaris organization.

Heydrich's ideas ran along unorthodox lines. To him, the direct approach was contemptible because it was too simple. His secret service was constantly teeming with weird plans for savage enterprises. Even those few he succeeded in translating into practice sufficed to establish Heydrich as one of the most insidious, but undeniably one of the most brilliant, spymasters of this nefarious age.

In a sense, Heydrich is the most misunderstood and underrated figure in the espionage history of World War II. Although it is Canaris' picture that is etched on the imagination of the world as Germany's master spy, Heydrich certainly gave him a run for first place. Some even think Heydrich surpassed Canaris in the efficiency and effectiveness of his operations, although this remains, in the nature of these things, a moot question.

Everything about this man was obscure or mysterious, including his origin. He was born in Halle in 1904 to the director of the Music Academy, whose name was listed in a contemporary directory as "Bruno Richard Heydrich (properly called Suess)." It was this parenthetical addendum in the old directory that made Heydrich reticent about his birth and youth. "Suess" was a common Jewish name in Germany.

Too young for war in 1914-18, he joined a terrorist youth organization after the peace and at the age of fifteen already had a reputation as a proficient assassin. He joined the navy as a cadet, advanced to the rank of lieutenant, but was then abruptly cashiered. He had several love affairs running simultaneously, including one with the daughter of a naval architect. When the young lady became pregnant, her father demanded that Heydrich marry her. The lieutenant refused in righteous indignation. He would never marry a woman, he said, who succumbed so easily to a seducer. The naval architect took the case to Admiral Raeder and Heydrich was discharged.

He entered the Nazi movement and found a place inside the Party's intelligence organization and an opportunity to rise through blackmail. He learned that a high-ranking Prussian official was secretly corresponding with Hitler's arch rival within the Nazi Party, the ill-fated party theoretician Gregor Strasser. Heydrich courted the official's wife and became her lover. Between amorous embraces in the lady's apartment, he discovered the hiding place of the incriminating letters and stole the correspondence.

Armed with these letters, he extorted a place for himself with the Munich Elite Guard. After that, his rise was rapid. He was not yet twenty-seven years old in 1931 when he was made chief of the Party's special intelligence division and commandant of its goons, raw-boned giants of blonde Nordic appearance and of ruthless, sadistic disposition.

Young as Heydrich was, he looked still younger; powerful as he was, he thirsted for still more power. He was tall, lean, with an excellent figure which made him look extremely well in the sleek, black SS uniform. His beardless face gave him a somewhat effeminate appearance, but that impression was quickly

destroyed by his eyes, which were frigid and mirrored a truly
cynical soul. Wilhelm Hoettl, who served under him in the SD,
compared Heydrich with Cesare Borgia. "Both men", he said,
"were imbued with the same complete disregard for all ethical
values, both possessed the same passion for power, the same cold
intelligence, the same frigidity of heart, the same systematically
calculated ambition and even the same physical beauty of a
fallen angel."

Heydrich looms large in the history of contemporary secret
service because, in an age of enlightened and mechanized intrigue, he was the only practitioner of medieval, brute cabal.
His life was an unbroken chain of murders. He had people put
to death on the principle that a dead enemy is better than a
live one, and he made no squeamish distinction between proven
foes and presumed friends. He liquidated people he instinctively
disliked, colleagues he thought might endanger his rise, Nazis
he regarded as untrustworthy.

His achievements even before the war were phenomenal,
but they were trivial compared with his later victories. The war
he helped to "justify" was to give him great opportunities. He
looked forward to it with a glutton's anticipation of an epicurean
meal.

3

Canaris Paves the Way

Hans Piekenbrock looked like a prosperous wine merchant, but he was a spymaster of superb competence. A fun-loving, jovial Rhinelander, he was a colonel of the German General Staff and the chief of Canaris' Section I, the branch of the *Abwehr* charged with espionage. He was a tall, heavy-set man, broad-shouldered, bluff and immensely popular with his subordinates, who called him "Pieki." There were few missions they would not undertake for him.

Because Canaris had little time or inclination to deal with the detail work of Section I, preferring the rarefied atmosphere of political and diplomatic intelligence, Piekenbrock enjoyed great autonomy and he made the most of it.

The vital secrets of Germany's actual and potential enemies were in his files. Because of the enormous difficulties of obtaining secret intelligence from inside the Soviet Union, Piekenbrock chose to neglect the U.S.S.R. He did manage from time to time to smuggle agents into the Soviet Union and a few of them did succeed in returning, but the bulk of his information was developed by reading between the lines of Soviet publications, by interviewing returning travelers and by that other effective means of remote control, desk-bound intelligence.

Piekenbrock had his difficulties in other sensitive areas as well. The Foreign Ministry, anxious to avoid friction with Britain, France and the United States (to lull them into complacency and keep them out of war), muted the Section's espionage activities in those countries. Until 1936, the service had been actually forbidden to maintain a network in Britain. Not until 1937, when Canaris personally appealed to Hitler, was the *Abwehr* permitted to spy against England without restrictions.

Less than two years sufficed to build up the *Abwehr* files on Britain, with exact details of the country's small peacetime army, the complex RAF and the sprawling Royal Navy. During those prewar years, the Special Branch of Scotland Yard and M.I.5 of the War Office's Intelligence Directorate (the two major British counter-espionage organs) managed to unmask a number of petty spies, but the big fish evaded them. The backbone of German espionage in Britain was not broken until the outbreak of the Second World War.

England was not even a major target of the *Abwehr*. France was considered far more important. It was the traditional enemy and the historic stamping ground of German spies.

The *Abwehr's* tactics against France were not new at all. Bismarck's secret agent, Dr. Wilhelm Stieber, prepared for the Franco-Prussian war of 1870 by moving thirty thousand spies into France in 1869. France was similarly pre-invaded on the eve of the First World War.

On the eve of the Second World War, the pattern was the same. Even Churchill was fooled. On August 15th, only nineteen days before the outbreak of the war with France, he was taken by General Georges, commander-in-chief of the French armies in the field, to inspect the Maginot Line. Upon his return, Churchill presented a confidential report to the War Office.

"The French Front cannot be surprised," he wrote. "It cannot be broken at any point except by an effort which would be enormously costly in life, and would take so much time that the general situation would be transformed while it was in progress."

But the Line Churchill described as "unbreakable" had already been broken—not by German *Landsers,* who were to accomplish this feat only a few months later—but by the agents of Pieki and Canaris.

A special branch was set up in Section I for the exclusive

purpose of cracking the secrets of the Maginot Line. Innumerable surreptitious approaches were made and several German agents, sent boldly against the target, were caught. The *Abwehr's* persistent efforts were finally crowned with success, due to the corruption of two French officers in key positions. One was a Captain Credle, aide to the commanding officer of the Metz sector of the fortifications, from whom—by way of an *agent de liaison*, an Alsatian named Paul Denz—the Germans received a partial blueprint of the Line. Conclusive information was procured from another French traitor named Georges Froge, an army captain in charge of provisioning the troops of the Line. By frequent travels up and down the system, and by access to maps and papers containing the vital statistics of those garrisons, Captain Froge gained extensive knowledge of the Maginot Line.

Froge was a strangely wayward man who looked with sympathetic eyes at the totalitarian system of the Nazis. With so much knowledge of his country's defenses and so little sympathy for its political system, he became a natural target for the Germans.

As soon as he had been "fingered" as a potential spy with invaluable information, the Germans embarked on "Operation Z," as the special maneuver to ensnare Forge came to be called. It was discovered that the captain was in straitened financial circumstances and loved money as much as he hated his country. After that it did not take long to land Captain Froge.

Confirmation of his information came into the *Abwehr's* possession accidentally, the morning after the occupation of Prague in 1939. Marching with the German army into the Czechoslovak capital were special agents of the *Abwehr* under orders to seize intact the files of the Czechoslovak General Staff, especially the archives of its Second Section. Contact was promptly established with a traitor in the Czech General Staff, Colonel Emanuel Morawetz, who took his *Abwehr* friends to a hidden safe in which the Czechs kept, not their own, but France's greatest secret—the complete blueprint of the Maginot Line.

How this blueprint came to be in that safe is a story in

itself. When the Czechs decided to build their own system of fortifications and to pattern it after the Maginot Line, a Czech technical commission was permitted to inspect the French Line and make detailed drawings of anything they liked. The Czechs had added their own estimates to the blueprint, annotated, analyzed and criticized the French system and, in one of those General Staff "exercises," even demonstrated how it could be pierced.

The second most important item on the *Abwehr's* shopping list was the French navy. With agents based in Belgium, Section IM (Piekenbrock's naval intelligence division) made a systematic survey of the French fleet and French coast, from battleships to speedboats, from the Channel to Cannes. The intelligence was supplied by a network of agents created especially for the purpose. A few of these were Frenchmen. One, a handsome young naval lieutenant of excellent family, fell into the arms of a pretty *Abwehr* decoy, a certain Lydia Oswald, who was delegated to seduce him. The lieutenant had access to the private files of Admiral Darlan, commander-in-chief of the French navy.

This source was remarkable, not only for the quality of the intelligence supplied, but for the speed with which it was transmitted. At one point during the crisis Darlan dictated an order to mobilize the fleet. The lieutenant got hold of it and four hours later the *Abwehr* received the order—before it reached the French fleet. And in 1939 an *Abwehr* agent named Otto Baltes had returned to Berlin with a list of every single French airport and a detailed report on the planes and men at each. The man from whom Baltes obtained this detailed intelligence was a young captain of the French air force, working in the cabinet of Pierre Cot, the Minister of Air. Like so many before him, he had turned traitor for love as well as money. He was lured into the trap by an attractive Alsatian decoy working as a *midinette* on Rue de la Paix. When she became his full-time mistress—a *liaison* that needed far more money than the captain earned—Baltes stepped in to supply the cash. In return he received the precious report.

This was the last scrap of intelligence Canaris needed to complete the French dossier. It now included everything the German High Command needed to know about France.

Despite this traditional preoccupation with France, the busiest desk of the whole Abwehr was the Polish Branch of Colonel Piekenbrocks' Section. Poland was an ideal hunting preserve. Many German nationals lived in Poland, and the colonel shrewdly organized them into a special *Meldedienst,* an *ad hoc* information service. He also established long before the war a so-called "covering network"—a veritable spiderweb of confidential agents. This was spread across the land and included every point of military interest. This was a dormant network. The agents had instructions to remain quiescent in order to avoid detection, and to go into action only in emergencies or when they happened to have information of extraordinary importance. They were to be saved for the coming war.

In addition, Piekenbrock organized a special group in Poland to report on the Polish army. Very few of these were Germans; the majority were native Poles who, with a variety of motives, had decided to betray their country to the Germans.

For several years before the war, Piekenbrock's talent scouts combed Poland for recruits. The colonel did not find it difficult to recruit a sizable army of traitors. A large number of senior officers and important officials actually volunteered their services. But the German-Polish espionage contest was not quite a one-way street. The Poles also displayed industry, ingenuity, and even some efficiency in espionage. Up to the war itself, they scored as many coups against the Germans as did the *Abwehr* against Poland.

Section II (Intelligence) of the Polish General Staff was a big and powerful organization. Housed in the heart of Warsaw in a battered, mystery-shrouded, gloomy old building on Pilsudskego Square, it had reports that presented as good a picture of

Germany and the *Wehrmacht* as the Germans had of Poland and the Polish army.

The major outpost of Polish Intelligence, specializing in Germany, was located in Bromberg, not far from the German border. It had eleven subsidiary branches, including one in Danzig. The Poles even succeeded in penetrating to the heart of the Danzig substation of the *Abwehr*. They achieved this with the hoary methods of old-fashioned espionage, using a pretty woman as a decoy—one Clara Shebinska. A comely Polish lady, as so many Polish ladies are, Clara lived in Danzig and held down a humdrum secretarial job with a firm that was above suspicion.

But she had been planted in the Free City for the specific purpose of striking up friendships with the gentlemen of the *Abwehr*. She was well-briefed and supplied with incidental intelligence about the personal habits of the Lotharios she was expected to entrap. Her major asset was, of course, her voluptuous beauty: she was a petite blonde with a round baby face, startled big brown eyes, sensuous lips, and a figure as well-rounded as her education. She was vivacious, infinitely charming, and evidently blessed with a romantic disposition.

She frequented the haunts of the *Abwehr* people, was picked up by several of them and soon enough was on intimate terms with the resident manager of the local *Abwehr* office. She knew how to coax from her lover abundant information about the *Abwehr's* activities in Danzig, and even inside Poland.

Behind the Danzig operation, and the generally brilliant performance of the entire Bromberg network, was a strange individual. He was called Zychon, although that may not have been his real name. He was a professional soldier, totally unknown to the world at large, but in the Polish army he was famous and respected. Even his enemies conceded that he was by far the best intelligence officer the Poles had. And yet (now in his forties), he was still only a major, a perennial major.

Zychon was always passed over when the promotions were

handed out because he was an eccentric and an iconoclast. He was constantly stepping on sensitive toes, crossing up the schemes of others, insulting his superiors, and in general making mockery of discipline and rules. In appearance, he looked like a hobo; in manners, he was a bum.

He would have been cashiered long before had he not been indispensable. Just when it was decided to retire or court-martial him for one or another of his astounding capers, he would come through with one of his phenomenal scoops. He didn't care. He was always drunk.

Zychon was a dipsomaniac and probably also a lunatic. He dispensed with secrecy in the most secretive of all professions. As soon as he arrived in Danzig, for instance, he would put in a call to his German opposite number to announce his presence in town. Sometimes he would chat amiably with the German, his shoptalk abounding in tantalizing loose ends. More often he would call his antagonist to curse him roundly in the most uncouth fashion. On these occasions, the German would say, "That damned fool Zychon is drunk again", and never was there more truth in a piece of incidental intelligence.

From time to time, the Germans tried to infiltrate the Bromberg network by exploiting one or another of Zychon's weaknesses, and once in a while they seemed to be on the verge of success. But just when the arrangements appeared concluded, Zychon would disappoint them. This caustic jester was no fool. He was a king of spies.

It, therefore, caused a profound sensation within the *Abwehr* when Subsection East reported to topside in Berlin that vague feelers had come from the Zychon organization that held out the promise of a real break. At first it appeared that Major Zychon himself was putting out the feelers, but when contact was established with the would-be traitor, he turned out to be Zychon's second in command, Captain Kasimir Tolodzietzki.

He offered a plausible explanation for his defection: hatred of his capricious boss. Tolodzietzki was Zychon's whipping boy and scapegoat. The major made life miserable for his hapless aide and gradually built up in him a blind rancor. Tolodzietzki may not have intended to harm Poland, but merely to hurt Zychon. His plot was simple. He would slip some intelligence to the *Abwehr* in order to get Zychon into hot water. He so arranged his treachery as to make it appear that the major was the real culprit. Then he wrote poison-pen letters to Warsaw hinting that Zychon was involved in sordid deals with the Germans. His zeal finally became so great that he put the Germans on their guard. The *Abwehr* suspected that Tolodzietzki was merely a plant through whom Zychon was trying to smuggle misleading information into the *Abwehr's* files.

Just as the Germans were set to drop Tolodzietzki altogether, the Poles stepped in and proved that the German suspicions were without foundation. His aide's defection had not escaped Zychon. Tolodzietzki was placed under surveillance and his treacherous activities were discovered. He was arrested and hanged. The Poles made the mistake of publicizing the hanging. The execution opened the Germans' eyes. The reports they had refused to regard as genuine were now vindicated, dusted off, and, in due course, made their contribution to the German triumph over Poland.

Another major source of information for the Germans was an officer of the Polish army whose identity is still clouded in secrecy. He managed to escape Tolodzietzki's fate, and the Germans, in their gratitude, still refuse to identify him. This man also volunteered his services to the *Abwehr* and offered to enlist a number of Polish officers to act as spies. He, too, was received with a great deal of suspicion and at first his offer was rejected. After the Tolodzietzki affair, however, the Germans realized their mistake and tried frantically to re-establish contact with the volunteer. What with the mills of espionage grinding rather slowly, they needed more than two years to regain contact, which was finally made at a most crucial time—on the eve of the Second World War.

After that, everything worked smoothly. The agent delivered to the *Abwehr* a number of Polish officers stationed at key posts and from them, bit by bit, the Germans acquired the entire Polish mobilization order and deployment plan.

Thus Canaris' organization delivered to Hitler all he needed to know about France and Poland. His Eastern flank was protected by the Nazi-Soviet pact. There was only one more thing he wanted—the neutrality of Britain.

4

Stagnation in the Allied Camp

In stark contrast to the sprawling secret services of Hitler, the democratic countries either had no intelligence services worthy of the name or maintained severely constricted, hibernating organizations. The French and British services were in the latter category. They subsisted largely on shoestring appropriations and coasted on past prestige with the inevitable consequences. To put it bluntly, both the French and British secret services were just plain bad, totally inadequate to the challenge and demands of those fateful years.

In France, which had produced Joseph Fouché, one of history's most nefarious spymasters, intelligence was a traditional instrument of power, but it was practiced as an art rather than an exact science. In line with the chaotic organization of the French government and the jealousy-ridden, predatory bureaucracy of its permanent officials, intelligence was decentralized and compartmentalized. Each service kept aloof from the others and actually frowned upon liaison or co-operation for fear that concord might compromise autonomy.

In 1939, France had a galaxy of truly brilliant ambassadors stationed at the key capitals. Men like André François-Poncet and Robert Coulondre, successive ambassadors in Berlin during these stormy days, were fully capable of procuring their own information and evaluating it in their reports to the Quai d'Orsay, but they had no control over what was done with their reports back home. In the French table of organization, intelligence per se was regarded as the responsibility of the armed forces; accordingly, the major intelligence services were lodged deep within the military establishment.

On the eve of the Second World War, France had four major intelligence services, but no agency to co-ordinate or synchronize them. The army had two, the Second and Fifth Sections of the General Staff; the former engaged in general intelligence and strategic evaluation; the latter, in espionage and counter-espionage. The navy had its parallel intelligence division. The Air Ministry had a somewhat smaller intelligence section, probably the best of the lot, because, being the youngest, it was not yet encumbered by traditional impediments.

By virtue of its age, influence and adeptness at arrogating power to itself, the army's *Bureau de Renseignement*—the Second Bureau—came to occupy a central position in this intelligence labyrinth. It was a cloistered, professorial organization whose distance from the realities of the day was somehow symbolized by its location. It was housed at La Ferète-sous-Jouarre, well away from the hustle and bustle of Paris and also physically separated from the Fifth Section.

Despite its gray pre-eminence, Army Intelligence suffered from various fatal handicaps. For one thing, it was headed by officers of relatively low rank. In 1939, its chief was Gauché, a colonel. Head of the Second Bureau was Baril, a major. Gauché and Baril happened to be men of marked personality and profound intelligence, but their influence did not reach far, even within their own organizations. They were constantly stymied by brother officers who sat closer to the commanding generals, and who were remarkably uninfluenced by hard information when arriving at their own judgments.

Gauché, for example, made several valiant efforts to funnel information about the Polish campaign up to General Gamelin, commander-in-chief of the army. He hoped it would induce the general to alter his outmoded, stolid strategy. He got as far as Colonel Préaud, a friend of Gamelin and head of the commander's Operations Bureau. Préaud found himself in disagreement with Gauché's conclusions and refused to forward even the intelligence on which they were based.

The generals themselves were inclined to disregard or dismiss the conclusions of their intelligence officers. When General Weygand was presented with a report on mechanized warfare that proposed a revamping of the French military machine, he scribbled on the margin of the document (which, incidentally, was prepared by Charles de Gaulle): "What you have written has deeply interested me, but I do not agree." That was the end of the matter.

Similarly, the Second Bureau differed from the senior French observers in its facts and evaluations of the lessons of the Polish campaign. But so great was General Gamelin's distance from intelligence that he did not find time even to leaf through the Polish *dossier* of the Second Bureau.

The Second Bureau was burdened by a number of officers forced down its throat because they happened to be friends or protégés of generals. Military attachés were so chosen and the Bureau had to depend on them for most of its intelligence. During the years immediately preceding the Second World War, Colonel Didelet—a man, who, like his aide and his predecessor, could not speak German—was French military attaché at the crucial Berlin post. Didelet received the appointment because he was one of Weygand's protégés. In Berlin he lived in a fool's paradise. The reports he sent to Vincennes read like fairy tales today. He failed to find out the actual strength, the doctrine, tactics and over-all purpose of the German armored divisions, the very divisions soon to be assigned the dominant role in vanquishing France.

And the *Deuxième Bureau* was frozen stiff in its own tradition. Despite men like Gauchér and Baril at the top, the organization was antiquated and inefficient. Its blunders ranged from minor tactical faux pas to major strategic errors. On the General Staff map put out by the cartographic branch, the

German city of Aachen (Aix-la-Chapelle) was placed inside
Belgium. The main Hamburg-Berlin railway line was marked
as a branch, capable of carrying only light traffic. The periodic
Intelligence Summaries contained fundamental errors of fact
and judgment, which in several instances had serious consequences. The historian Marc Block, who served as an intelligence
officer during World War II, maintains that the gross errors in
the *Intelligence Summaries* were, in part, responsible for the
disastrous defeat of France in 1940.

"It should be the business of Intelligence," Block wrote in
his melancholy post-mortem, "to anticipate . . . needs, and to
provide the required facts even before they are demanded. It
should circulate to each, all the relevant information as soon
as it is available. But instead of this being done, Intelligence
scarcely ever moved outside the narrow limits prescribed for it
by a tradition that knew nothing of the needs of mechanical
warfare."

In France, it may truly be said, the intelligence service
both mirrored the confusion of France and contributed hand-
somely to deepening that confusion.

England was only a little better off.

To the outsider the British secret service is a vague, almost
chimerical organization. The government steadfastly refused
either to confirm or deny its very existence, to blame it publicly
for its blunders or to claim credit for its successes. The very motto
of the Secret Service is: "Never explain, never apologize." All
attacks upon the Secret Service are mutely absorbed and no
charge, however preposterous or damaging, is ever dignified with
an answer or denial.

The ironclad secrecy in which Britain wrapped its Secret
Service was part prudence and part whimsy; to a large extent,
the latter. It was a romantic masquerade that appealed to
Britons, a grandiose pageantry of espionage that in 1939, on
the eve of another world war, was anachronistic, even childish.

Growing exasperation with this confidential strong arm of

His Majesty's Government induced members of Parliament to breach the sacrosanct tradition and openly discuss the apparent decay of the Secret Service.

In the House of Commons, Geoffrey Mander bemoaned "the frequent appalling ignorance of the British Government on the subject of what is going on abroad." Mr. Lees-Smith demanded that the Secret Service be removed from the aegis of the Foreign Office because its traditions and methods were "not suited for dealing with the particular methods which have to be adopted with a regime of the Nazi type."

Most outspoken and eloquent, as usual, was the Cassandra of those days, Winston S. Churchill, who voiced the most direct criticism of the Secret Service. On April 13, 1939, in the wake of Hitler's occupation of Czechoslovakia, he said: "After twenty-five years' experience in peace and war, I believe the British Intelligence Service to be the finest of its kind in the world. Yet we have seen, both in the case of the subjugation of Bohemia and on the occasion of the invasion of Albania, that Ministers of the Crown had apparently no inkling, or at any rate, no conviction, of what was coming."

The stagnation of the Secret Service was evident both at home and in the field. It was most glaring within the Foreign Office and suffered from all the shortcomings of British diplomacy of that period. Members of the Secret Service adopted the hoary Victorian mannerisms of British diplomats and their penchant for both decorum and intrigue. Political intelligence became a tool abused by department heads, the middle-layer of permanent officials. Anarchy was rampant and the traditional secrecy cloaked, not only confidential transactions, but the anarchy as well.

In time of war, Britain reaches out and enlists the very best brains of the Commonwealth in the secret service. Great writers such as Maugham and Mackenzie; outstanding scholars like Ewing, Hogarth and Lawrence; brilliant politicians of the stature of Wilson and Cox were brought into the service to serve as intelligence specialists in areas they knew best.

But in the lazy and leisurely days of peace, British intelligence falls back on the "corps," a handful of lifetime professionals. Some of these men prove excellent technicians, well trained, in the legendary "Black Castle" which allegedly houses the Imperial General Staff's college of spies, but usually they are men with little savvy or imagination. They go by the textbook. They incline to think, along with Falstaff: "Pray that our armies join not in a hot day; for, by the Lord, I take but two shirts out with me, and I mean not to sweat extraordinarily."

Then there was the question of money. In emergencies Britain can be lavish, but in time of peace she is often unusually miserly.

On the eve of the First World War, His Majesty's Secret Service received the niggardly appropriation of some forty-seven thousand pounds, as compared with the seventy thousand pounds which Cromwell allocated to John Thurloe two centuries earlier, when the purchasing power of the pound was enormously greater.

The result of this was disastrous. The Foreign Office was forced to dismantle the Political Intelligence Department, to let its best men go, and to get along as best it could. By 1938, the budget of the Service had been increased to more than four hundred and fifty thousand pounds. But most of it had to be spent on combating foreign agents swarming all over the British Isles and the empire. It was not until the Czechoslovak crisis that the Foreign Office suddenly decided to revive the Political Intelligence Department (called P.I.D. or, colloquially, "Pids") and appointed a brilliant career diplomatist, Rex Leeper, as its chief. This department did not go into actual operation until September 10, 1939, a week after the outbreak of the war. Leeper set it up at Woburn, the estate of the Duke of Bedford—an intelligence service, as Bruce Lockhart remarked, fifty miles from the center of intelligence.

The revival of "Pids" compounded the anarchy, for now the Secret Service complex became even more complex. For one thing Leeper, despite his qualifications, did not become chief of

the Secret Service. In fact, his own department was hardly
secret at all. The actual chief of the labyrinthian service was
hidden somewhere deep under cover and conveniently so, because he had nothing to be proud of or to shout about.

Anarchy and confusion were not confined to London; if
possible, they were even worse in the field.

It is the practice of secret services to cover sensitive areas
with networks of operatives prepared long in advance; some of
these networks are never used. They are supposed to provide
assurance that in critical situations they can supply whatever
intelligence is needed.

What with its curtailed appropriations and its world-wide
commitments, the British maintained the barest skeleton network; even so, both the Foreign Office and the War Office's
Directorate of Intelligence had their own operatives in Germany.
These were full-time, indoctrinated, trained espionage agents in
the exact sense of the term, working on a preconceived plan
and on a long-range basis, quite independent of *ad hoc* informants and volunteer helpers.

Their presence was evident; from time to time Reinhard
Heydrich's SD and other organs of German counterespionage
managed to catch British spies red-handed. In 1938-1939, they
executed twenty-three common, garden-variety spies, all of them
German nationals. Among them were several rather minor agents
in British employ, working as train-watchers or as local observers
of airports, barracks, railroad junctions and the like.

These men and women were managed by either the service
attachés at the Embassy in Berlin, or by the British consuls
scattered across the Reich, but chiefly by the so-called Continental Secret Service. It was never thought advisable to maintain the headquarters of the Continental Secret Service in the
country which was the major target of espionage. The practice
was rather to establish this central office under some plausible
cover in a nearby friendly country that was expected to remain
neutral.

Until midsummer of 1938, the chief Continental base was

in Vienna. It operated behind the front of the British Passport Office, traditionally a *dependence* of the Secret Service. The Passport Officer was Captain Thomas Kendrick, one of the foremost career officers of the British Secret Service.

Kendrick's position became untenable when, in March, 1938, the Germans annexed Austria, occupied Vienna and instituted a manhunt for spies. It did not take them long to get around to Kendrick who was arrested on charges of espionage. The Foreign Office went through the usual motions of protestation, but all it really wanted was to get Kendrick out of jail and back to London. On August 22, he was expelled. Though he was not any the worse for the experience, his network, of course, collapsed.

After that, the center of British espionage activities against Germany shifted to Copenhagen, but, in November, 1938, this shift also suffered a serious setback. The Danes, disturbed by the increased espionage activities of foreigners on their soil, started an elaborate spy hunt and one Waldemar Poetzsch was caught in the net. At that time all espionage agents were *ipso facto* presumed to be in German service, but Poetzsch's interrogation developed the startling fact that he was working for the British. The Danes were most reluctant to interfere with the operations of a British agent, but, since his arrest had been publicized, they had to salt him away. His trial was held *in camera,* but the Germans managed to procure Poetzsch's confession, and thus learned a lot about the management and the operations of the Continental Secret Service.

Additional damaging information reached the Germans from another Danish source, the police, which had a special department for counter-espionage. Section III-F of German military intelligence managed to infiltrate this department and enlist the confidential assistant of the chief of police. From this source, the Germans obtained exact information about the activities of the Continental Secret Service, not only in Denmark, but in all of Scandinavia.

After the Poetzsch debacle, Continental Secret Service

shifted its headquarters to The Hague. This office was headed by a "lifer," a professional spymaster named Henry Richard Stevens. He was a major in the British Army who had been trained for espionage in the "Black Castle." He managed a sizable organization that operated in more or less independent sections. There were political and economic branches, a counter-espionage department and military and naval sections, each under a chief who had considerable autonomy. The Military Section was under an apparently retired officer of the British Army, Captain Payton Sigmund Best, who had first come to Holland in World War I.

Best operated a network of agents inside Germany. They supplied him with whatever *military* information they could lay their hands on. His chief liaison with this net was an excitable little "refugee" who called himself Dr. Franz and who supplied authentic intelligence about the rapid development of the *Luftwaffe*. Best confined his interest to espionage proper and, until the outbreak of the shooting war, kept aloof from operatives in the field.

The Holland field office attained an importance second to none. Its excellent prewar performance was largely due to the efficiency of the intelligence department of the Netherlands Army under General van Oorshot, with which the British worked, and to the competence of a single man, the Dutch Military Attaché in Berlin. He was a soft-voiced, pleasant-mannered, self-effacing colonel of the Netherlands army named Jan G. Sas, an outstanding figure in this twilight world of espionage.

Sas had many good friends within the *Wehrmacht* and was on especially intimate terms with Colonel Hans Oster, chief of staff of the German Military Intelligence, a determined and energetic anti-Nazi within the *Abwehr*. Oster was by nature rather suspicious, but about Sas he had no qualms. He talked to him even more freely than to his fellow conspirators. The two colonels would meet in Oster's house in Zehlendorf, usually after dark, for nominally social visits. During those calls Oster supplied Colonel Sas with all the intelligence to which he had access and part of this material eventually found its way to London.

Britain had still another field office in Berne, Switzerland, but it did not come into its own until after the invasion of Holland in 1940.

The contribution this checkered field service could make was somewhat hampered by the aging of the dormant network. Much of it had been in existence for years, if not decades, and its members had become lazy and stale. Another deficiency was inherent in the quality of the very men who were supposed to manage the various rings.

Britain was unfortunate in having in Berlin an ambassador to whom espionage was repugnant (likely to interfere with his policy of appeasement) and whose preconceived notions precluded the proper evaluation of even the most reliable information if it ran counter to the grain. This was Sir Nevile Henderson, a rather stiff career diplomatist, befuddled by the intricacies and chicanery of the unorthodox Nazi diplomacy. Actual espionage was not in his domain. It was managed in part by the anonymous delegate of the Secret Service and in part by the service attachés, but they nevertheless came under the spell of this pathetic envoy.

Thus on February 15, 1939, exactly one month before the German occupation of Bohemia and Moravia, Group Captain J. L. Vachell, the British Air Attaché in Berlin, reported to London: "I feel that it is unlikely that Germany will undertake any military operation for the next two, or possibly three, months." And on February 28, when the German troops were already at their battle stations for action against Czechoslovakia, Colonel [later General Sir] Frank Mason-Macfarlane, the military attaché, answered queries with the following double talk out of which no intelligence estimator at home could make head or tail:

"The German army is passing through a phase of its evolution in which very much that would normally be abnormal is in point of fact normal. . . . The great difficulty—even to skilled observers—is to decide when 'normal abnormality' merges into something more significant. Up to date [fifteen days before the march on Prague] I have no reliable information whatever to indicate that mobilization in any form has commenced, but I cannot say more than that."

With so-called "information" of this kind coming in, it is hardly surprising that the evaluation work of the bumbling Blimps back in London was worse than useless.

On August 15, German preparations were practically complete and a tentative date—August 26—had been chosen for the commencement of hostilities against Poland.

And yet, on this same day, in a confidential dispatch to the British Minister in Warsaw, Foreign Secretary Lord Halifax still ventured the opinion: "I have the impression that Herr Hitler is still undecided, and anxious to avoid war and to hold his hand if he can do so without losing face."

5

The Trojan Horses

At the dawn of war, Colonel Piekenbrock had given to the *Wehrmacht* the vast store of *military intelligence* it needed; yet, even in the face of such abundance, Hitler's knowledge of his foes was incomplete—in fact, fatally deficient. The glittering, pampered and flamboyant German secret service combine also had its Achilles' heel. It was totally inadequate in the vital sphere of political intelligence.

This function was claimed primarily by the Foreign Ministry, but it was also usurped by Heydrich's organization and by two quasi-official agencies: Foreign Minister Ribbentrop's private bureau (the notorious *Buero Ribbentrop*) and by the Foreign Affairs Bureau (*Aussenpolitisches Amt*), a quasi-diplomatic arm of the Nazi party, headed, in a whimsical manner, by Alfred Rosenberg, the Party's mystic theoretician and frustrated diplomatist.

These agencies vied with one another in a mad scramble for diplomatic information. In their efforts to establish separate networks of their own, and in their competitive greed, they got into each other's hair. The result was that Hitler received an enormous amount of political intelligence whose quality was not matched by its quantity.

From the very outset of the Nazi regime, *political* intelligence had been endowed and encouraged. How the network was built and cultivated in England was described in a candid report to the Fuehrer by Rosenberg: "Efforts," he wrote, "to find persons in England who were favorably inclined toward the

German cause date back to 1929. Our English agent, R., in
Berlin, arranged my first trip to London as early as 1931. There
a number of contacts were made that worked out well in a
practical fashion in bringing about an Anglo-German understanding."

If Rosenberg's account is true (and it presumably is, since
British prosecutors at the Nuremberg War Crimes trial allowed
it as evidence), it is clear that his organization was successful
in creating an unprecedented British network of sincere friends,
misguided dupes and mercenary spies. "Most important of all,"
Rosenberg wrote, "was Group Captain W., a member of the
Air General Staff, a firm believer that Germany and England
should stand together in the defense against the Bolshevik danger.
As we succeeded in spreading this opinion, we expanded our
circle within the Air General Staff. The Royal Aero Club
became a centre of Anglo-German co-operation. In 1934, Group
Captain W. came to Germany and was received by the Fuehrer."

Rosenberg's network also included a secretary of Prime
Minister Ramsay MacDonald; a consultant of the War Office
named Captain McCaw (one of Lord Kitchener's aides); the
aide-de-camp of the Duke of Connaught; a certain Archibald
Boyle, whom Rosenberg described as "an adviser to the Air
Ministry"; and "a great number of other contacts" among
British politicians, officers and Members of Parliament. His
influence extended even into the Royal Family. On at least one
occasion, Rosenberg was received in clandestine audience by
the Duke of Kent, who volunteered to present Germany's case
sympathetically to his brother, the King.

The sympathy and concrete co-operation of so many prominent Britons blinded dilettante diplomats like Ribbentrop and
Rosenberg to the realities of the situation. They believed these
Britons were plotters like themselves, figures in a vast conspiracy, the members of which preferred *Mein Kampf* to the
Magna Carta. Some of these Britons were fools or dupes, to be
sure, but they were not traitors.

After the occupation of Czechoslovakia, men and women who had championed Hitler's cause suffered the horrible hangover of the morning after, with the bitter taste of Hitler's perjury in their mouths. Overnight, the Nazis lost virtually all of their celebrated English friends, yet somehow this did not become apparent to Ribbentrop or Rosenberg.

The estimate prepared for Hitler by the Foreign Ministry and Rosenberg's bureau was explicit. It stated unconditionally that Britain was bluffing and that Hitler need not fear intervention. This estimate was put in writing by Ribbentrop: "England will never dare to oppose the Fuehrer, or else she will be smashed as was Poland and thereby suffer the loss of her empire; while France, should she intervene, will be bled to death at the Westwall."

To keep Hitler on this one track, Ribbentrop issued strict orders that only his point of view and his information be presented to the Fuehrer. He actually went so far as to issue a directive: "Should it come to my attention that any of the officials expressed a different view, I will personally shoot him in his office and assume the responsibility for the act vis-à-vis the Fuehrer."

It is hardly surprising that those agents of the German diplomatic service who had some respect for their own skins began a hasty rewriting of their dispatches—or that the misguided Hitler felt safe in going to war.

But while the Nazis mistakenly believed they had an effective Trojan horse inside the British citadel, there was really just such a horse within their own camp; this was an invaluable opportunity which the British muffed badly. There was a gold mine of potential espionage within the highest councils of the Third Reich. It was a heterogeneous group of professional men, church leaders, high officials and officers, members of the upper classes and a sprinkling of Social Democrats, all of them bitterly anti-Nazi and pro-Western in their orientation.

Among them were: the valiant and invaluable Oster;

Ulrich von Hassell, ex-ambassador to Italy, who became the diplomatic adviser of this secret opposition; General Ludwig Beck, the recently dismissed chief of the General Staff; Carl Friedrich Goerdeler, ex-mayor of Leipzig; and many more—generals on the active list, like Witzleben, Falkenhausen and Thomas; officials in the various ministerial departments, like Dohnanyi, Moltke and Popitz, all of them fretting and frustrated because their hostility to Hitler did not attract British imagination.

Foremost in the younger generation of German dissidents was an attorney named Ferdinand von Schlabrendorff. Since his student days in Halle he had been fighting the Nazis. As early as 1928, he had stood up in their meetings, heckled their speakers and endured beatings at the hands of the Storm Troopers.

Schlabrendorff had historic family ties with England. He was a descendant of Christian Friedrich Baron von Stockmar, the Anglo-Belgian statesman who was Queen Victoria's mentor and the matchmaker of her marriage to Prince Albert. Schlabrendorff was, therefore, chosen by this underground to alert Britain to the danger confronting her. He was actually sent to London to carry vital secret information to Whitehall. But in London, Schlabrendorff found both sides of Downing Street strangely closed to him. He finally managed to get through to Lord Lloyd, an important Conservative politician outside Neville Chamberlain's government, and to Winston Churchill. He was received in Charwell by the man who was the true voice of Britain, but who at that stage had neither authority nor responsibility.

Schlabrendorff was somewhat ill at ease as he sought to justify his mission to Churchill. After all, he was a German, yet there he was, betraying his government's most momentous secrets. Facing Churchill in the idyllic environment of his country home, he began by saying: "Sir, I want you to understand that I am not a Nazi. I am a patriot." A broad smile came over

Churchill's cherubic face. In a voice mellowed by that smile, he told Schlabrendorff, "So am I."

As he later recalled, Schlabrendorff told Churchill that "the outbreak of the war was imminent, and that it would be unleashed with an attack on Poland, no matter what efforts might be made to mediate the crisis.

"Moreover," he said, "I could advise him that an English rapprochement with Russia would be doublecrossed by the conclusion of a pact between Hitler and Stalin. Hitler sought to protect his back with such a pact."

But there was nothing Churchill could do to act upon the information. Schlabrendorff's mission ended in total failure.

Once the war had actually begun, however, Whitehall at long last bestirred itself to exploit the unprecedented opportunities it had so long neglected. Oster, from the very heart of the *Abwehr*, had been supplying immensely important information in a roundabout fashion through the Dutch, and London had made no real attempt to establish a proper liaison between its intelligence services and the vital source which he and his friends constituted. Now Stevens and Best in Holland were instructed to establish contact with the German anti-Nazi underground. At this point the Germans, hitherto ignored by Britain, came to occupy a paramount position in the Chamberlain government's strategic designs. Whitehall believed that the war, which the German plotters so bitterly opposed, would enable them to oust Hitler and to end hostilities before they really began.

Chamberlain himself addressed a conciliatory proclamation to the German people via the plotters, telling them that Britain would not hold them responsible for Hitler's sins if they rose up and overthrew him. Things were so far advanced that a D-day was set. The conspirators were to go into action early in November, assassinate Hitler, overthrow his regime and make peace with the West. Several plans were drafted to ambush the Fuehrer and it looked as if the war would be over before Christmas.

Unfortunately, Britain and the German plotters were no longer alone in the conspiracy. Just when Britain decided at last to deal directly with the plotters, there appeared in the background an intruder, Reinhard Heydrich. The contours of the plot were known to him, but at this stage he did not know enough of the details to strike. And, from a propaganda point of view, it was not propitious to expose the dissidence of such highly-placed Germans and thus destroy the myth of German unity.

Heydrich, therefore, decided to strike at the conspiracy indirectly, by hitting the British Secret Service, which sponsored it. The existence of Best's organization and the nature of British activities in Holland were known to him in detail through the revelations Waldemar Poetzsch had made at the time of his arrest in Denmark the year before.

The Germans had additional information about the Stevens-Best organization from an unexpected source: Commander Richard Protze, the remarkable ex-head of the *Abwehr's* Section III. Protze was in his late sixties when Canaris was forced to retire him, but Canaris invited him to settle in Holland and while away his retirement by spying on British spies. So in 1938 "Uncle Richard" moved to Wassenaar, a suburb of The Hague, ostensibly representing the German state railways.

In the summer of 1939, Uncle Richard looked out of the window of his villa and saw a stranger loitering outside. When he spotted him again several times during the next few days, he decided to invite him inside. The loiterer turned out to be a Dutchman named Walbach. He confided to Protze that he was indeed a British agent, working for Stevens and Best. He was a thickset man with a massive head and a piercing stare, and he was evidently for sale.

"What do the British pay you?" Protze asked, and when Walbach said, "Seven hundred guilders a month," the German made him an offer. "I will pay you another eight hundred, in addition to what you are getting from them. Your job will be to keep me posted about the British Secret Service here in Holland."

Soon afterward Walbach identified Stevens as the head of the Continental Secret Service and Best as the officer in charge of military intelligence. Walbach was diligent and, during those days, Canaris told an officer in his *Abwehr*, "I think Uncle Richard has penetrated the British Secret Service. He is sending me embarrassing reports from that quarter." Among Best's contacts was the mousy little German who called himself Dr. Franz and posed as a refugee from the Reich. Best had no reason to trust him unreservedly, if only because Franz was extremely loquacious, but the abundant information he supplied about the *Wehrmacht* invariably proved accurate.

Early in September, Franz, who until then had dealt with Best through a go-between, demanded to see the captain in person. He had some momentous information that he would entrust only to the boss himself. Contrary to his normal practice and somewhat against his better judgment, Best agreed to meet Franz. Franz revealed that the invaluable information he had been able to funnel to the Secret Service originated from a *Luftwaffe* major named Solms who was a member of the anti-Nazi underground. Now Solms had information about certain events that could lead to the downfall of Hitler, but he refused to entrust them to Dr. Franz. He had instructed the little doctor to arrange a meeting with Captain Best.

Best agreed and suggested that the major come to Amsterdam or The Hague. Solms replied through Franz that he could not come so far. Best then agreed to meet him at Venlo, an obscure little village on the Dutch-German frontier.

Solms turned out to be a big, bluff, self-confident, excitable Bavarian who talked as big as he looked. It soon became evident that he was only an errand boy for more important people. A second meeting was arranged for the following week, again at Venlo. This time the major was calmer and less boastful. He talked coherently of his mission, which was to get British support for an ambitious plot, headed by an anonymous general, to overthrow Hitler. Best made a minimum effort to check up on the man's *bona fides*. He asked him a few technical questions and, when Solms answered them precisely, Best was satisfied that his man was on the level. No other efforts were made to check up on Solms or, for that matter, on Dr. Franz. Both men were accepted at face value.

During the second meeting a code was devised in which Solms would communicate with Best, via Franz and a mail-drop in the Netherlands. A few days later Franz told Best that he had received a call from another officer in Germany who informed him in the code that a letter had been sent to the drop for Best's eyes only. The letter arrived and in it the anonymous correspondent advised Best that the mysterious leader of the plot, "the General," was prepared to meet him in person, provided Best could convince him that he was, indeed, a top-ranking British agent. Attached to the letter was an ingeniously worded news item, which Best was to have broadcast by the BBC on its German beam. The item was broadcast twice on October 11.

Solms had faded out of the picture, with the explanation that the Gestapo had him under surveillance. The general was to handle things in person. As the plot thus moved to higher echelons, Best thought it advisable to draw Major Stevens into the maneuver. The developing drama was also revealed to General van Oorschot, director of Dutch military intelligence, who assigned a young Dutch intelligence officer, Lieutenant Dirk Klop, to act as his liaison.

At last, Franz told Best that the General was ready to meet him. A rendezvous was arranged for 10:00 a.m. on October 19, this time at the small frontier village of Dinxperlo.

The Germans arrived at noon, two hours late. There was no general in the group, only two officers, both in their early thirties, who introduced themselves as Lieutenants Seydlitz and Grosch. Franz vouched for them. Best drove the party to an isolated roadside café, and there treated them to lunch. An undefinable tension arose during lunch and Franz in particular seemed to become very excited.

The party attracted attention, the worst thing that could have happened in a clandestine palaver. Best thought it advisable to remove to safer surroundings, called a friend in nearby Arnhem, and continued the conference in the friend's dining room. Throughout proceedings thus far, many of the rules of good espionage had been violated. Best's handling of the venture showed little professional skill. Now it seemed the whole enterprise would come to an untimely end.

The party had attracted the attention of a Dutch soldier who called the police and told them that a bunch of German spies were having a meeting, first at the café and then in the Arnhem house to which he had tracked them. Police surrounded the house, broke in and demanded an explanation. Klop explained everything to the policemen and they withdrew, but the basic security of the enterprise had been breached. During this episode the two Germans were in a panic and even tried to escape through the windows. Little Dr. Franz came close to passing out. Still, nothing kindled Best's suspicions.

To a great extent, all of the excitement was in vain. The two Germans had brought no information. They were simply authorized to arrange another meeting, holding out the phantom general for bait. Best agreed and the next meeting was planned for October 25, then postponed to October 30. On that day, Klop alone went to Dinxperlo with instructions to bring the Germans to The Hague.

The general was still not in the group, but this time there were three officers instead of two. Seydlitz was missing, but Grosch was present, with a man who identified himself as Colonel Martini, and a Major Schemmel, who was apparently the leader of the group. He was a stocky young man in his late twenties, his baby face furrowed with dueling scars, making him far too conspicuous for such a secret mission. Although he looked like a dullard, he turned out to be exceptionally well-informed; he had a decisive manner and a firm control over the situation.

Schemmel gave a clear and concise exposition of the internal situation of Germany and told Best that, on behalf of the general, he could guarantee an end to the war, provided the British were willing to give Germany an honorable peace. Stevens and Best gave Schemmel a non-committal answer, pending instructions from London.

Best had given the Germans a clandestine wireless set to facilitate communication. The Germans radioed their messages to the communications center of British Intelligence in London, where they were received by two wireless operators who identified themselves as Inman and Walsh. From London, the messages were relayed to Best.

Best and Stevens were instructed by London to "pursue the matter with energy" and to deal with the Germans sympathetically, but cautiously, to save His Majesty's Government embarrassment in the event of failure. Another inconclusive meeting was held at Venlo on November 7 (there was still no general) and still another was arranged for November 9. This one was to be decisive.

The morning of that day was dull and cold; rain hung in the autumn air. The weather dampened Best's enthusiasm and he was also disturbed by the fact that for the last few days he had been trailed by an unpleasant looking stout man, though he did not connect this shadow with the plot.

At 10 o'clock he went to Stevens' house and found that his colleague was also uneasy. The major went to a drawer, took out two Browning automatics, loaded them, gave one to Best and slipped the other in his pocket. While they waited for Klop to arrive, the Germans came in on the radio, on a direct beam instead of via London. Best expected another cancellation, but this turned out to be a routine request for a change in the hours of transmission. Best concluded everything was going well.

Klop arrived and, driven by Best's driver, a Dutchman named Jan Lemmens, the party proceeded to Venlo at a leisurely pace. As they drove, their conversation drifted to the possibility of invasion and Stevens did a most unusual thing, especially on this sort of mission. He took a pencil and a piece of paper and jotted down a list of the contacts he would have to get out of Holland in the event of invasion. Whether or not the list was still on him at the climax of this adventure only Stevens knew. Best *thinks* Stevens succeeded in destroying it.

It was shortly after four when the party arrived at the rendezvous, the red-brick Café Backus, just two hundred yards from the frontier. Nobody was in sight, but Best noticed that, for the first time in his experience, the frontier barrier on the German side had been lifted.

Best spotted Major Schemmel on the second-floor veranda of the Backus and saw him giving a signal with a sweeping move of his right arm.

He thought the major was beckoning him to drive up to the café but, just as he was bringing his car to a stop, he heard an outburst of shouting and shooting. A large, green, open car drove up to the café, and stopped as it hit the bumper of his own automobile. It was packed with men, two of whom sat on the hood firing submachine guns.

Stevens leaned over and said: "I am afraid our number is up, Best!" Next moment both Britons were subdued and handcuffs snapped on their wrists. With little courtesy, they were marched into Germany, as the frontier barrier slowly came down behind them.

The driver, Lemmens, brought up the rear, but there was no sign of Klop. In the commotion, the young officer tried to escape, but just as he was vanishing under a bush, a German spotted him. A machine gun opened up and the youthful "Cloppens" was mortally wounded.

What Best and Stevens should have suspected long before, since the Germans had managed their end of the plot with remarkable clumsiness, was now made abundantly evident: their fabulous plot was a German trap. The idea had originated in Heydrich's fertile brain. Its execution was assigned to a rising young star in the *Sicherheits Dienst*, Werner Schellenberg, only twenty-eight years old, a cold and calculating intellectual with a consummate talent for secret service work.

Schellenberg was "Major Schemmel." "I admit," Best later wrote, "that he had completely taken Stevens and me in when we met him in Holland, but this was not really surprising since he was exceptionally well-informed and had been well-briefed for the occasion. Besides, the man was a natural conspirator, who, as events showed, kept faith with no one."

Heydrich had scored a fantastic scoop although he failed to reach the German Opposition. Stevens and Best were merely at the fringes of the greater plot, knew none of its real leaders and few of its details, so they could reveal nothing about it during their prolonged interrogation by Schellenberg. But they were at the very heart of conventional espionage efforts aimed at Germany, the *spiritus rectors* of the British spy network operating inside the Reich.

The incident exposed the inadequacy of the British secret service, which was due to the incompetence of key personnel. The naïveté with which Stevens and Best fell into Schellenberg's trap indicated that they were by no means the ideal choices for such delicate jobs. They were tired adventurers, over-ripe for retirement.

The blow Schellenberg had dealt had a frightful impact on Whitehall's approach to the secret war in that it dissuaded the disillusioned and embittered British Secret Service from ever again dealing with even the most deserving Germans who came bearing such gifts. But at the same time, it also had a salutary effect. It led to the long overdue, complete reorganization of the British intelligence setup.

The whole incident shook British complacency to its roots, but the ultimate shock came from a venomous little touch administered by Schellenberg. Even as Stevens and Best were being safely salted away in the Gestapo cellars in Prinz Albrecht Strasse, Schellenberg used the wireless set-up they had created to send one last message to London. It read:

"Communication for any length of time with conceited and silly people is dull. You will understand, therefore, that we are giving it up. You are hereby heartily greeted by your affectionate German opposition.

The Gestapo."

In London the message was duly set down by the British operator who acknowledged it with a polite "Thank you" and, as usual, added his name—Walsh.

6

The Great Carillon

Early in 1937, Hitler had given Canaris the green light to establish an espionage network in Great Britain, and the delighted admiral set to work at once. Operating responsibility fell to Colonel Karl Busch, a veteran intelligence officer who headed the *Abwehr's* Anglo-American branch.

Busch set up not one, but two, separate rings in Britain. The first was made up of relatively petty agents. It included hundreds of German *maedchen* who were planted as domestic servants in the homes of important Britons. Like other spies, these girls were trained at the *Abwehr* school in Hamburg where they learned such diverse things as how to prepare English roast beef and how to operate a wireless transmitter.

Busch regarded this ring as useful, but expendable. It would gather handy information, but its major purpose was to act as a gigantic decoy. Busch expected that it would so absorb the attention of the woefully-undermanned British counter-espionage agencies that the second, and far deeper, ring would go undetected.

Most of the members of Ring No. 2 were dormant. They were to establish themselves in key positions in Britain but to do no peacetime work unless they came across something of the utmost importance. Only when war itself came were they to unpack their ingenious transmitters and go into action.

By 1939, both rings were functioning according to plan. And both were known to British counter-spies, thanks to a little hairdresser of Dundee, Scotland. Mrs. Jessie Jordan, a middle-aged, middle-class widow, led a humdrum middle-of-the-road life on Kinlock Street in Dundee. She was a Scotswoman, and average in every respect: homely, industrious and insufferably dull. Her beauty parlor was quite a favorite with the ladies of the neighborhood.

Mrs. Jordan was also a favorite of the mailman because she was always most generous with tips. She had reason for being so open-handed. People like Mrs. Jordan usually receive very little mail, but hers was exceptionally heavy, a fact that the mailman reported to his superiors. His report wound up on the desk of a big, bluff, broad-shouldered, stern-looking man, Colonel Hinchley Cooke, in Room 505 of the War Office. It was the room which housed MI.5, the counter-espionage service.

Mrs. Jordan was put under discreet surveillance, and soon Cooke learned some interesting facts about her. He found out that she was the widow of a German who had died fighting for the Kaiser in the First World War. Then it transpired that several times in 1937 she had gone surreptitiously to Germany. Although she said all of her relatives lived on the British Isles, she was receiving letters from the United States, France, Holland and even South Africa; and she was forever posting letters to all sorts of faraway places.

Mrs. Jordan's mail was quietly opened, and what Colonel Cooke read in those letters convinced him that the trim widow was the central maildrop of a broad German espionage net. She was arrested, tried and given a four-year sentence.

As is usual in such cases, suspect cards were prepared of people supposed to be in the ring; their identity was revealed by the surveillance of Mrs. Jordan, though they were not arrested. These persons were then shadowed and led the counter-espionage agents to still other suspects. In due course, the Jordan case yielded scores of suspects and Colonel Cooke was breathing a bit easier.

Fortunately for Cooke, Busch's formidable rings were showing their hands in still other ways. In Portslade, in Sussex Downs,

lived a retired officer of the British army, Ervine Batley, who
had an unusual hobby. An enthusiast of Sussex Downs, he
became an expert of the region and spent years preparing a
series of unique contour maps which became famous.

One day in 1938, a young man knocked at his door, and in-
troducing himself candidly as a German tourist on a hiking tour,
asked Captain Batley for some of his famous maps. The captain
tipped off the constable at Portslade and MI.5 was called.
Nothing was done to interfere with the young tourist's hike, but
he was shadowed from then on. He led Colonel Cooke's men
to a cluster of German agents.

At about the same time, a British subject named Joseph
Kelly was caught red-handed spying for the Germans. He was
a bricklayer and helped in the construction of several new
defense installations. He had access to blueprints and sold some
of them to the Nazis. Before he was arrested, he also led MI.5
to several of his associates. Among them was Walther Reinhardt,
a German intelligence director serving as consul in Liverpool.
Reinhardt was expelled in due course, but before he left he also
helped to enlarge the file of cards in the office of Colonel Cooke.

Far more important than these and similar haphazard leads
was a source MI.5 developed laboriously as an inside job. From
the fallen spies, Colonel Cooke found out that German agents
were trained in the *Abwehr* school in Hamburg. MI.5 decided
to smuggle a plant into the school. The man they picked for the
job was a young British linguist.

He managed to get a job in the *Abwehr* school, teaching
colloquial English to German spies about to go to England.
From then on, of course, MI.5 was able to accord every new
German agent arriving in England the reception due such special
tourists. They were not arrested, but all were placed under
surveillance. A known spy-at-large can be watched and can be
fed misleading information, whereas, if he is arrested, he is
likely to be replaced and it may take some time before his
replacement can be identified. In this particular case, a wholesale

detention of the youthful linguist's pupils would have made the *Abwehr* suspicious of the tutor himself.

This daring young man had several means of alerting MI.5 to incoming Germans. His favorite method of warning developed out of his native sense of humor. Agents going on a resident mission had to take a course from him in English habits and customs. He told them that those staid Britons were suckers for respectability, and, being a nation of shopkeepers, measured respectability in terms of pounds, shillings and pence.

He suggested, therefore, that when they arrived in Britain, they take their money to the nearest post office and open a postal savings account. But, he cautioned, it was not enough to do just that. One's respectability had to be demonstrated, and the people who were the most important to convince were the police. Therefore, he suggested that they lose their passbooks and report the loss to the police, who would thus learn they were men of means. At least a few of his pupils followed his advice. For this reason, anyone who was unfortunate enough to lose his savings book and to report it entered the select suspect list of MI.5.

From such diverse sources, MI.5 compiled a roster of German spies. On the eve of the war, MI.5 and Scotland Yard's Special Branch had a fairly good idea of the makeup of the two rings. All told it was estimated there were a minimum of three thousand German espionage sharks in Britain, of whom some four hundred journeymen belonged to Colonel Busch's Ring No. 1 and thirty-five key agents to his Ring No. 2. The rest were minor agents, spies-at-large, free-lancers, informants, pro-Nazi busybodies or dupes.

If MI.5 and the Special Branch were doing such a superb job, it was partly because the old system was well oiled, and partly because those who now administered it were exceptionally competent men. MI.5 was headed by one of Britain's outstanding espionage specialists, the formidable Staffordshire squire Sir Vernon George Waldegrave Kell, one of the authentic mystery men of the world. Though he spent some forty-odd years (some of them very odd, indeed) in his country's service, he remained totally unknown to his fellow countrymen.

At New Scotland Yard, Sir Norman Kendal and Commissioner Ronald Howe, stern-faced, fish-eyed, thin-lipped bosses of the Criminal Investigation Department, were General Kell's opposite numbers. Out in the field, the real nemesis of foreign spies was Cooke, along with Assistant Commissioner Albert Canning, who headed Scotland Yard's Special Branch, the organization that comes closest to the British idea of a secret political police. Addicted to striped suits and polka dot ties, and to an oversized Homburg pulled down over his brow, Canning could have been mistaken for a barrister.

When Hitler attacked Poland, both MI.5 and the Special Branch were alerted to stand by. On September 3, shortly before the expiration of the British ultimatum, the code word was flashed to the War Office and Scotland Yard. The great spy hunt was on. The job was superhuman. The suspect lists had grown to almost seventy-five thousand entries. Not all of these were spies, by any means, but the spies were in that crowd.

During the night from September 3 to 4, inspectors and special agents of Scotland Yard, with some two thousand detectives and uniformed policemen, made thousands of calls. Before the night was out, four hundred and thirty-five persons received polite invitations to accompany the officers to various centers prepared for their reception. In subsequent days, weeks and months, the cases of seventy-three thousand two hundred and thirty-five secondary suspects were scrutinized and five hundred and sixty-nine additional foreign agents were spotted.

With regard to some six thousand individuals, MI.5 and the C.I.D. were not quite sure, but these were not the times to give such people the benefit of the doubt. *Habeas corpus* was suspended for the duration. These suspected enemy agents had their movements strictly curtailed.

And the number of spies Canaris had sent to Britain was not much greater than the number of German spies Kell and

Canning managed to catch. Colonel Busch's two phenomenal spy rings were unceremoniously smashed, just when they were needed most. It was Canaris' first major defeat.

Back in Germany, there was a man who looked exactly like a Hollywood actor playing the role of a German intelligence officer, Captain Herbert Wichmann. He was big and bluff, with a Prussian cropped head and dueling scars, heavy-set but agile, heavy-handed but alert, not exceptionally brilliant but industrious and efficient; the very prototype of the competent, hard-working, self-effacing German staff officer. He was chief of the British desk at the *Abwehr*. Within a few moments after the outbreak of war, Wichmann was sitting in a guarded communication room of the Hamburg wireless center, breathing down the neck of the radiomen who flashed prearranged signals to agents in Britain and France. The code word, repeated again and again at intervals, alerted his men to go into action at once, and to operate henceforth to the best of their abilities and according to their instructions, for better or for worse.

Captain Wichmann could not imagine, and had no reason to suspect, that virtually his whole British network was sitting, not at their wireless sets, but behind the bars of Wormwood Scrubs, the famous prison that MI.5 had taken over for the duration. So he was not surprised when answers began to come from their transmitters operated by radiomen of the British Secret Service. In long hours of meticulous practice, these Englishmen had learned to imitate the highly individualistic touch of each German on the Morse key. This characteristic touch is the basic identification mark of agents who operate transmitters. So perfect was the mimicry of the British substitutes that the *Abwehr's* radio operators never found out the ruse.

The continued operation of a fallen spy's radio is one of the favorite tricks of espionage, a ruse that is both old and common and yet hardly ever fails to be effective. The Germans coined the word *Funkspiel* for it; literally this means, "radio game." That translation, however, does not express the picturesque quality of the German term. The word implies a mysterious carillon that rings out in the ether, sounding a Lorelei tune to mislead or entrap men who listen to it.

The great carillon resounded at the hands of British bell-ringers. The English continued this game for fifteen months, during which time Canaris felt safe and smug. He even boasted to Count Ciano of Italy of his formidable network in England and mentioned with particular pride a certain agent who was making up to twenty-five transmissions a day. As far as the Germans knew, only one of their key agents had been lost and even that, they thought, was due to an unfortunate accident.

During the great round-up in early September, a broker who lived in a London suburb tuned in his radio to listen to BBC's 9 o'clock news and was irked by some strange interference that came and went on schedule, lasting exactly seven minutes, from 9:02 to 9:09, four nights in a row. He called the police, and Scotland Yard sent a detector van to the suburb. It did not take long to locate a lonely house on a sideroad from which, it seemed, someone was sending faint Morse signals on an unlicensed transmitter.

The owner of the house was a meek little Government clerk, "a very 'umble person," as Dickens would have said. When detectives searched his house, they found that the source of those crackling sounds was a wireless transmitter of a type that they had never seen. It had but a single tube and operated on three small batteries. The whole set, including its tiny Morse tapper, weighed only four pounds. It was the famous Afu, a little "whispering box," sending out the faintest of signals. They were virtually inaudible in England but could be picked up by a special *Abwehr* station near Hamburg.

The clerk was soon salted away in Wormwood Scrubs, but his set was left undisturbed. A Secret Service signaler continued to send messages in his code. One day, in great excitement, the substitute agent radioed Wichmann that he had succeeded in procuring information of the utmost urgency, so important, indeed, that he was most reluctant to put it on the air. He asked the captain's permission to come to Germany so that he could bring the message in person.

This was an unusual request and required high level consideration. Transportation was not a simple matter. The best means of getting an agent out of England was by submarine, but Doenitz's boats were badly needed elsewhere. Nevertheless, Canaris coaxed from Hitler an order to place a U-boat at the *Abwehr's* disposal.

Early in October, the agent was radioed his instructions: he would be picked up on the next totally moonless night in a lonely, rock-encrusted bay on the Welsh coast.

At 2:00 a.m. on the night fixed for the operation, the vague flickers of a flashlight's staccato signals sent thin ribbons of light from the shore out to the black water. At intervals of ten minutes each, those vague lights flickered. An hour later came the answering light. The submarine had arrived.

Abruptly a bright light flashed. A moment later the air was filled with the din of battle. British destroyers had been lying in ambush for the U-boat and they sank it in a matter of minutes.

Captain Wichmann never found out what had happened. When nothing more was heard from either the sub or the agent, it was presumed that both had been lost after the boat had succeeded in the pick-up. It was a long time before Doenitz again consented to loan one of his U-boats to the confounded *Abwehr*.

7

Straws in the North Wind

In the book of traitors, Major Vidkun Quisling occupies a page to himself, partly because his treachery was so enormous and partly because his motives were so puzzling. Quisling *was* a traitor on a staggering scale, but he himself never conceded it. He regarded himself as a reincarnation of Harald the Conqueror, destined by Divine resolve to lead his people into some kind of promised land. What that land would be exactly, and how he would get there, Quisling did not quite know.

He was born in 1887 in Tyrdesdal, Norway, the son of a village preacher. It was still a wild region; bears roamed the countryside. Quisling abandoned the valley quite early, but the impact of his "barbarian birthplace" left him with feelings of inferiority and delusions of superiority. He was imbued with broad humanitarian impulses: "As a young boy," he once said, "I wanted to preach on Sundays and heal on weekdays." He became a professional soldier instead.

At the military academy, he was a superbly industrious and brilliant student, but he was stubborn, taciturn, and he secluded himself in an impenetrable shell. Before he was thirty, he was a captain in the Norwegian Army's General Staff; then he became a military attaché at St. Petersburg and Helsingfors. The Russian revolution caused an upheaval within him, and in 1922, he turned his back on the army, became an assistant of Fridtjof Nansen, the great humanitarian, ministering to the needs of Russian refugees. In 1927, he was back in the Norwegian Legation in Russia and, during the break of Anglo-Soviet relations, he represented British interests in the U.S.S.R.

Despite the admitted brilliance of his work, Quisling never ceased to puzzle even those who seemed to be closest to him. When asked about his assistant, Nansen remarked, "I don't know Quisling, because I cannot fathom him."

In the late Twenties, Quisling's career slowed to a standstill. Gradually he came to feel he was the victim of a conspiracy. From his morose, truculent, self-imposed isolation, he groped his way to others like himself and formed a clandestine fraternity of disgruntled patriots. One of them was a certain Hagelin, a prominent Oslo merchant; another was a colonel named Konrad Sunlo, commandant of the Narvik garrison, a dreamer of totalitarian dreams at his Arctic outpost.

Quisling became obsessed with a hatred of Bolshevism, which he viewed as a Jewish conspiracy, and he formed the National Unity Party. In 1931, he was made Minister of War in a hodge-podge coalition government, and promptly moved to bend the office to his personal ambition. He became involved in all sorts of nebulous conspiracies until his schemes proved too much for the tolerant Norwegians and he was kicked out.

It was at this loneliest stage in his career that the Nazis, looking for allies abroad, spotted him. Quisling was discovered by Alfred Rosenberg, the intellectual *condottieri,* who was always on the lookout for unemployed plotters.

In 1938, Rosenberg's secretary, Thilo von Trotha, visited Oslo, ostensibly as a tourist, and called on Quisling. The self-styled Norwegian Colossus impressed von Trotha as a lone wolf, difficult to handle, so nothing developed then. But the situation changed abruptly; in 1939, Quisling decided to revive contact with Rosenberg. Upon Rosenberg's invitation, Quisling made a trip to Berlin and met him in his house in Dahlem where the major was driven in a curtained car amidst theatrical secrecy.

His tongue loosened by generous portions of aquavit, Quisling treated his host to a dissertation he was never to forget.

The Norwegian candidly censured Germany for her lack of interest in his homeland. "He pointed out," Rosenberg later reported to Hitler, "the decisive geopolitical advantage of Norway in the Scandinavian region and the advantages gained by the Power in control of the Norwegian coast. . . ." Quisling also requested support for his party and press in Norway, basing his request on the "Pan-Germanic" ideology. Rosenberg agreed to lend him this support.

In August, twenty-five members of Quisling's *Nasjonal Samling* were secretly brought to Germany for a fourteen-day course, to learn the methodology of Nazi activism. At the same time, Rosenberg tried to peddle Quisling's services to various German agencies. He tried to interest Hitler's confidential secretariat in the Norwegian, and also Goering, the latter with the bait of Norwegian real estate as possible landing fields for *Luftwaffe* aircraft. For a while, there were no takers. Rosenberg was embarrassed because he had promised Quisling money and his own Bureau had no appreciable funds.

At last, in the fall of 1939, he found a customer for his client: Admiral Schniewind, Grand Admiral Raeder's chief of staff. Raeder had long been yearning for an outlet to the North Sea and eyed Norway as an ideal base. As early as October 10, 1939, the Grand Admiral tried to coax Hitler into an invasion of western Scandinavia, but Hitler was too busy with other plans. The admiral then detoured into a conspiratorial side alley and was most receptive when Schniewind told him of Quisling's availability. Rosenberg bolstered the case with a memo in which he spoke of Quisling in glowing terms and outlined what the fellow could do for the German navy.

"According to this plan," he wrote, "a number of picked Norwegians will be given training in Germany for this particular task. They will be told exactly what to do, and will be assisted by seasoned National Socialists who are experienced in such matters. These trained men are then to be sent back to Norway as quickly as possible, where details will be discussed. Several focal points in Oslo will have to be occupied with lightning speed, and simultaneously the German Navy with contingents of the German Army will have to put in an appearance at a prearranged bay outside Oslo in answer to a special summons from the new Norwegian Government [presumably that of Quisling]. Quisling has no doubt," Rosenberg added, "that such a *coup,* achieved instantaneously, would at once meet with the approval of those sections of the Army with which he now has connections."

Raeder asked Rosenberg to produce Quisling. Rosenberg took Quisling and Hagelin, the Oslo merchant and Quisling's co-conspirator, to see Raeder on December 11. Quisling urged his German partners to act quickly lest the British move in ahead of them.

Raeder undertook to sell Quisling to Hitler. On December 16, the major was presented to the Fuehrer. It was a moist, sentimental meeting—the spirit of Nordic brotherhood dripping like dew—but it was not quite satisfying to Quisling. He found the Fuehrer evasive, even negative. Above all else, Quisling was appalled to find that Hitler took his pact with Stalin rather seriously and refused to be drawn into talks about a possible Russo-German clash.

Behind Hitler's hesitation was both ignorance and ruse. He knew little about this fellow Quisling and had not thought seriously of an extension of the war in the direction of Norway. He did not want to show his hand to this foreigner about whom he knew nothing except Raeder's and Rosenberg's word. Quisling might be a double agent, an Allied tool to obtain information about his plans—straight from the horse's mouth.

When Quisling returned to the Chancellery two days later, he found Hitler in a more accommodating spirit. He now agreed that a special staff be appointed under Raeder to explore the potentialities of Quisling's military recommendations. The political exploration was to be done by Rosenberg. In Oslo, Commander Schreiber, the Naval Attaché, was to do the plotting with Quisling. From the Norwegian's point of view, the Fuehrer's most important concession came at the end of the second meeting. He promised two hundred thousand gold marks for Quisling from the secret funds managed by Counselor von Grundherr in the Foreign Ministry. But the Foreign Ministry still refused to subsidize Quisling whom they regarded as a crackpot, willing to sell his country but incapable of delivering it. Rosenberg never managed to pry the funds loose.

For all practical purposes, the Quisling story ended there. He lingers on in odium as the man who handed his country to the Nazis on a platter, but, in reality, Quisling had no share in the rape of Norway when it came, not because he was not willing, but because the Germans did not need him.

Until January, 1940, Admiral Canaris knew little if anything of Quisling's perambulations, so closely was the wayward Norwegian held by Rosenberg and Raeder. The *Abwehr* entered the conspiracy against Norway as the result of a report from one of its V-men stationed at Metz in France. On January 4 this agent discovered that the *Chasseurs Alpins,* a division of crack mountain troops, had been withdrawn from the Maginot Line and shipped to England on the first leg of a trip to somewhere in Northern Europe—possibly to Finland to aid the Finns in their war with the Russians, or to Norway to seize Narvik.

The report was brought to the attention of the chief of the Hamburg outpost, Franz Liedig by name, a Navy commander on the retired list. Liedig immediately carried it personally to Canaris who, in turn, took it to Hitler. This piece of information may well have sealed the fate of Norway since, as we have seen, Hitler had not been much interested in that country, but he was determined to keep it out of Allied hands at any cost.

From then on, Canaris kept a finger in the Scandinavian pie. In February, when planning for the "Operation Weser Exercise," as it was called, got under way in earnest, and a special task force of planners was set up at *Wehrmacht* headquarters—camouflaged as "Commando for Special Employment No. 31"—the admiral managed to plant Commander Liedig as the top intelligence officer of the enterprise.

Liedig had an efficient network going in Norway. Its members were chiefly coast watchers at Oslo, Bergen, Christiansand, Stavenger, Narvik and other ports. Their job was to observe the movement of ships and especially to report promptly the departure and routing of convoys bound for England. This was no easy task. Convoy information was dispensed only to the skippers of the ships and then only a few hours before sailing. But Liedig's network operated with phenomenal skill and success. He boasted that reports from his agents enabled the *Luftwaffe* and the U-boats to sink one hundred and fifty thousand gross tons of Allied shipping within a few months in 1939-1940.

Upon receipt of his instructions from Commando 31, he went to Norway and personally organized an expansion of his network. The old coast watchers had to go to work also as collectors, and a second network was set up to procure additional information. Commander Liedig soon had Norway well covered.

While preparations for the "exercise" progressed, the over-inflated balloon of Quisling was losing air rapidly. Even Rosenberg had to concede that much and there was little he could do about it. Hitler probably did not even think of Quisling when on March 1, 1940, he ordered the *Wehrmacht* High Command to prepare for the occupation of Norway and Denmark; and he certainly acted without the slightest consideration for the hapless Norwegian when on April 1, he ordered the invasion to begin at 5:15 a.m. on April 9. On the contrary, a puzzling last-minute development in Oslo must have recalled to him his original doubts about Quisling.

On March 26, Commander Schreiber, the German Naval Attaché, reported from Oslo that Norwegian anti-aircraft and coastal defense units had been suddenly given permission to open fire without waiting for higher orders. Schreiber, who had kept more or less aloof from Quisling, suggested that there must have been a leak somewhere and hinted vaguely that it could have been in Quisling's circle. After Schreiber's report, Quisling was cut off from any information. On April 4, he hurried to Denmark for a secret meeting with a senior German officer. The general forced from him the confession that his own grandiose plans had failed to mature. After his initial bluster failed to move the German, Quisling went down on his knees to plead with the general to hurry up and start the invasion. Until then, the general had regarded him only as a crank—now he turned away from him with contempt: even he could not stomach such abject treachery.

Both Quisling and his mentors lost their influence on the operation. Rosenberg was eliminated and Raeder was superseded by General von Falkenhorst who refused to have anything to do with "that crackpot." Minister Braeuer, following his instructions from the Foreign Ministry, conspired on a far higher social level. He tried to draw King Haakon VII into a pro-German plot and cultivated Foreign Minister Koht whom he thought to be sympathetic to the German cause and who might form a pro-Nazi coalition government.

At 4:00 a.m., on April 9, Commander Schreiber, the Naval Attaché, donned his uniform and went down to the harbor to greet the incoming German warships. "Everything that I can do here," he wrote in his diary before he left, "has been considered and prepared down to the smallest detail." On his drive to the harbor, Schreiber passed the British Embassy and saw a thin ribbon of smoke rising from the garden. "They are burning their papers," he said to himself with a smug smile.

He waited in vain. Far out in Oslo Fjord, the Norwegian batteries heeded their instructions and challenged the Germans as soon as they sailed into view. The ships which Schreiber had come to greet were at the bottom of the fjord or stopped cold with mortal wounds.

At 9:30 a.m., Schreiber despaired, rushed back to his office and tried to raise Berlin by radio, but he could not establish contact. Schreiber now issued orders to burn his papers. He expected the police to break into the house momentarily because Quisling had failed to come through with his vainglorious *coup*.

At last, after noon, a *Luftwaffe* airlift brought in German soldiers who occupied the stunned and sullen city. The government fled toward the north. The King went with the government.

At 5:00 p.m., when Oslo was virtually secured by the Germans, Quisling came out of his hole. So minor was his influence that most of the German generals did not even know he existed. When General Eberhardt arrived and established himself in the Grand Hotel, he found Quisling in a suite on the third floor of the hotel, claiming that he was the new Premier of Norway. Eberhardt had never heard of the man before. He called Braeuer in the German Legation and said, "There is a crank here on the third floor who says he is the chief of a new Norwegian government. Shall I throw him out? Or shall I arrest him?"

But by then, Braeuer's own game was also played out. The King was gone and Koht refused the Nazi invitation with indignation. There was nobody left but Quisling. Braeuer told General Eberhardt: "It is all right. He's a fellow named Quisling. He *is* the new Premier, so leave him alone."

The terror regime over which Quisling presided actually became a liability to the Germans. It did not subdue the Norwegians and so he proved a flop for the second time. Without Quisling's terror, there would probably have been no effective resistance; as it was, the people of Norway rose to harass their oppressors without a moment's let-up and eventually to evict them, leaving Quisling alone to be shot.

When Philip of Macedonia, the father of Alexander the Great, was told that a certain city in his army's path was impregnable, he asked: "Is there not a pathway to it wide enough for an ass laden with gold?"

It was the fate of Vidkun Quisling to be nothing but an ass.

In Denmark the Germans had no Quisling; they had someone far better, Commander Franz Liedig. Liedig went far beyond the usual scope of a mere intelligence officer; he blossomed out in the role of the conqueror.

Liedig was an avaricious reader of everything that bore on

the work of the secret service, and among his favorites was a little book published in 1931 by the Italian Curzio Malaparte, called *Coup d'Etat: The Technique of Revolution.* The first chapter of this book, entitled "The Bolshevik Coup d'Etat and Trotsky's Tactics," presented a largely apocryphal account of the seizure of Petrograd by the Bolsheviks in October, 1917.

According to Malaparte, Lenin planned to overthrow the Russian democratic regime that had followed the Czar by mass demonstrations and the conventional means of revolution; but Trotsky claimed he could achieve the same result with a handful of terrorists and saboteurs, simply by paralyzing the government through cutting it off from the outside world. In his account of Trotsky's *coup,* Malaparte described in fascinating (though fictitious) detail how Trotsky accomplished the task; how he sent out his men to practice the *coup* in "invisible maneuvers"; how his agents located the sensitive focal points of the government—telephone exchanges, power stations, even pinpoints like individual railroad switches—and how they eventually struck. Instead of moving the masses, as Lenin proposed, Trotsky's men blew fuses, threw switches, and within a couple of hours they had completely isolated the government which had to surrender in its impotence.

This was exactly how Liedig planned to conquer Copenhagen. In a report of one of his agents he discovered that the nerve center of the whole Danish Army was in an ancient fortress on the outskirts of the capital. He figured that if he could seize the fort right at the outset of the campaign, he would be able to paralyze the Danish Army completely and make resistance impossible.

Liedig's plan was accepted and this was, in fact, how Copenhagen was "captured." He needed only a small contingent of soldiers for the *coup,* and a few agents to assure that the roads leading to the fortress had not been mined. He put the troops into a floating Trojan Horse, a German freighter which sailed peacefully into Copenhagen harbor with nothing to indicate that her "cargo" consisted of German storm troopers specially trained for the *coup* à la Trotsky.

One thing could have wrecked Liedig's scheme. A colleague of his within the *Abwehr,* the determined anti-Nazi Colonel Oster, was exasperated by the prospect of Hitler's continuing aggrandizement, and betrayed, not Liedig's shrewd design of which he knew nothing, but the imminent invasion of Norway and Denmark. On April 1, only eight days before the projected D-day, Oster sneaked information to the Danish Naval Attaché in Berlin about the invasion plans; and on April 4, he alerted the Norwegian Military Attaché.

The Norwegian was apparently incredulous, at best, since he did not even forward the information to Oslo. The Dane relayed the message to Copenhagen but his superiors simply refused to believe it.

On April 9, 1940, Denmark fell to the Germans, exactly as Commander Liedig had planned and scheduled it.

In capturing Copenhagen, the Germans also fell into possession of something which might have been the most important booty of the war—had they only known it. That "something" was a laboratory at the Copenhagen University, directed by Dr. Niels Bohr, the celebrated Nobel Prize physicist. To the Germans he was just an egghead and they let him alone. Dr. Bohr on his part, busied himself with teaching and lived quietly to encourage the Germans in their indifference. But behind closed doors, in the utmost privacy of his private laboratory, he worked on a mysterious project whose secret would have been worth millions to the Nazis. He was collaborating with his American friends on a program of atomic research. The Bohr laboratory was as important a way-station on the road to the atomic bomb as anything that then existed anywhere in the United States and Britain. It was, indeed, an integral part of the project, except that it was behind the brown curtain, within the reach of the Nazis.

For years during the occupation, Dr. Bohr continued his

fantastic double life in science. He had a small supply of heavy water, a precious possession for this particular research. Had the Nazis found out about it, they would probably have been alerted to Bohr's secret. To conceal it, he kept the heavy water in a large beer bottle and stored it in his refrigerator with the rest of his beer.

As Bohr's work advanced, it became necessary to bring him out of Denmark. By then, it was 1944. The British secret service organized the escape. The scientist was told to be at a pier at a given hour after dark where a small boat would meet him and take him to Sweden. He startled his companions when they saw him lugging along a large bottle of beer. They decided for themselves that the funny scientist must be a beer addict. In Sweden Dr. Bohr went straight to the Nobel Laboratory for a reunion with Dr. Lise Meitner, a colleague who had preceded him there, and handed her the precious bottle for safekeeping. Dr. Meitner examined its contents more for sentimental than scientific purposes, and she exclaimed in a voice of real anguish. It was real beer. The bottle with the heavy water still reposed in Bohr's Copenhagen refrigerator.

For the next twenty-four hours that confounded bottle became the most important target for the Allied secret services. A team of the Danish underground sneaked into the abandoned Bohr house, reached the icebox without incident, took the important bottle and smuggled it safely to Bohr in Sweden.

They never did understand why they had to go to so much trouble just to get a bottle of Danish beer for a bibulous old professor.

8

Behind the Battle of Europe

Between the fall of Poland and the opening of the Norwegian invasion lay one of the strangest periods in history—the months of the "phony war". Standing on the ruins of Warsaw in September, 1939, Hitler appeared to be satisfied with the carnage he had wrought, but deep within himself he was perplexed. What to do next?

He toyed with both peace and war. On October 6, 1939, he invited Britain and France to talk peace, but was rebuffed. Groping for something else, he kept his generals on pins and needles while he played with half a dozen ideas; for each they had to design a possible campaign. "Sunflower" was the name for a possible campaign in North Africa aimed at Tripoli. "Alp Violet" was to be aimed at Albania. "Felix" contemplated crossing Spain to seize Gibraltar. And "Operation Yellow" was to conquer the Low Countries.

Traveling salesmen flocked to Berlin—native conspirators from Holland, Belgium and Norway—peddling their countries to Hitler. From Holland came a fluffy, shifty-eyed philistine named Anton Mussert, a puppet dangling from strings held by the *Abwehr*. From Belgium came a scheming, pampered dandy, Leon Degrelle. Before long, Hitler succumbed to their siren songs. He pushed "Yellow" to the top of his shopping list and issued top-secret Order No. 4402/39, instructing Army Group B of General von Bock "to make all preparations according to special orders, for immediate invasion of Dutch and Belgian territory if the political situation so demands". Shortly afterwards, A-Day (as it was called) was fixed for the invasion. Weather permitting, it was to be November 12. A phony war, indeed!

This pending campaign was consistently jeopardized by the twin scourges of the secret service, delays and leaks. The invasion had to be postponed again and again, and, during the procrastination, details of the design came to be known.

Among the first to learn of the plan were the Italians, many of whom hated the Nazis in spite of their formal alliance. The Italian military attaché in Berlin tipped off both his Belgian and Dutch opposite numbers. (The Dutchman, Colonel Sas, already had the information from Oster.) In Rome, the Foreign Minister, Count Ciano, also warned the Belgians and Dutch. At great personal risk, a leading member of the German opposition, Minister von Buelow-Schwante, went to Brussels and, in a clandestine audience, delivered a warning in person to King Leopold. Both the Belgians and the Dutch skeptically shrugged off the warnings.

Just then something quite extraordinary happened that should have lent weight to these scattered storm signals. On January 10, 1940, a *Luftwaffe* plane, piloted by a Major Hoenemanns, was on a flight to Cologne with a copy of the Dutch-Belgian deployment plan for the command of Army Group B. Hoenemanns was unaware of the exact nature of the papers he carried and took his mission somewhat lightly. For one thing, he took a hitchhiker along, a General Staff officer; for another, he was somewhat careless in plotting his course. He lost his way and came down in a field near Machelen on the Meuse inside Belgium.

Hoenemanns and his hitchhiker were duly alarmed when they found out where they were and decided to burn the papers. It so happened that both men were non-smokers and they had no matches on hand. The first man to reach the spot was a Belgian and Hoenemanns immediately asked him for matches. He complied and they set to burning the papers. Before the two men could get too far with it, a Belgian patrol closed in, extinguished the blaze and arrested the Germans. Interrogation revealed that Major Hoenemanns belonged to the 7th *Luftwaffe* Division of parachutists with headquarters in Berlin and that he was attached to the *Luftwaffe* Unit 220, whose plans were to transport the 22nd Infantry Division by air to points of attack. British combat intelligence identified the division as specially trained for the landing of airborne troops in Belgian territory.

Although badly charred, the documents could still be salvaged. They were three in number, containing instructions for the *Luftwaffe's* VIII Aviation Corps, describing in detail the impending attack on Belgium and the role parachutists and airborne infantry were to play. It was a complete blueprint of the campaign.

Although they became somewhat apprehensive, the Belgians were not unduly alarmed. They evaluated their find from all angles and finally decided that the whole incident was a clever ruse staged by the Germans to drive fear into Belgian hearts in order to tighten their neutrality. Anxious to avoid any complications, the Belgians hastily repatriated their unwelcome guests, returned the stray plane and closed the incident.

In Germany, Hoenemanns' ill-fated mission created understandable consternation and led to another postponement of the operation. What's more, it induced the High Command to redraft the whole plan.

While this was going on, Allied intelligence preoccupied itself with fantastic projects rather than with the business at hand. Some efforts were made to establish the order of battle of the German Army, but virtually nothing was seriously undertaken to discover the intentions of Hitler or to cover the movements of his forces and to conclude from these movements the direction in which he planned to go. While Germany was feverishly preparing for the campaign in the West, Allied intelligence concluded, from the apparent idleness of the *Wehrmacht*, that

Hitler had shot his bolt and was bogged down in melancholy confusion, accompanied by growing dissidence within the *Wehrmacht* High Command.

French *Service de Renseignement* was now headed by General Rivet, an excellent and a gallant officer, but a stranger to the specific problems of a secret service at war. The deficiencies of the organization baffled those in the field. "To be perfectly frank," wrote the historian Marc Block, then serving as a reserve officer in the field, "more than once, I found myself wondering how much of this muddled thinking was due to lack of skill, how much to conscious guile. Every officer in charge of an Intelligence section lived in a state of constant terror that, when the blow fell, events might blow sky-high all the conclusions that he had told the general in command were 'absolutely certain'. To put before him a wide choice of mutually contradictory inferences ensured that no matter what might happen, one could say with an air of triumph—'If *only* you had listened to my advice!' Officers whose job resembled mine never got any information at all about the enemy, save what they were lucky enough to pick up in general conversations, or as a result of some chance meeting—in other words, almost exactly nil."

French combat intelligence officers in the field tried to take matters into their own hands, but their efforts were sabotaged from above. For example, it was imperative to establish what stocks of motor fuel the French could expect to find on the spot should they be forced to move into Belgium to meet the Germans. The Belgian General Staff, inspired by the King's devotion to strict neutrality, proved highly un-cooperative. A French intelligence officer with General Blanchard's army heard of a certain Belgian fuel dump and established contact with a confidential informant who gave him the required data about the capacity of the tanks. Moreover, the man volunteered to keep the tanks filled to capacity if that was what the French General Staff wanted. "This would make your supply problem easier," he said, "in the event of your finding yourselves constrained, some day, to move your troops into the territory in which they are situated. Alternatively, I can maintain the bare minimum necessary for the requirements of peaceful commerce, thereby avoiding the danger of having to abandon the valuable resources to the Germans. It is for the French General Staff to decide. As soon as I know what they want done, I will take the necessary steps."

The matter was referred to a higher echelon of intelligence, but the officer in charge said, "Our job is to collect information, not to make decisions", and refused to have anything to do with the matter. The young officer was shunted from one office to another and in each he heard the same formula. Thus rebuffed, the young man decided to resolve the issue on his own level. He sent his contact a coded message, "Don't fill the tanks," justifying his insubordination with a melancholy rationalization: "Unbroken silence on our part," he said, "would have betrayed to this foreigner the shilly-shallying state of mind of the French General Staff. It was bad enough to know it ourselves."

The German preparations, of course, were moving rapidly ahead. One problem plagued the top brass: how could the Germans prevent the bridges over the River Maas and the Albert Canal from being destroyed? If they could be seized intact, the army could sweep over them and seal the fate of the Low Countries in a matter of days. Early in November, a conference was held in the Chancellery to discuss this problem. Hitler presided and Canaris was in attendance. The *Abwehr* was ordered to prepare a plan for the seizure of those bridges by a *ruse de guerre*, by sabotage troops dressed in Dutch and Belgian uniforms.

Back in the *Fuchsbau*, Canaris called the keeper of his depot at Quenzsee to inquire how the *Abwehr* stood with Dutch army uniforms. He was told Quenzsee had some, but they were out of date. The *Abwehr* needed a few up-to-date pattern uniforms to enable the tailors (inmates of concentration camps) to make enough uniforms for the adventurous admiral's little land army.

The problem was referred to Commander Kilwen, head

of the Dutch desk of the *Abwehr,* and he in turn got in touch with Mussert in Holland. The Dutch Fuehrer decided to steal the uniforms, but to camouflage the theft as common, garden-variety burglary. Mussert handed the job to a trusted member of his bodyguard who was a professional burglar in private life.

The raid on the Dutch army depot was reminiscent of what New York burglars call a "Seventh Avenue heist." Mussert's burglars got what Canaris needed, but the thief was caught on Belgian soil with the uniforms in his possession and the cat was out of the bag: he confessed that he had been in the process of doing a "job" for the Germans and that Canaris was the mastermind behind the burglary.

Strangely enough, the incident struck the Dutch and the Belgians as extremely funny. They were far more amused at the plight of the clumsy burglar than alarmed by the implications of the burglary. A Flemish newspaper published a cartoon showing a grinning Goering, dressed in the uniform of a Brussels street car conductor, admiring himself in front of a mirror.

Canaris was called on the carpet by Hitler and Goering. He went to the meeting well prepared, with newspaper clippings and agent reports, assuring his bosses that the Dutch and the Belgians suspected nothing or else they wouldn't have treated the whole thing as a joke.

But Canaris still did not have the uniforms. He sent to Holland one of his best agents, whose specialty was surreptitious entry. Where the burglar failed, the *Abwehr* thief succeeded brilliantly. With the help of the Mussert organization, he sneaked into the depot—on a night when it was guarded by a Dutch soldier who was a Nazi sympathizer—picked a full selection of Dutch uniforms and sent them, in the German Military Attaché's bulging pouch (which, of course, enjoyed immunity from search), to Quenzsee. From there on, General von Lahousen, a former Austrian intelligence officer who was taken over by the *Abwehr* after the *Anschluss,* did the planning. Lahousen had his own sabotage troops, the Brandenburg Regiment, but it was not big enough to handle such a complex operation. Lahousen flew to Breslau and from that location with *Abwehr* volunteers organized Special Battalion 100 to take care of the Maastricht bridges, with one of his officers, Lieutenant Hocke, in command. From his regular sabotage troops he then formed Special Battalion 800, with Lieutenant Walther in command, to carry out the operation at Gennep.

At Gennep a platoon of Battalion 800 was to be "captured" by agents of Mussert disguised as Dutch frontier guards; the German "prisoners" were then to be escorted to the bridges, which they were to seize with the active co-operation of their hosts. On A-Day, May 10, 1940, well before zero hour, Walther led his Battalion 800 to the rendezvous with the Mussert agents. The Dutch traitors apparently disarmed their "prisoners", but left with them handgrenades and automatic pistols concealed under unseasonable greatcoats. With the help of their "captors", these "prisoners" pounced upon the Dutch guards at the Gennep bridges, who did not even know the war was on. The operation was a resounding success.

Things did not go as well at Maastricht, perhaps because (1) those *Abwehr* volunteers from Breslau did not have the savvy of the men of Battalion 800; (2) they lacked the assistance of Mussert's men; and (3) because the Dutch regulars guarding the bridges were not paralyzed by the sudden appearance of transparently phony Dutch soldiers driving up in cars. The bogus Dutchmen were greeted by volleys of shots. Lieutenant Hocke was killed and, in the ensuing confusion, the real Dutchmen managed to blow up the three bridges.

The mishap stunned Canaris. He drove to the spot and was visibly depressed when he realized he could not hand up to Hitler this special invasion-day gift. He found whole columns of German tanks and trucks jammed on the roads, waiting while engineers were building pontoon bridges. Even so, Dutch resistance was crumbling rapidly. The fiasco was forgiven and forgotten when, only five days later, Dutch resistance collapsed and the campaign was over.

Canaris had been busy elsewhere, too: his *Abwehr* organized an attempt to abduct Queen Wilhelmina. She was to be quarantined at the moment of the invasion to prevent her from leaving Holland. Hitler had been gravely disturbed by King Haakon's flight from Norway, an unexpected move that led to certain political complications, serious in aspect, during the consolidation of that conquest. Now, in the Netherlands, he was determined to foil any such attempt on Queen Wilhelmina's part, lest she become, like the King, the focal point of resistance. Commander Protze in Wassenaar and Klewen of the *Abwehr's* Dutch desk were ordered to pin down the Queen at The Hague. The plans went astray; she was gone by the time a delegation of Protze's thugs reached her palace to carry out Hitler's order.

The Queen had no intention of leaving Holland and was absent by a misunderstanding. She had asked the British to send some fighter planes to go into action against the German bombers. Her telegram was garbled in translation and in London it was thought she was asking for a plane to fly her out of Holland. No plane could be sent, but a destroyer was diverted to take the Queen on board.

The Queen embarked and told the captain to take her to Flushing in Holland; no matter how he tried, however, the captain could not enter the harbor. In the end, he told the Queen there was nothing to do except to head for a British port. She arrived at Buckingham Palace at 5 p.m. on May 10, wearing a tin hat, bedraggled and worn, still moaning that she could not stay with her people in their darkest hour. So if anybody succeeded in kidnaping Wilhelmina, it was the British, but whether or not there was any premeditation in the act, nobody will say, even today.

The Netherlands resisted for only five days. The King of the Belgians, refusing to leave despite Churchill's entreaties, surrendered his armies on May 28. France's turn came next, and then the Battle of Europe was over.

9

Churchill At the Helm

The outbreak of the war had ended the isolation of Churchill, and on September 3, 1939, he was brought back into His Majesty's Government as First Lord of the Admiralty. Hardly was he settled in his old chair in front of the wooden map stand he had placed in the First Lord's spacious office way back in 1911, when the signal was flashed to the Fleet: "Winston is back!" His electrifying presence was felt instantly by all. It was felt especially by Intelligence.

Throughout his colorful career, Churchill was an advocate and adherent of the Intelligence Service. In World War I, his relations with the Admiralty's Naval Intelligence Division were intimate. Later, when he held no official position, he maintained a secret service of his own that enabled him to talk on the issues of the day with specific knowledge.

Virtually his first act in the Admiralty was to review the intelligence set-up. What he found did not displease him. The intelligence services of the armed forces were not afflicted by the anarchy and impotence that paralyzed the secret service of the Foreign Office. Although badly understaffed, as was every branch of the military establishment, they had an excellent core of officers serving under capable directors. The algebraic MI (Directorate of Military Intelligence) of the War Office was headed by the popular, forty-six-year-old Major General Frederick George (Paddy) Beaumont-Nesbitt. Air Intelligence was under Group Captain K. C. Buss, a gallant RAF officer who, after the war, attained a high position in the Foreign Office's intelligence set-up.

In the person of Admiral John Henry Godfrey, Naval Intelligence had an able and experienced, energetic and imaginative director. Godfrey's staff was small to begin with, but it was rapidly augmented by newcomers, most of them officers of the reserve. A great many were foreign correspondents who brought to their new assignment the ability to smell out the news.

Only a few hours after his arrival at the Admiralty, Churchill personally penned his first note to the D.N.I., asking him for detailed information about the German U-boat force. Churchill was pleasantly surprised by the promptness with which the information was supplied (within twenty-four hours) and its convincing authoritativeness. The D.N.I. told him that Germany had sixty U-boats available for immediate action and that she would have a hundred early in 1940. This was but three boats off the mark; in fact, Germany then had fifty-seven submarines built and forty building.

Churchill continued to bombard the D.N.I. with a flow of notes. On September 6, for instance, he inquired about the situation on the west coast of Ireland, which he accurately expected to become an important area for some of Canaris' clandestine machinations. "Are there any signs of succouring U-boats in Irish creeks or inlets?" he asked, and then suggested: "It would seem that money should be spent to secure a trustworthy body of Irish agents to keep most vigilant watch." This was a timely warning, because, as we will soon see, neutral Eire became a lively battlefield in the secret war.

At one point, Mr. Churchill recommended to the D.N.I. that confidential documents and manuals be printed on a special paper made of cellulose nitrate that would explode when lighted. Another suggestion that he put forth was to reduce secret papers to tiny proportions that could be read only by some powerful projecting apparatus. Though nothing yet was known of the *Abwehr's* phenomenal microdot system, Churchill correctly anticipated its existence. How his keen mind deduced vital information from telltale evidence was shown on the eve of the Battle of Europe. On March 30, 1940, he read a brief item in the *Daily Telegraph* reporting that some twenty German ships stranded in Dutch ports were apparently getting ready to run the British blockade. Churchill assumed that such a mass exodus foreshadowed an imminent Nazi move on Holland and promptly aroused the D.N.I. to the possibility.

When the fortunes of war brought Churchill to the Prime Minister's chair, he wasted not a moment in moving to revamp and rebuild Britain's intelligence operations. One of his first moves was to appoint, as his personal aide for intelligence, Major Desmond Morton, his next door neighbor at Charwell and his longtime adviser on such matters. The two men had first met during World War I when Morton, then on the staff of Field Marshal Haig, served as Churchill's guide during his visits to the front. When Churchill became Secretary for War and Air in 1919, he named Morton to an important post in secret intelligence.

Their friendship survived Churchill's eclipse in power and, between the two wars, Morton remained, with official permission, the source of much of Churchill's confidential information. Morton was Churchill's personal adviser on intelligence matters throughout World War II and at the end of the war was rewarded with a knighthood.

On the Cabinet staff, two men performed important intelligence functions and linked the political leadership to the Secret Service. They were Sir Edward Bridges, secretary to the War Cabinet, and Colonel Edward Ian Claud Jacob, military assistant secretary.

However, the appointment of good men to such positions as these was far from enough, and in June, 1940, Churchill proceeded to break the stifling domination of the Foreign Office over the Secret Service. He created two new top-echelon groups at the apex of a new pyramid.

A civilian triumvirate, officially called the Committee of Three and nicknamed by insiders "the Secret Three of Whitehall", was appointed under the chairmanship of Lord Swinton, a former Secretary for Air. This was supposed to be the highest British agency dealing with espionage, responsible solely to Churchill and reporting directly to him. The committee had, according to Stanley Firmin, "absolute and co-ordinating control over every single phase of British Intelligence work, wherever and however it was carried out." In practice, however, its major influence turned out to be in the field of counter-espionage.

The second top group was the Joint Intelligence Committee, composed of the directors of the various service intelligence agencies. The directors were to meet, co-ordinate and evaluate the material that had been gathered by their agencies and funnel it, with conclusions, to the Prime Minister and the War Cabinet on the one hand, and to the Imperial General Staff and the heads of the services on the other.

It was the J.I.C. which, in the perilous summer of 1940, kept Churchill almost hourly informed of German plans to invade England in defiance of Napoleon's melancholy experience. Churchill was not always happy with the material he received from J.I.C. He rarely disputed the facts, but he frequently disagreed with the conclusions. He was always impatient when others sifted and digested intelligence for him and preferred to see "authentic documents in their original form" so that he could make his own deductions.

Under these committees Intelligence began to function with a unity of purpose and in an orchestrated manner. There was the Secret Service proper, with a revamped apparatus and rejuvenated personnel; the Directorate of Military Intelligence with some eighteen or nineteen branches, including a special branch for espionage and sabotage in MI.6 (Special Operations); the Division of Naval Intelligence that was soon to come under the expert leadership of Commodore Rushbrook (who was to head it until the end of the war); Air Intelligence under Buss; the security branches of Military Intelligence (MI.5), Scotland Yard (C.I.D. and Special Branch), the Royal Air Force, and the Foreign Office.

Throughout its history, the quality of the British Secret Service had been inexorably tied to the man who headed it, the director-general of the whole complex organization. His identity is never officially revealed, not even after his retirement —not even in his obituary notice. Britain was fond of making quite a show of the secrecy in which it traditionally shrouded the supreme spymaster of the Empire. Paul Dukes, who was knighted for his brilliant espionage work during the Russian Revolution, wrote, "It was eighteen months before I was allowed to know his real name and title, and even then I was careful never to use it."

In an organization like the Secret Service, which, because of its tight discipline and ironclad secrecy is well-nigh totalitarian in character, this supersecret chief plays a dominant role. The whole secret service is molded in his image. It reflects his qualities and character, indeed, his whims.

Now, a new star appeared in the firmament of the secret service, Stewart Graham Menzies by name. At the time of his appointment he was forty-nine years old, a proper gentleman and a gallant soldier. The son of Lady Holford, he was the product of three of those British institutions which are supposed to mold men for this kind of job: Eton, the Grenadier Guards, and the Life Guards. He was married and was related to Anthony Eden by one of his two marriages.

Just what else qualified Colonel Menzies for his important new job was difficult to ascertain. Yet Britain was fortunate in having him. He revamped and revitalized the moribund secret service until it again became worthy of its prestige and tradition. He served with exceptional distinction and gallantry, throughout the Second World War and during the difficult years of the Cold War, until his retirement in 1951. Grateful England made him a general and a knight twice over.

Menzies was also made a grand officer of the Belgian Order of Leopold and was awarded Poland, Holland and Norway's highest decorations. The United States bestowed upon him the Legion of Merit. As we shall see, he well deserved these honors for services, which, however, were not specified in the citations.

Old General Kell retired from the War Office, and his place at the head of the vastly enlarged MI.5 was taken by Sir David Petrie, a policeman with a brilliant record of service in India. Although only a few years younger than Kell, this dour Scot brought to MI.5 a youthful drive combined with the methodical investigating practice of the veteran policeman and the stern discipline of the colonial official.

In addition to the renovation of the old agencies, however, new ones were needed to fight this new kind of war, and they began to blossom overnight: the Censorship Division of the Post Office; Wireless Intelligence; a special Anti-Sabotage Division composed of acrobatic young daredevils under the dreamy-eyed, soft-voiced and elegant Lord Rothschild, scion of the famous banking family who abandoned finance for science.

Even before the fall of France, Churchill had envisaged the need of organizing the Continent for continued resistance. He wished for a special force that could harass the enemy at his soft points, inflict sudden and painful damage, collect vital information and move instantly in the defense of Britain, if necessary. "There ought to be," he wrote to General Ismay, his military aide, "at least twenty thousand storm troops or 'Leopards,' drawn from existing units, ready to spring at the throat of any small landings or descents."

At the same time, Colonel Dudley Clarke, an officer of the General Staff, thought of guerrilla warfare and remembered the Boer Commandos. He jotted down his ideas on a single sheet of paper, which eventually reached Churchill's eyes and obtained immediate approval. Clarke and a staff were installed in a private house in Grosvenor Crescent, where, in civilian clothes, they posed as the board of trustees of a mythical charity.

There was much about the effort that was grimly hilarious. Churchill had proposed that each of the twenty thousand "Leopards" be equipped with a Tommy gun, and it turned out that there were exactly forty Tommy guns available in the whole of Britain. Only half a dozen boats could be found to ferry the raiders across the Channel, and in two of those the engines failed. When it was decided that the Commandos should blacken their faces in night action, no black greasepaint could be found in the entire military establishment. It had to be bought from a Wardour Street stage costumer.

It was hardly surprising that their first raid, near Le Touquet, was no great shakes. In the words of the official historian of the Commandos, "It had accomplished little and yet, at the same time, much. The military information brought back had no very great value, but the raid had a most heartening effect upon the people of England."

A later raid was far more successful. Radar was becoming a vital weapon in the battle for air supremacy, and the Germans had established a major station at Bruneval on the French coast between Fecamp and Le Havre. A resident British agent discovered its existence and a team of specialists was sent to reconnoiter and make sure of its importance. On the basis of their report, a team of one hundred and twenty Commandos was dropped from the air on the night of February 7, 1942, while thirty-two others were landed from the sea in support. They succeeded in dismantling and taking away the important parts of the apparatus intact and in blowing up what they left behind. The equipment they brought back revealed to England some of Germany's most jealously-guarded electronic secrets.

In due course, however, the intelligence function of the Commandos was largely superseded by its military activities and so its detailed history, fascinating though it is, would be out of place here. The intelligence work fell largely to another brand new organization created in the Ministry of Economic Warfare, the Special Operations Executive, or S.O.E., for short.

The S.O.E. developed from a brief note Churchill had sent to General Ismay on June 24, 1940, after France's total collapse. "It seems most important," he wrote, "to establish now before the trap closes an organization for enabling French officers and soldiers, as well as important technicians, who wish to fight, to make their way to various ports. A sort of 'underground railway' as in the olden days of slavery should be established and a Scarlet Pimpernel organization set up. I have no doubt there will be a steady flow of determined men, and we need all we can get for the defense of the French colonies." The Prime Minister could afford to propose such unorthodox ideas to the hidebound military Tories of the War Office, but when lesser lights came forward with similar suggestions, they were frowned upon and even punished.

How dangerous it was to voice such ideas was shown by the fate of a lieutenant colonel of the First Royal Dragoons, named A. D. Wintle. At the time of Dunkirk, he hit upon the idea of dropping in at French airfields to recruit airmen for continued resistance to the Nazis. His idea scandalized his senior officer. It came to a bitter quarrel, the end of which found Colonel Wintle in the Tower of London on charges of insubordination and threatening a senior officer. He was later acquitted, but, in the light of his experience, few of his contemporaries dared to annoy Colonel Blimp with original ideas.

But where Wintle was put in his place, Churchill prevailed. The War Office added a special operations division to Military Intelligence and, beyond that, on a far broader and more unorthodox scale, S.O.E. was created. Major General Sir Colin McVean Gubbins, who headed it, described its purpose in a lecture on January 28, 1948, at the Royal United Service Institution:

"The shock of initial German success was profound, particularly in the occupied territories of Western Europe. France, Belgium, Holland, Denmark and Norway lay as if stunned; only the Poles, toughened by centuries of oppression, were spiritually uncrushed. Yet in all these countries there were hundreds of thousands of individuals who refused to accept defeat and who prayed for the means to continue the struggle.

"The British Commonwealth was on the defensive and it was clear that it would be years before invasion would be possible; what could, however, be done in the meantime was to attack the enemy by unorthodox methods: attack his war potential wherever it was exposed and at least create some running sores to drain his strength and to disperse his forces. This would give the maximum of assistance to the forces of liberation when invasion of the Continent finally did take place. To undertake this task, an organization, Special Operations Executive, was created."

According to General Gubbins, this was the plan: "To encourage and enable the peoples of the occupied countries to harass the German war effort at every possible point, by sabotage, subversion, go-slow practices, *coup de main* raids, etc., and at the same time to build up secret forces therein, organized, armed, and trained to take their part only when the final assault began. . . ."

Churchill's (or, for that matter, Colonel Wintle's) original idea was subsequently broadened. On July 23, Churchill wrote to the Secretary for War: "It is, of course, urgent and indispensable that every effort should be made to obtain secretly the best possible information about the German forces in the various areas overrun, and to establish intimate contacts with local people, and to plant agents. This, I hope, is being done on the largest scale, as opportunity serves, by the new organization [S.O.E.] under M.E.W. [Ministry of Economic Warfare]."

Called affectionately the "Old Firm" by its habitués, S.O.E. was housed in two buildings on Baker Street—the brass in Michael House, and the rank and file in Norgeby House, close to Sherlock Holmes' fictitious dwelling. To passersby, the agency was the "Inter-Service Research Bureau", or at least that was what the sign said on the door of Norgeby House. Other sections of S.O.E. were scattered throughout London, behind screens of similar secrecy; one occupied premises from which a famous circus had just been gently evicted.

By the whimsical placing of S.O.E. under the Ministry of Economic Warfare, its supreme chief became a man one would never have normally associated with the melodramatic pursuits of espionage and sabotage. He was the Right Honorable Hugh Dalton, son of a prominent clergyman, Eton-bred barrister and an economist with a doctorate from King's College. He was the Labor Party's outstanding budgetary expert, former Chancellor of the Exchequer. Dalton condescended to the management of S.O.E. with a certain professorial aloofness and the righteous indignation of a canon who has wandered by chance into a house of ill-repute. Someone in S.O.E. once said that Dalton reminded him of one of those large dinner gongs which stand on wooden legs in old country houses. "When you beat it with a stick padded with chamois leather," the quipster remarked, "it gives out a deep, booming sound. That's Dr. Dalton—but there's no dinner at the end of it."

But Dalton's mental and physical vigor impressed even the most intellectual and athletic members of this organization, which was composed in equal measure of brain and brawn. "I found him," Bruce Lockhart remarked, "very receptive to new ideas, decisive and quick in action, and a tiger for work. We christened him Dr. Dynamo, and he deserved the compliment."

Aside from S.O.E., Dalton supervised another alphabetic combination, the P.W.E., the initials standing for Political Warfare Executive. It was headed eventually by Bruce Lockhart and was to do in the propaganda sphere what S.O.E. was to achieve in espionage and sabotage, to harass the enemy at home and abroad. Its purpose was to attack people's minds and move them to controlled action.

It was P.W.E. that produced the outstanding propaganda appeal of the war: the V-symbol with all its ingenious sideshows, the Morse beat, the opening bars of Beethoven's Fifth Symphony, the V-signs scribbled on enemy walls and Churchill's enthusiastic participation through the display of the sign on all opportune occasions.

The campaign was thought up by Victor de Laveleye and Douglas Ritchie, assistant to the director of B.B.C.'s European Services, who became well known during the war by his *nom de radio*, Colonel Britton. One night in the winter of 1940, de Laveleye, a former member of the Belgian Government, found an intriguing item in an R.A.F. intelligence summary. It re-ported that Belgian patriots were defying the German Field Security Police (a branch of *Abwehr* III) by writing the three letters "R.A.F." on the walls and shutters of their houses. De Laveleye got the idea to substitute the letter "V" for the three letters "R.A.F.", partly because it was more meaningful with its connotation of victory or *victoire,* and partly because it en-tailed reduced risk, because it could be written more swiftly.

De Laveleye was then in charge of the B.B.C. broadcasts in French to Belgium and mentioned his idea in passing on one of his broadcasts. He thought no more about it until he heard that the "V" was cropping up in increasing numbers on Belgian walls.

At about the same time, and quite independently of de Laveleye's historic brainwave, Ritchie also thought of a symbol that could, through its powerful visual appeal, inspire and en-courage the subjugated Europeans. Eventually, as John Baker White put it, Ritchie's and de Laveleye's suggestions came to be fused in the phenomenal "V" campaign. Haphazard though the original idea was, the campaign was executed with the utmost efficiency, and before long the symbol swept occupied Europe.

By 1942, the activities of the Old Firm leveled off, and Dalton was replaced by the noble lord in whose charge the S.O.E. remained for the rest of the war: Major the Earl of Selborne. At the time of his appointment as Minister of Eco-nomic Warfare, he was fifty-five years old, and a cement man-ufacturer by profession.

Both Dalton and Selborne were, in the final analysis, only nominal heads of S.O.E. Its actual chief was a seasoned and flexible young officer of the British Army's General Staff, the legendary Colin Gubbins, then forty-four. He is the forgotten man of the secret war, the least known chief of wartime secret service (and that largely by his own choice). As soon as the war ended and he collected a string of decorations (including the Legion of Merit from the United States), the newly created knight, Sir Colin Gubbins, retired from the Army. He went into seclusion on the Isle of Harris, where he found the peace and tranquility he needed after "the long years of dreadful night", as he put it.

Gubbins directed a fantastic clandestine war that was, in his own words, "a day-to-day battle with the Gestapo, the Quislings and the Japanese secret police, one long continuous struggle, with torture and unbelievable suffering and death waiting around every corner at every moment."

No problem equal to his faced any other commander of the late war. He had no precedents, no experience on which to build; the Second World War was the first in history in which organized resistance in occupied territories was mounted on this scale, and was directed and supplied from outside. His task was vastly complicated by the multi-national character of his composite force and by the conflicting interests, ideas and aspirations of the émigré governments with which he had to work in close cooperation.

S.O.E. experienced both misery and grandeur, scored amazing victories and suffered heartbreaking defeats. After all, S.O.E. had to cope with the pitfalls and risks of a hazardous coalition war waged by rank amateurs against seasoned and ruthless professionals. It was by sheer necessity composed of a miscellany of modern buccaneers.

Ian Colvin, a foreign correspondent whose conscientious coverage of German dissidence took him deep into the bowels of the secret war, remarked that virtually the only survivors of S.O.E. were officers who held wartime jobs in London. It is true that the life expectancy of S.O.E. agents was distressingly brief. In one of his books, Peter Churchill listed some seventy fellow agents, of whom only twenty escaped capture or death. "Hundreds of men like me were sent to the occupied countries," he wrote. "Some were captured on the very fields where their parachutes landed; some lasted for weeks; some for months; some were captured on the eve of victory, whilst a few were lucky enough to survive the entire war."

The high mortality rate of these agents reflected not only

the occupational hazards, but also some of the inner shortcomings of S.O.E. As Colvin pointed out, many of its operations were gallant but ill-founded.

Most of S.O.E.'s history is still suppressed by the application of the Official Secrets Act; the chances are that the whole
of its story will never be told. A few of the narratives whose
publication was authorized depict the Old Firm as a house
occasionally divided against itself, rampant with jealousies, chaos
and ignorance, its dissensions and bickerings endangering the
men and women whose survival depended on the organizers at
home. Jean Overton Fuller's story of "Madeleine," a pathetic
young woman of the Resistance, abounds in complaints and re-
proaches, accusing S.O.E. of criminal blunders. Some of these
mistakes were so monumental and sustained, so costly in the
lives they claimed, that critics of S.O.E. averred there was more
than just stupidity, disorganization, jealousy and carelessness
behind them. "But corroboration or denial of these facts," Colvin wrote, "even the investigation by Inter-Allied Commissions
of Enquiry, of the possibilities of gross carelessness or treason
had, in such instances, been frustrated by an order to burn the
documentary records of Special Operations Executive after the
war."

The influence of S.O.E.'s operations on the future stability
of Europe was also questioned, notably by Captain Liddell Hart,
who ventured the opinion that their long-range residue effect
was deplorable. F. O. Miksche, wartime operations chief of a
Gaullist secret service, agreed as stated below:

"The People's Underground War [which S.O.E. was called
upon to promote and stimulate] destroys the soul of a nation,
systematically leading it into disobedience and disrespect of law
and order. As in all revolutions, the People's War means complete chaos, a savage struggle in which the end justifies the
means, and vengeance, trickery, and even treachery, play a great
part. Each action provokes a reaction, and the consequent re-
prisals engender hatred to a degree hitherto unknown. The
Second World War has already proved all this, and we see in

contemporary Europe the dire consequences of the war-time underground struggles."

Despite all its shortcomings, S.O.E. made a substantial contribution to victory, and undoubtedly saved many lives. Bruce Marshall, in his account of the White Rabbit, a famous operative of S.O.E., tells how agents "disrupted the enemy's communications by blowing up railway tracks or hindered his war production by destroying pylons, electricity generating plants and machinery in factories. This form of warfare was both more accurate and benign than aerial bombardment. An agent insinuated into a factory could sabotage effectively and without loss of human life a piece of essential machinery that a squadron of bombers would be lucky to hit by chance."

Even the bloodletting caused by S.O.E. blunders, I submit, proved salutary in the end. I, for one, firmly believe that only austerity and anguish and pain can produce the determination and bring forth the sacrifice needed to win the secret war, while pampering and bribery will lead to stagnation and failure.

10

The Bitter Weeds of England

In the summer of 1940, the *Abwehr* had reached its peak and was imperceptibly deteriorating; British Intelligence had moved out of its stupor and clumsiness, and had become, virtually overnight, a crucial arm of His Majesty's Government. These changes exerted a decisive influence on history: Hitler needed the *Abwehr* more than anything else to smooth his way to his next destination; Churchill needed the counsel of his Intelligence Service to prevent the Fuehrer from reaching it.

After the conclusion of the French campaign, Hitler was again somewhat uncertain about his future course. For a few days he toyed with peace feelers. Among others, the King of Sweden appeared behind the scenes and proffered his services to mediate some sort of a peace arrangement that would have enabled the Nazi to keep his loot. The services of Gustaf V were rejected by both sides; in indignation by Churchill, in puzzlement by Hitler. After that, Hitler no longer hesitated.

On July 2, he sent orders to the Abwehr to start the assembly of intelligence needed for plans for an invasion of England.

On July 16, he issued "Directive No. 16/40", entitled "Preparations for a Landing Operation Against England." The last sentence of the document's preamble read: "The enterprise is to be referred to by the cover name, Sea Lion"—as transparent a cover name as there ever was, reflecting Hitler's conceit and self-confidence.

However, extreme measures were introduced to screen the

operation. Only seven copies of the directive were prepared, one each for the supreme commanders of the Army, Navy and Air Force; one for General Jodl, chief of Hitler's own general staff; and two for Section L (*Landesverteidigung*) in Jodl's bureau, whose officers were to draft the plans. The seventh copy was locked up in Hitler's own files.

Despite this secrecy, however, the British managed to penetrate to the very core of Sea Lion. As early as June 27, an intelligence report arrived on Churchill's desk indicating that Admiral Schniewind's operations section in the German Admiralty was preoccupied with drafting invasion plans against England. The entire British Intelligence combine was alerted at once.

Late at night on July 6, Colonel Jacobs presented to the Prime Minister the first of a series of invasion dossiers. It contained abundant data that, however, appeared to be somewhat contradictory. It had several reports from confidential informants indicating that England was, indeed, the Fuehrer's next goal. But hard intelligence—reports of coast and train watchers and aerial reconnaissance—showed no evidence of German activity in preparation for an invasion.

This uncertainty lasted until about the third week in July, when Military Intelligence began to identify *Wehrmacht* units apparently marked for the assault on England. Two mountain divisions, in particular, intrigued the British officers. They had been observed by agents during vigorous exercises with mules at the rocky French coastline near Boulogne. An agent by the name of Bruno was forthwith sent to Boulogne, and it was ascertained that those divisions were training in preparation for scaling the Folkestone cliffs.

Among other invasion forces, the British succeeded in identifying two regiments of the 7th Parachute Division that were to descend, five thousand men strong, at the southern Downs. Elements of thirteen additional divisions were identified, deploying quietly all along the Channel coast from Ostende to Boulogne. At the same time, train watchers reported troop concentrations in the Pas de Calais and Normandy. Coast watchers noticed a large number of self-propelled barges and motor boats creeping along the French coast; aerial photographs presented a graphic demonstration of the gradual growth of danger.

It became imperative to land agents on the French Channel coast to discover from close quarters what aerial reconnaissance inevitably missed, a string of painstakingly camouflaged coastal guns. French informants in the area were not yet available, so agents had to be found in Britain. One of the men who seemed to qualify was a prominent Westminster politician named R. E. Hutchinson, who used to visit the area around Cap Gris Nez year after year and also knew a lot about coastal artillery. But he was too well known in that part of France, and it was feared he might be recognized and betrayed. Hasty plastic surgery was performed to alter his features. He was still wearing the bandages over his new scars when he landed in France on his first mission. His journey was justified. He returned with detailed intelligence about those long-range coastal guns around the Cap.

Then the secret service came through with a phenomenal scoop. Information was procured that Hitler had definitely decided to mount the invasion on September 15; and that it was to be where the Channel was narrowest, to hit the area between Folkestone and Eastbourne, and the beaches both south and north of Brighton.

The decision was made on July 31. Information about it reached Churchill early in August, together with reports that the Army High Command was by no means enchanted with the prospects of the enterprise. On August 7, General Halder, chief of the Army General Staff, actually remonstrated with Hitler, suggesting that the invasion project, as envisaged by the German Admiralty, was tantamount to putting the army through a meat grinder. After that, some of the German generals referred to Sea Lion by a far less dignified name, Operation Meat Grinder.

Tension mounted steadily. On September 7, British intelligence reported that the German barges and small ships had begun their move to staging points. The *Luftwaffe* was being augmented to striking strength. Several observers noticed that

concentration of short-range *Stukas,* the *Luftwaffe's* dreaded
dive bombers, at advanced airfields had increased.

In the possession of its vast intelligence dossier, Britain was
able to make its dispositions prudently and well in advance. The
situation was entirely different on the German side. This confused state was primarily due to the fact that the planners, including Admiral Schniewind and Jodl's bright young men in
Section L, had to make their designs in the woeful absence of
up-to-date, comprehensive and trustworthy intelligence. On
July 7, Field Marshal Keitel expressed the consensus when he
described Sea Lion as "an extremely difficult operation that must
be approached with the utmost caution" because, he said, "the
intelligence available on the military preparedness of the island
and on the coastal defenses is meagre and not very reliable."
Hitler was eyeless, like Samson in Gaza.

When Hitler had commanded the *Abwehr* to obtain the
necessary information for the invasion, Colonel Busch ordered
what he still believed to be his network in Britain to drop everything else and get to work. What he got back was the ringing
of the British carillon, a mass of data that was either useless or
misleading. Hence Piekenbrock and Busch decided to send a
new crop of agents into England and also to work with a ready-
made network, the Irish Republican Army. This latter idea had
a double aim: Ireland could be used as a point of entry for
spies into England, and some information could be obtained
directly there; also if an I.R.A. rebellion could be co-ordinated
with Sea Lion it would provide an extremely handy diversion for
further harassment of the British.

For its first crack at Ireland, the *Abwehr* decided to employ
a most unusual tactic—the use of a spy who had already fallen.
He was a certain *Herr Doktor* Hermann Goertz, a disbarred
Hamburg lawyer who had drifted into espionage because he
could succeed at nothing else. As early as 1935, Goertz had been
sent into England with a pretty "secretary," Marianne Emig,
to spy out the RAF airfields ringing London. It was a far-sighted

move, since some of the information he procured helped to guide the *Luftwaffe* during the bombing of the city years later. But Goertz was soon nabbed and served four years for espionage. After his return to Germany in 1939, Busch decided to send him to Ireland. He was dropped by parachute, but through an error of navigation by a clumsy pilot, he came down in Northern Ireland and was spotted. He barely managed to get over the border into Eire a jump ahead of the Royal Constabulary and had to leave his radio and other equipment behind, which was soon discovered. The British promptly posted a price of three thousand pounds on his head. Since a substantial section, even of the I.R.A., was opposed to co-operating with the Germans, Goertz was both a hunted and a haunted man, and he was actually relieved when he was finally arrested. He served some years in an Irish internment camp, and was eventually scheduled to be turned over to the British. The night before the proposed transfer he committed suicide with a capsule of cyanide.

Goertz wasn't the only Irish card in the *Abwehr's* hand by a long shot. A celebrated I.R.A. exile, Sean Russel, had been brought from the United States to Germany where a nucleus of other I.R.A. men were in training at Quenzsee. Since the Germans feared that the British might eventually occupy the Free State—or that the government would flee there if Sea Lion succeeded—it was important to promote an I.R.A. rebellion. A U-boat was commandeered to take Russel home, but by the time he arrived at the French port of Lorient to embark, he was a very sick man with an old ulcer flaring up. The Germans shipped him off anyway, but he had a hemorrhage and died at sea.

The *Abwehr* had a third important Irish link, this one in London. He was a prominent Irish businessman who claimed to have some association with the I.R.A.; he himself, however, was not a member. This man was sought to serve as liaison between his contacts in the Free State and the *Abwehr* in

Germany, but, with the outbreak of the war, it became extremely difficult to manage this three-cornered operation or even to get in touch with him.

An agent was sent to him via Spain, with a set of codes and some radio equipment. The courier managed to get to London, but when he called on the Irishman, he so frightened him that this chosen leader of the *Abwehr* espionage at first refused to go through with his original deal. Using the effective argument of blackmail, the courier told the reluctant spy that he would be denounced to the British if he persisted in his refusal. Under such pressure, the hapless Irishman agreed to continue to work for the *Abwehr*, but he refused steadfastly to operate a wireless. Arrangements had to be made for other couriers to visit the man in London from time to time and pick up whatever material he had; they would then continue on to Ireland and collect more reports directly from the man's contacts there. How effective this link became may be seen from the *Abwehr's* own admission that "throughout the course of the war only a single Irish courier ever reached Germany."

Important as this Irish loophole could have been to the *Abwehr*, little had been done before the war to prepare it, and now everything had to be improvised. Canaris found it difficult to coax planes from Goering to drop his spies in Ireland. So, early in June, 1940, a German sailing enthusiast, a man named Nissen, tied to Canaris by their common hobby, received a summons to report for duty at once with General von Lahousen's Special Duty Battalion 800, the combat sabotage unit. The *Abwehr* wanted him to take secret agents to Britain and Ireland, and even to the Western Hemisphere and South Africa, if need be.

Nissen was given the freedom of the Channel coast, to requisition any boat or yacht that seemed suitable to him, train the crews, organize the missions, do anything at all, but do it quickly, for Heaven's sake.

Then, as work on Sea Lion progressed, Nissen, still far from having completed his preparations, was called to the *Abwehr* office at Brest and told to take three spies to Ireland, on the double. He decided to make the journey by sail alone. "After three days sailing," Nissen reported later, "I landed my passengers by dinghy under cover of darkness in the gulf of Baltimore, near the Fastner Rock in the southwestern extremity of Ireland."

But though the journey was a success, the mission ended in failure. Nissen's three clandestine passengers were two inexperienced young Germans born in South Africa, and an Indian ship's chandler. They were supposed to make their way to England from Ireland, procure information in advance of Sea Lion, send it by wireless to Germany, and then turn into saboteurs. The Indian got cold feet. He conveniently denounced himself and sat out the war in internment. The two young Germans tried to get into England but they were picked up, and joined their colleague behind bars.

With failure piling upon monumental failure, the *Abwehr* grew desperate. In panic they combed their files and screened their schools, but all the manhunt produced was a single man who was able, willing, even anxious to go to England. He was a professional spy named Jose Rudolph Waldberg.

What a miserable discovery he was! At that time working as a stool pigeon in a camp for prisoners of war, he did not speak or understand a word of English! He was a trained spy who had performed well in Belgium and France, but he was overworked and now showed signs of fatigue.

Three more were turned up in Holland, one of them a German discovered by Mussert. He was Karl Meier, twenty-four, a professional Nazi, who agreed to go when he was told that he would be followed within forty-eight hours by the invaders, including a paymaster who would hand him a royal remuneration.

The other two were petty Dutch smugglers who had to be blackmailed into the mission. They were offered the choice of England or of a Nazi concentration camp. "I knew what it meant to be taken to Germany," one of them, Sjoerd Pons, said later. "I was willing to do anything just to get out of this pickle."

So was his companion, Charles Albert van den Kieboom, a twenty-six-year-old clerk whose features bore the unmistakable evidence that his mother had been Japanese.

The frantic search at last yielded three more recruits: a thirty-four-year-old German merchant named Karl Theo Drueke; a young, slow-witted Swiss chauffeur named Werner Heinrich Waelti; and an enigmatic, anonymous woman. Like Kieboom and Pons, Drueke and Waelti spoke very little English, knew even less about the business of espionage, and agreed to the trip only under some duress.

The only intriguing figure in this little mob was the woman. She was in her early twenties, a bewitching, blonde, Nordic beauty, athletic yet graceful and feminine, the kind of unlikely apparition you see on the travel posters of ski resorts. She was as smart as she was handsome, and she had nerves of steel.

What was such a woman doing in this dismal company? Nobody seemed to know who she was or whence she came. She called herself Madame Erikson and said she was Norwegian, but the name was an alias, and the fact that she spoke English without a trace of an accent belied her Norwegian nationality. Her companions knew nothing about her, not even her alias. They referred to her as the Fraulein, but they treated her with a healthy respect, for there was no doubt that Fraulein was the boss.

Now Admiral Canaris had his handful of spies—six men and one woman versus England. Even in espionage, this would not necessarily mean an uneven struggle. Sometimes an exceptional spy can score fantastic successes single-handed, but there was nothing exceptional about this particular crew except for their complete unsuitability. Only utter desperation on the part of the *Abwehr* can explain the selection of these Sad Sacks.

Lord Jowitt, who came to know these people better than anyone else either in Germany or in England, could only say, "If the cases of which I had experience were a fair sample of German espionage, then that espionage must have been remarkably inefficient."

The *Abwehr* had no time to be finicky. Kieboom, Pons and Meier were taken to Brussels. The two Dutchmen were put up in a small boarding house, but Meier, who was a volunteer, was settled in style at the Hotel Metropole. They were given a month's training in the handling of a special wireless transmitter and in Morse code. Meier's training went a bit further than that. As he himself described it, "They gave me lessons in the structure of the English Army—divisions and brigades, what they are formed of, what were important things to tell; for instance, where battalions were situated and how we could recognize them. Go to the cafe and listen, for soldiers always talk. Make friends. There were more things than that; if you see tanks or something pass, give their exact number if possible; also about troops marching through towns, remember their direction and destination."

The seven spies were split into two groups: Waldberg, Meier, Kieboom and Pons were to go to the south of England. Scotland was chosen as the destination for Drueke, Waelti and the woman. On September 2, the first group was ready to leave. Waldberg was "to find out what divisions and brigades were on the south coast, what were the nature of the fortifications, and what were the type of guns, both coast artillery and anti-aircraft artillery." Meier was to collect information about the economic situation and the morale of the people, but also information about the R.A.F. Kieboom and Pons were told to snoop in a general way: "How the people is living," as Pons put it in his inimitable English, "how many soldiers there are, and all the things."

They were to report their findings by wireless between five and eight in the morning, and eight and two at night. At last, they were handed their gear, put aboard a fishing boat and ferried across. They rowed the last part of the way in dinghies and landed in the area of Romney Marsh. By 4:00 a.m., they were all ashore and Waldberg rigged up an aerial between a tree and a bush, got out his wireless set, and signaled to his employers, "Arrived safely, document destroyed."

A few hours later, he sent still another message, but it was no longer triumphant. It read, "Meier prisoner, English police searching for me, am cornered, situation difficult." He somehow felt the jig was up because he concluded the message with a pathetic "Long live Germany."

Waldberg started the chain reaction that led to their doom by becoming thirsty. Since he could not speak English, Meier had to go to fetch him a drink—some cider, if possible. Meier made his way to nearby Lydd, found a pub and asked the woman inside for some cider and cigarettes. The proprietress was no fool; she recognized Meier for a bloody foreigner at once, because, you see, it was only nine o'clock in the morning, before the legal opening hour. Meier was told to come back later, and when he returned at ten o'clock, he found an official waiting for him. At the Lydd police station, he conceded that he had just landed from a boat, but insisted he was a Dutch subject and had come from France to join the new Dutch resistance organization. He said nothing about Waldberg, and the British had to find his partner through their own efforts. It did not take them long. Early in the morning of the next day (September 4), Waldberg's thirst drew him out of his hideout and straight into the arms of the police.

The downfall of Kieboom and Pons was even more abrupt. They landed near Hythe shortly after 5 a.m. on September 3, ignorant of the fact that a unit of the Somerset Light Infantry was stationed nearby. At five o'clock sharp, Private Tollervey saw the silhouette of a man on the far side of a road. He challenged the elusive shadow and that did the trick. Kieboom came forward and surrendered.

At 5:25 a.m., another soldier caught Pons, quite literally with his pants down. Pons was engaged in exchanging his soaking wet trousers for a dry pair. He gave himself up before he could finish buttoning up his pants.

Waldberg and Meier died on the scaffold together at Pentonville on December 10, 1940. They were followed by Kieboom a week later. Pons was acquitted and survived the adventure.

The British promptly exploited the *coup* by putting a lively new tune on their carillon. Contrary to the usual practice, they immediately announced the capture of the spies, and even went so far as to release pictures of their precious wireless sets. They wanted to give the impression that these were the first such sets to fall into their hands, and thus to quash any possible suspicion that they were operating those sets that had been captured earlier.

While previously their carillon had worked but sluggishly, now the British opened up with a flood of information to make the Germans think the old network was working well again. The British put on the air an intricate pattern of fake information, including a few items larded with some truth. The *Abwehr* swallowed everything gluttonously and rejoiced that the famine had ended. After that, much of the German High Command's planning for Sea Lion was based on intelligence they received from the *Abwehr,* which in turn had procured it from British Intelligence.

D-Day for Sea Lion had to be postponed until October, and since the second batch of spies, Drueke, Waelti and the woman, had finished their training, the *Abwehr* decided to send them to London via Scotland. Drueke and Waelti were shipped off to Norway where they reported to the "Fraulein." At dawn on September 30, the three of them boarded a seaplane and flew to a point in the North Sea off the Banffshire coast. They transferred to a dinghy, but had to wade ashore, because the water was too shallow for their rubber boat. The fact that they had to set wet feet on British soil was to hasten their downfall.

When they reached land, they realized they did not know where they were. Such ignorance is not conducive to an agent's survival. They were to operate separately anyway, so they decided to grope their separate ways to inhabited places. Following his luminous compass, Waelti walked to a nearby whistle stop on the Aberdeen-Edinburgh line.

Drueke and the woman made their way to another railway station. As a security measure, the British had removed all signs

from the train stations, and so this wayward couple had to ask
the stationmaster where they were! The official told them this
was Port Gordon, whereupon Drueke stepped to a timetable on
the wall, picked a station at random, and whispered to his
companion to buy two tickets for Forres. The peculiar conduct
of these strangers induced the stationmaster to put in a call to
the police. A few minutes later, Constable Grieve ambled in to
ask a few questions. His inquiry was soon continued by Inspector
Simpson at the stationhouse and it brought forth a strange
assortment of clues: a Mauser with six rounds in its magazine,
nineteen additional rounds in Drueke's overcoat, a flashlight
marked "Made in Bohemia," a few other incriminating odds
and ends and a sausage with the German brand name on it.

Simpson locked the pair up and called Special Branch in
London. He told about Drueke and described the girl, who
looked prettier than ever in her neatly cut two-piece suit, except
that her elegance was somewhat marred by wet shoes and
stockings.

When the man at the other end of the wire heard the
girl's description, he turned to another employee. "She has
arrived," he said. The other leaned back in his swivel chair and
a broad smile came over his face. He merely replied, "Great
work."

What was behind that cryptic exchange the British still
refuse to say, except for Lord Jowitt's laconic remark that "it
may be [Madame Erikson] was able to be of some use to our
authorities." In point of fact, she was a British agent who had
been insinuated into the *Abwehr* in the hope that she would
guide German spies into the arms of the British authorities, as
she did, most successfully.

In the meantime, Waelti managed to reach Edinburgh by
way of Buckpool and Buckie. He arrived at five o'clock in the
afternoon, checked his baggage and went to get a haircut and
see a motion picture. He had time on his hands. He was to
meet his contact—a man in a gray flannel suit with a scar on

his forehead—the following morning at Victoria Station in London.

While Waelti was at the cinema, Inspector Sutherland of the Edinburgh Special Branch, acting on a tip from the Erikson woman, picked up his trail. He opened the suitcases left by the young Swiss in the baggage room and found in them a complete espionage laboratory. When Waelti returned to the baggage room, he suddenly felt on either side of him two big men, one of them catching his hand as it was moving quickly toward his hip pocket. It was evident that Waelti would have been willing to fight for his life. As it was, he had to go to the scaffold in Wandsworth Prison in August, 1941, without a struggle, accompanied only by his partner in misfortune, Drueke. Madame Erikson was unable to attend the executions. She was extremely busy elsewhere.

After Waelti's downfall and as long as Sea Lion was alive, the bulk of the information the *Abwehr* received from England was sent out by British Intelligence. As time went on, the artificial fog in which the Germans were wrapped became increasingly dense, until the *Abwehr* lost all sense of direction. As more and more doctored intelligence arrived from England, the size of Britain's defenses appeared increasingly great while Germany's chance for success seemed smaller and smaller.

The first victim of the *Abwehr's* gullibility was the High Command's Department of Foreign Armies-West which was supposed to develop the enemy's order of battle. On the eve of the first Sea Lion D-Day, the Department estimated that Britain had a total of thirty-five divisions available for her defense, of which sixteen had been deployed along the coast and nineteen kept in strategic reserve. In actual fact, Britain had only twenty-six divisions altogether. The German agents reported that British ground forces totaled one million, six hundred and forty thousand officers and men, while in reality their real strength was still below the million mark.

The inflated figures could not fail to influence the High

Command, but it soon became evident that the increasing German uncertainty was due to something more than fear of just the usual risk involved in such an ambitious enterprise. Behind the mounting Nazi apprehension was a big lie, a lie so monumental, indeed, that it aided in the defeat of one of history's most ambitious military ventures even before it could start.

Lies may be dead and damned, and rumor may be what Shakespeare called it, nothing but long-tongued, babbling gossip, but in times of war, lies are powerful weapons in the arsenals of secret services. All secret services have special branches whose wartime job is to concoct lies and to spread useful rumors.

On a summer day in 1940, a young man of twenty-eight, working at humdrum intelligence jobs in the War Office in London, was called to the office of "Paddy" Beaumont-Nesbitt. The young man was John Baker White, a junior major in MI. He was ordered to conduct psychological warfare, not against the Germans in general, but specifically against the German Army.

Baker White was sent to lovely St. Margaret's Bay near Dover to see for himself what Britain had in tangible weapons. The Sea Lion scare was at its height and what Baker White found made his heart sink. The beach was defended by a rifle company with two Bren guns and an old Vickers machine gun. Their supporting artillery consisted of a few ancient French 75mm guns, with only ten rounds of ammunition for each gun. Behind that thin line there was nothing else for twenty miles. "We're damn thin on the ground," an officer told him; Baker White thought it was a masterly understatement.

And yet Major White found something interesting. Running along the beach were pipes with holes punched into them at regular intervals. There were fuel tanks and pumps behind the pipeline, feeding a mixture of gasoline, fuel oil and creosote into the pipes. The contraption operated like a garden sprinkler; it spewed flames along the beach and down to the water line. "In operation," Baker White remarked, "they were a frightening spectacle, with clouds of thick, blinding black smoke through which shot great jets of red flame."

On the drive back to London, he could not get that flaming spectacle out of his mind. Suddenly he had a vision. He saw flames extending beyond the water line, setting the Channel itself on fire. "Setting the sea on fire," he repeated again and again all the way home to London. How about spreading a rumor that Britain was, indeed, as Tennyson had put it, a looming bastion fringed with fire?

Baker White consulted experts and they assured him that an operation like this would be extremely difficult and prohibitively expensive, but was feasible. Armed with this expert opinion, he worked up a memo and submitted it to the committee that was to pass on all such concoctions. Back came the committee's okay, with the remark: "No objection, but we think it a pretty poor effort."

The rumor now floated out of Baker White's hands and was planted by other organs of the British secret service in the usual spots: in the lobby of the Grand Hotel in Stockholm, the bars of the Avenida in Lisbon and the Ritz in Madrid, in Cairo and New York, Istanbul and Buenos Aires, wherever the Germans had their listening posts.

There was not much more that Baker White and his associate rumor-spreaders could do, except to sit back and wait for the playback. For a while nothing happened. Then, abruptly, the first faint echo was heard. A German pilot, shot down in Kent, mentioned during his interrogation at the Cockfoster "cage" something about Britain's "burning sea defenses." A few days later, another *Luftwaffe* prisoner spoke of them again. After that came the deluge. Promoted and stimulated by elaborate instruments of political warfare, the rumor was sweeping the world.

Two fortuitous events gave the rumor the plausibility and impetus it still needed to be devastatingly effective. An R.A.F. flight of bombers, on a routine mission against a concentration of German invasion barges, caught a battalion of *Landsers* at an exercise near Calais. A rain of incendiaries was showered on them and the men of the battalion were severely burned. The brand new French underground was already spreading the rumor. Now they could point to the *Landsers* in hospitals in France and Belgium as "evidence."

At about the same time, forty-odd German soldiers arrived in England. They were corpses washed up along the coast. They were members of another invasion battalion engaged in embarkation practice. A few of the barges had put out to sea, strayed into foul weather and sunk. The coming of these German bodies was quickly linked to the floating tall tale.

"This was," Churchill wrote, "the source of a widespread rumour that the Germans had attempted an invasion and had suffered very heavy losses either by drowning or by being burnt in patches of sea covered with flaming oil. We took no steps to contradict these tales, which spread freely through the occupied countries in a wildly exaggerated form, and gave much encouragement to the oppressed populations."

In France, as soon as a German soldier would enter a café, at least a few young men or women would usually get up and ostentatiously warm their hands at the stove. In Belgium and Holland, people would stop Germans politely on the streets, ask them for lights and then hold the flame of the match or lighter suggestively under the German's nose.

To the German High Command, this was no longer a joking matter, especially when the *Abwehr* received foolproof confirmation from its agents in England. Needless to say, it was again British Intelligence which supplied the corroboration.

To at least some of the German generals, like Halder, the rumor was a godsend because they could use it as an argument against the whole maneuver. Even those who had thought it practicable now stopped thinking so, seeing the whole venture in a new light, the light of those imaginary flames. Sea Lion's D-Day was again postponed, pending tests.

Several tests were made, two of them on an elaborate scale. One was conducted at Fécamp in Normandy, the other on a secluded lake near Friedland in East Prussia. The experts had orders to make their tests as realistic as possible and they took the instructions literally. They covered prototype barges with asbestos sheets, filled them with soldiers, then poured oil on the water, ignited it and steered the barges into the pools of burning oil. All on board were burnt to death.

Far from alleviating the rumor, these tests merely added to its plausibility. The experts reported to Hitler that the British could create a wall of fire, completely impenetrable, by pouring oil on the waters of the Channel from specially-constructed fuel planes and by igniting it with incendiary bombs.

The test at Fecamp was still another proof. A few of the dreadfully charred bodies from the test barge drifted out to sea and were washed up along the French coast. The burned bodies provided the final convincing proof.

How decisive the rumor was on the course of Sea Lion is difficult to say, but those who were close to Hitler during those days believe the rumor unnerved him.

At any rate, Sea Lion was postponed from September to October and then indefinitely. Hitler no longer bawled out General Halder when the Chief of Staff told him on December 5 that he considered the execution of the enterprise no longer possible. On January 9, 1941, Hitler ordered his High Command to suspend all preparation for an invasion of England, but to continue to go through the motions as a feint to keep the British jumpy. He was fooling only himself.

But even without Sea Lion, Britain was under savage attack. She was pounded from the air by Goering's enormous *Luftwaffe,* which had begun the Battle of Britain on August 12. On the night of August 24-25, the first bombs fell on central London. Hitler proclaimed in a broadcast, during which his voice broke with hysteria: "The hour will come when one of us two will break, and it will not be National Socialist Germany." Late in the afternoon of September 7, the all-out Battle of London was joined. It was ushered in with a statement by Goering that it will continue "day and night until the R.A.F. has destroyed itself in vain attempts to stop us, and until the people's will to resist is broken."

But Goering, who should have known better, was whistling in the dark. In spite of his stupendous intelligence service, he did not know what the British had and how they were taking it. He looked to Canaris' *Abwehr* and to his own chief of intelligence, Colonel Joseph (Beppo) Schmid, for the knowledge he needed so badly, but all he got from them was double talk they had picked up from the British carillon.

In their ignorance, his generals bickered and made contradictory arrangements for the big battle. Early in September, Hans Sperrle insisted that the R.A.F. still had a thousand fighter planes left. Albrecht Kesselring said they had next to nothing. Beppo Schmid set the "absolute maximum figure" at three hundred and fifty Hurricanes and Spitfires. They were all wrong. In actual fact, the British had six hundred and fifty fighter planes.

Throughout the Battle of Britain, the Germans were fatally handicapped by such faulty intelligence. "It was a battle of chance and force against science and skill," wrote Chester Wilmot. "There was no shortage of courage on the German part, though their pilots lacked the zest of the British, but their confidence was undermined by the knowledge that in comparison with their opponents they were blind, deaf and dumb."

The British flooded the Germans with contradictory information, now claiming that things were going badly and morale would break momentarily, then insisting damage was slight and morale was better than ever.

These "blossoms" were scattered throughout the world. A British agent in Washington leaked information to General Boetticher, the German Military Attaché, that London was on the verge of collapse, traffic at a standstill, famine widespread and epidemics rampant. The German Minister in Lisbon reported exactly the opposite, claiming he had received his information from a prominent Portuguese banker who had just returned from London—in fact, another British agent. The German

Military Attaché in Sofia then confirmed Boetticher's information, while his colleague in Rio de Janeiro corroborated the Lisbon envoy's statements.

German intelligence tried to tap the intelligence services of the neutrals. The British anticipated this and enlisted the aid of their diplomatic friends. The Duke of Alba, Spanish Ambassador at the Court of St. James's, played the game as did the Swedish Minister, sending hopelessly contradictory reports to their respective Foreign Ministries whence they expected the Germans to procure them.

The British received additional help from an unexpected source. The Hungarian Military Attaché in London was an ardent Nazi sympathizer and one of the very few dependable sources the Germans still had in England. He opened his own clandestine radio system in the attic of his house on Grosvenor Place, signaling to the Hungarian General Staff first-rate intelligence. A German agent in Budapest funneled the information on to Berlin.

But the Hungarian Military Attaché in Stockholm was as close to the British as was his London colleague to the Nazis. The Stockholm attaché tipped off the British to the illicit radio; the British seized it and continued to operate it.

So much was at stake and so little was known, that on September 17, at the height of the battle, Goering flew to England in person, to survey from the air what his agents failed to report from the ground. He found out precious little.

But Goering thought he had another ace to play. For some months in the late spring of 1940, a funny German word kept cropping up in radio intercepts and captured documents. To British ears it sounded like the bark of a Katzenjammer kid, though in German it connoted a polite ritual. The word was *Knickebein* which is the German for "curtsey," the colloquial application of "weak-legged" or "weak-kneed." It was assumed that *Knickebein* had something to do with electronic beams that guided German planes to British targets. These were radio beacons which the Germans had erected in various parts of the

Continent. Using directional radio, the *Luftwaffe's* pilots could obtain the desired fixes by the angles from which any two of these transmissions came.

In due course, the British countered these beacons with a system of electronic interference they named "meacons." The "meacon" picked up the German signal, amplified it and returned it from a different angle. The results were gratifying. The "meacon" helped to lead the Germans astray. Once a *Luftwaffe* bomber, homing on the doctored British beam, came down in what its pilot confidently thought was France. He had the surprise of his life when he was told he had just landed in Devonshire.

The British did not expect this to last forever and they decided that *Knickebein* must have been the cover name for a network of secret agents the Germans had planted in England to neutralize the "meacon." Agents of the net, it was thought, were to plant in the various English cities secret beacons on which the Germans could home. The entire British counterespionage organization was mobilized, and a frantic hunt began for those suspected German spies and their secret beacons. None could be found.

What, then, *was* this *Knickebein*? The question was answered by the forces of what Churchill called "the Wizard War." "This was a secret war," he wrote, "whose battles were lost or won unknown to the public, and only with difficulty comprehended, even now, by those outside the small high scientific circles concerned. No such warfare had ever been waged by mortal men. The terms in which it could be recorded or talked about were unintelligible to ordinary folk. Yet if we had not mastered its profound meaning and used its mysteries, even while we saw them only in the glimpse, all the efforts, all the prowess of the fighting airmen, all the bravery and sacrifices of the people, would have been in vain."

Churchill had prepared for the "Wizard War" in advance. He assigned Professor Frederick Lindemann of Oxford as his scientific adviser and organized, under him, two groups of scientists: one to promote and stimulate war-essential scientific research at home; the other, to find out as much as possible about similar developments abroad, especially in Germany.

On June 20, 1940, Churchill's foresight paid enormous dividends. Lindemann came into his office to say, "We have found the secret of *Knickebein*."

Churchill's elation turned to shock when Lindemann told him what it was. *Knickebein* appeared to be the cover name of a new German device that was supposed to enable their bombers to attack day or night, irrespective of weather conditions. This was the deduction of a certain Richard V. Jones, Deputy Director of Intelligence Research in the Air Ministry.

Dr. Jones was summoned to a meeting with Churchill the next day. He spoke for twenty minutes in quiet tones, "unrolling," as Churchill put it afterwards, "his chain of evidence, the like of which, for its convincing fascination, was never surpassed by tales of Sherlock Holmes or Monsieur Lecoq."

Jones was, for all practical purposes, a spy on the grand scale, sitting behind a desk, and yet procuring data about the innermost secrets of the enemy with a sure hand. His raw material was varied. He was fed transcripts of prisoner interrogations, captured documents, radio cable and telephonic intercepts, censorship reports, all the mass of papers produced by a war's secret service.

A German bomber had been shot down, and in its wreckage R.A.F. intelligence officers found a far more complicated apparatus than seemed to be needed for night landing by the beam. The apparatus was shown to Dr. Jones and appeared to be a step toward a new system of beams by which the Germans expected to navigate and bomb. Jones tried to envisage the new system and perceived it in the form of an invisible searchlight whose beam would guide the bombers to their targets.

Jones then combed the interrogation centers for a *Luftwaffe* prisoner who might know something about this projected system. A few days later, he found the man he sought. Cross-examining him along the lines of his own reasoning, Jones received confirmation. The German broke down and conceded that the *Luftwaffe* was, indeed, experimenting with this new system and that it was expected to be ready for practical use by the start of the great air attack on England.

Jones' report started a chain reaction, with much of Air Intelligence and several secret agents devoting all their efforts to the procurement of additional data about *Knickebein*. Before long, several *Knickebein* stations were located near Dieppe and Cherbourg, and stone by stone, the entire frightening mosaic of the new system was brought together.

No sooner had Jones left the Cabinet Room than Churchill ordered Lindemann to develop a counter-weapon. *Knickebein* was put to work for the first time on August 23, when the Dieppe and Cherbourg stations trained the beam on Birmingham. As soon as the German stations opened up, the British started up their counter-stations. The supposedly infallible *Knickebein* beam was twisted and jammed. The *Luftwaffe* flew in, confident that nothing could go wrong this time, and was startled to find that well-nigh everything was going wrong again. This *Knickebein* phase of the air war was not much different from the bad old "meacon" days.

For two whole months, nobody dared to tell Goering that his beams were being twisted and jammed. When General Martini summoned the courage and told him at last, Goering refused to believe it and told his scientific chief, "That is impossible!" By then it was October, 1940. It was past the Q-hour by which the R.A.F. had to be defeated to win the Battle of Britain.

11

Barbarossa

In June, 1940, Hitler celebrated the fall of France with his little jog at Compiègne and then retired to his mountain retreat, the Berghof, where he could brood best. It was there, less than a month later, on July 19, that he invited General Alfred Jodl to lunch. Jodl was chief of Hitler's personal operations staff which was headquartered aboard a special train, "Atlas," so that it could follow the Fuehrer wherever he went and always be on hand.

Almost casually, between luncheon courses, Hitler instructed Jodl to begin drafting plans for an invasion of Russia. Back aboard "Atlas," which lay on a siding at Reichenhall, a nearby spa, Jodl called in his planning chiefs, Colonels Warlimont and von Lossberg, Commander Junge and Major Baron von Falkenstein, and issued the necessary orders.

Within a few days a preliminary plan was sketched out, but of necessity it had to be based on what intelligence was then available, and that intelligence was skimpy. Even cursory study of the plan showed that far more information was essential.

On September 7, 1940, the Battle of Britain was all but won by the *Luftwaffe,* had the Germans only known it. Crippled and nearly smashed, her only real weapon, the R.A.F., in splinters, Britain had her back to the wall. She and the rest of the West were preoccupied with the apparently impending Sea Lion which might signal the final end of the war in the West.

And on that day an officer arrived at the *Fuchsbau* with a message which he said he would deliver only into the hands of

Admiral Canaris himself. It was a document numbered 150231/
40, signed by Jodl, instructing the *Abwehr* to open operations
against the Soviet Union, Hitler's unsuspecting ally. Jodl urged
extreme caution: "These moves," he wrote, "must not create
the impression in Russia that we are preparing an offensive in
the East."

Canaris was caught by surprise. Relations with Russia had
been friendly; the intelligence organs of the two countries had
even exchanged information on occasion. And after the 1939
treaty, the *Abwehr* had been specifically told to drop espionage
efforts against the Soviet.

Canaris had received that earlier order with relief; he had
never been able to establish an effective network inside Russia.
That incredible Iron Curtain stretched for thousands of miles
from the Arctic Ocean to the Black Sea. First came a barbed
wire fence, spotted at close intervals with watchtowers. Behind
that lay fifteen yards of bare earth, ploughed and raked to show
the lightest footprint. And behind that was twenty miles of
deserted countryside, inhabited only by the frontier guards of
the N.K.V.D.

The only way to get an agent into Russia was through a
legitimate port of entry, where travelers were closely scrutinized
and thence watched throughout their stay. Moreover, the Russians used a system of infiltration inherited from the days of the
Czar. Prospective spies against Russia were recruited all over
Europe and smuggled into the Soviet Union, where they immediately fell into the arms of the secret police. The recruiters were
agents provocateurs.

In the face of such barriers, Canaris did not relish his new
assignment. Such information as the Abwehr had was being
obtained from four sources: from study of the few clues that
appeared in Soviet publications, from legitimate returning travelers, from various exiles, and from Herr Klatt.

This inscrutable man (whose real name and true identity
were never established) was *the* Secret Agent Extraordinary of
the *Abwehr* against the Soviet Union. Who he was, how he

looked, and what made him work for the *Abwehr,* aside from purely mercenary considerations, I do not know. He was one of those wayward adventurers one encounters everywhere in the Balkans, making an obscure but lucrative living from all sorts of deals, some legitimate—most of them shady. Klatt lived in Sofia in the 1930's. There he was engaged in business that apparently had nothing to do with systematic espionage until suddenly he blossomed out as a secret agent on a massive scale. He gained access to Soviet secrets and looked around for some organization on which he could unload them for the greatest profit. A survey quickly revealed to him that nobody but the Germans would be his customers; all others, interested as they were in his material, had no substantial funds to pay for it.

At that time, in 1938, the *Abwehr* was not yet in residence in Bulgaria, so Klatt had to go all the way to Austria to make the initial contact. Shortly after the *Anschluss,* the Munich branch of the *Abwehr* was moved to Vienna and given expanded jurisdiction over the whole of southeastern Europe. It operated under a General Staff officer, Colonel Marogna-Radwitz, a devoutly Catholic, dignified and decent, Bavarian nobleman.

In August, 1938, Klatt arrived in Vienna and was taken by a mutual friend to the colonel. He impressed Count Marogna, not so much with his personality (colorful but obnoxious), as with the material he had brought along and with his *bona fides.* He came to the first meeting with a startling amount of intelligence, especially about the innards of the Soviet Air Force. He claimed to have a link to the Soviet Legation in Sofia and said he was receiving the bulk of his information from the Soviet Union via short-wave radio. Although he was extremely accommodating, he steadfastly refused to reveal anything more about his sources, but he did volunteer to leave his material with the *Abwehr* so that it might be examined closely before a deal was made. Marogna promptly forwarded the *dossiers* to Berlin where they created a sensation. This was exceptional material and Klatt was greeted as the first gusher in an otherwise barren field.

His material stood the test of the most painstaking checking. The discovery of this remarkable agent was considered so important that it was reported directly to the Chief of the General Staff, an unusual step, and, from then on, the Klatt material was handled with top priority by special officers in Berlin. His data became the basis of German planning against the U.S.S.R. on the highest echelon, something few spies in history could claim.

When the deal was made (and it was fantastic in terms of money; Klatt was extremely expensive), the new master spy returned to Sofia to become the top ranking secret agent—and virtually the only direct-action spy—the *Abwehr* had working full-time in this important sector of the secret war. This phenomenal spy never disappointed his employers. And he never ceased to intrigue them. Marogna tried everything, as did Section III of the *Abwehr*, to penetrate this man's secret. All efforts over a period of years to disclose anything at all about Klatt personally, and about his sources, proved in vain, and so in due course the usual suspicion arose that he was probably a Soviet intelligence officer planted with authentic information so that he could palm off misleading intelligence on the Germans when it really mattered.

The suspicions seemed confirmed when several of Klatt's claims were proven false. A day-and-night surveillance showed that, contrary to his statements, he had absolutely no contact with the Soviet diplomatic mission. Whenever he claimed he had received material from the Soviet Union by short-wave, the *Abwehr* monitors could find no trace whatsoever of such traffic. And yet, the intelligence was there and it proved authentic in all instances.

A special effort was made to infiltrate the Soviet secret police for the sole purpose of finding out something about the suspected double agent. It was a complicated and costly affair, but all it revealed was that the Russians had some inkling of a monumental leak somewhere, but knew nothing about Klatt or his activities.

Had the Germans searched for Klatt's secret in Bucharest instead of Sofia, they would have read at least part of the riddle. The spy's actual source was neither the Soviet Legation in Sofia nor some mysterious informants in the Red Army General Staff, but solely the obscure correspondent of a Tokyo newspaper, Isono Kiyosho by name, who had his headquarters in the Rumanian capital. From the correspondent the lines led straight to a house in a Toyko suburb, to the residence of Dr. Richard Sorge, the Soviet's own master spy. Not that Sorge acted as a double agent, working also for the Germans, not directly, that is. Yet indirectly, without his own knowledge, he was doing exactly that. His network extended all the way from Tokyo to New York, with many way-stations along the route, including one in Bucharest. In the Rumanian capital, Kiyosho was his agent, receiving information for Sorge and relaying it to Tokyo, and sometimes even directly to Moscow.

And, Kiyosho-*san* had still another assignment from Sorge. In Bucharest was located one of the major European outposts of the Japanese Intelligence Service specializing in Soviet matters, and so, Kiyosho's assignment was to infiltrate that outpost, establish himself within it as a confidential informant, to find out what the Japanese were getting on Russia and from whom.

Kiyosho did a thorough job. He told Sorge some of what he found out, but most of it he sold to Klatt. It was in this roundabout manner that Klatt could function so phenomenally; he received the intelligence about the Soviet Union from the files of the Japanese secret service through a Japanese newspaperman working for the Soviet Union via a German Communist, and sold it to Germans in the end. Klatt's success was a testimonial to the superb cunning of that remarkable man, but also to the efficiency of the Japanese secret service, and especially to the utter baseness of the espionage game.

Klatt served the Germans to the bitter end, because his sources never dried up. Even when Sorge fell down in 1941, Kiyosho continued to function, and, in 1943, Klatt moved to

Bucharest on some pretext to be closer to his source. He never succeeded in gaining the unqualified trust of the Germans and was frequently on the verge of being unceremoniously sacked, not because his material was not satisfactory (it was uniformly excellent) but because his mystery continued to disturb his employers. Once, in 1945, only the personal intervention of General Heinz Guderian, then chief of the General Staff, saved his life; the Germans, totally exasperated by Klatt's impregnable secret, decided to get rid of him for good by sending him to a concentration camp. Guderian was scandalized; the information the man was supplying was so invaluable that the General Staff Chief gave orders to leave Klatt alone, or else, he said, the best source of information about the U.S.S.R. would be lost.

What happened to Klatt is a matter of conjecture. In March, 1945, when the collapse of Germany was imminent, he arrived in Vienna and appeared at the German secret service office there. He pleaded frantically for aid, trying desperately to escape from the onrushing Russians. He also asked protection for someone else who, however, never showed up: Kiyosho-*san*. The day after Klatt sought the help of the Germans, he vanished and was never seen again.

Unlike the Germans who had to put virtually all their Russian eggs into Herr Klatt's basket, the Poles worked massively on the Soviet Union and were generally regarded as best informed about the Red Army. It was, therefore, with considerable anticipation that Admiral Canaris followed the *Wehrmacht* into Poland in 1939. He was keenly interested in a house on Pilsudskego Square: headquarters of the Polish Intelligence Service.

On October 1, 1939, the *Abwehr* occupied the house and found it to be in relatively good condition, with a hundred or more large safes intact. *Abwehr* locksmiths were flown in from Berlin and they went to work with everything from hairpins to blow torches, only to find that most of the safes were empty. Nothing of value was found about Russia, not even the names of individual Polish spies whom the *Abwehr* could have taken over.

Shortly afterwards, a German officer on a daily constitutional near the ancient Polish fortress Leigonov noticed that the
door to one of the old fort's casements was wide open, and he
entered to inspect the inside of the crumbling relic. He was
surprised to find that the place was a vault and contained a
number of steel cabinets. It was a part of the archives of Polish
Military Intelligence. A hungry crowd of *Abwehr* specialists
descended upon the find, but it also proved disappointing. Much
of the data they found about Russia was stale; more of it was
glaringly inaccurate; what good there was, the Germans had
better.

Efforts were made nevertheless to locate Polish agents who
specialized in the Russians; soon enough, several of them volunteered their services. A special *Abwehr-Kommando* was set up
to organize and direct these people, but their management
became too much of a job and disgusted even the *Abwehr* officers. Most of these volunteers were ordinary scoundrels—un-
scrupulous, depraved and irresponsible individuals—whose low
personal qualities inevitably showed up in their work. Many of
them were mainly interested in revenge. They abused their privileged position under the Nazis to settle old accounts, murdering
their enemies and especially venting their wrath on helpless Jews.

More promising agents were imported from Finland and
the Baltic states; the *Abwehr* desired to utilize the surviving
intelligence officers of the armies of these countries destroyed
by the Russians. Some of these men and women proved valuable
recruits, but most of them were also disappointing.

So the best the *Abwehr* could do was to smuggle agents
across the new demarcation line in Poland and to find out whatever they could about the Red Army occupying the country.

Most of the Russian equipment the *Abwehr* spies managed
to identify was antiquated stuff in a badly neglected condition.
From this, the *Abwehr* concluded that the Red Army's armament
was generally poor.

Aside from these *Abwehr* efforts in the field of tactical intelligence (a low-level activity, whose preoccupation with humdrum

technical detail never appealed to Canaris and which, therefore, was woefully neglected in the *Fuchsbau*), there was an agency within the General Staff that specialized in technical information with emphasis on the Red Army. It was called *Fremde Heere Ost* (Foreign Armies East, with a sister agency called Foreign Armies West, concentrating on the French Army). It was headed by a gaunt, stone-faced ascetic intelligence perfectionist, Reinhold Gehlen by name.

Gehlen was an authentic genius at the game, potentially capable of great things in intelligence, but he was badly hampered at this stage by the usual impediments to intelligence work within General Staffs: low budget, inadequate personnel, limitations of jurisdiction, and incompetence. The strictly restricted authority of his agency was reflected even in Gehlen's rank. The head of this potentially all-important branch was a mere major.

On the eve of Barbarossa, and in preparation for it, Gehlen and his specialists had to work solely with the tools available to desk-bound intelligence officers, the reports of military attachés, sources such as newspaper clippings and the oral reports of returning travelers.

While later in the campaign, Gehlen succeeded in building his organization into an important cog in the German war machine, at this stage, his Foreign Armies East was performing just a little better than the *Abwehr* and much of the intelligence it succeeded in developing proved as inadequate as that of the Canaris organization. Moreover, his reports rarely reached echelons higher than Gehlen's own. It never reached the level of Hitler, who urgently needed whatever information he could get.

This led to a strangely inaccurate assessment of the Russian forces. Most of the Red Army equipment the *Abwehr* spies and Gehlen's chair-borne analysts managed to identify in Poland was antiquated stuff in a badly-neglected condition. From this, German Intelligence drew the conclusion that in general, Soviet equipment was inadequate. Later, when the Germans found much high-quality material in the hands of the Red soldiers,

Hitler thought the concentration of the old equipment in Poland had been a deliberate Russian ruse to mislead the *Abwehr*. Whether or not this was true cannot be determined, but after that, Hitler refused to believe virtually anything Canaris or his representatives told him about the Russians. *Abwehr* agents correctly identified seventy-seven Red Army divisions in Poland, but Hitler's own intelligence officers questioned that, too. Still later, when he was deep in the Soviet Union, during one of his inconclusive offensives, Hitler was heard to remark ruefully:

"Look at those Russian Panzers! How good they are, and how little we knew about them beforehand! If the Russians are ahead of us in anything," he said with scorn, "it is espionage!" These few words reveal his contempt for what he called the *Abwehr-Kram*, the "hodgepodge rubbish" supplied by his own military intelligence service.

Where mass was so important, and strategy decisive—in the historic onslaught on the Soviet Union on June 22, 1941— intelligence and espionage necessarily played subordinate roles. For once, the Germans embarked upon a campaign with inadequate information about the enemy, but, for the time being, the effects of that inadequacy did not become evident. The situation was different in the Soviet camp, where good intelligence and espionage were a vital weapon, and at first, a sadly-neglected one.

There was in Berlin in those days a rather obscure American, a forty-eight-year-old Texan named Sam E. (for Edison) Woods, an amazing many-sided man, educational expert, engineer, businessman, diplomat, a self-effacing cosmopolitan with a knack for making friends with men in the know. He had been serving since 1934 as commercial attaché-at-large to the United States Embassy, and he had proved extremely effective as a collector of secret intelligence, with his unassuming ways and his passion for anonymity. In fact, the Germans, who watched several members of the Embassy with eagle eyes, never paid the slightest attention to this "unimportant Mr. Woods."

In August, 1940, Woods received in his morning mail a

single ticket for a reserved seat in a Berlin movie house, although he had ordered none. He went to the movie house and found in the next seat an acquaintance of his, a prominent German with close links to the High Command via Dr. Hjalmar Schact's Reichsbank. Woods knew the man as a confirmed anti-Nazi who, however, understood how to conceal his real sentiments.

They gave no signs of recognition, just sat next to one another, apparently engrossed in the screenplay. The two men went their separate ways when the show was over. At home Woods removed from his pocket a piece of paper that had not been there when he went to the movie house. It informed him that "conferences were then taking place at Hitler's headquarters concerning preparations for war against Russia."

Woods forwarded the information to the State Department, where it was received with considerable skepticism, if only because, as Cordell Hull put it, the intelligence "was in marked contrast to the considerable evidence that Hitler was planning an invasion of Britain." Woods was instructed, however, to follow up his lead, and several clandestine meetings followed in various movie houses in Berlin. The German assured the American commercial attaché that his information was absolutely reliable; it had come to him from someone in the inner sanctum of the *Wehrmacht* High Command. "In fact," he advised Woods, "the air raids on England served as a blind for Hitler's real and well-calculated plans and preparations for a sudden, devastating attack on Russia."

His friend gave Woods details of the rapidly developing "Build-Up East." Among other things, he advised the American attaché that "an organization of the *Wehrmacht* had been formed for the old twenty-one Russian Czarist regional governments, and that the economic staffs for these territories had been appointed." He tipped him off, too, when the Germans began to print bales of Russian banknotes.

On December 18, Hitler issued his historic Directive No. 21, cloaked under the code name Barbarossa. Even this was distributed only to a small circle of officers, who had to know about it. It contained instructions for elaborate camouflage and deception, with misleading maneuvers going by separate code names—Shark and Harpoon—to give the impression that the build-up was for intensified operations against England from Scandinavian bases.

No amount of deception could keep the secret from Sam Woods. No sooner was Barbarossa issued than he was given its explicit details by his German friend: the German strategic plan was to drive simultaneously three savage wedges into Russia, the decisive one being in the center, stabbing at Moscow. He was also advised that Hitler had ordered all preparations to be concluded not later than the spring of 1941.

This was January, 1941. By then, Secretary Hull had no reason to doubt the accuracy of the intelligence. Woods cabled that his information could be corroborated by a prominent German exile in the United States. Assistant Secretary of State Breckinridge Long was sent to interview the refugee, who confirmed the information. In January, Hull placed the reports before President Roosevelt.

The State Department was then holding a series of confidential conferences with Russia in an effort to loosen the tie between Stalin and Hitler. At the conclusion of one of these meetings, Under Secretary of State Sumner Welles revealed to Ambassador Konstantin Oumansky the information the Department had about Hitler's intentions. This was the very first warning the U.S.S.R. had received, but Stalin simply refused to believe it. He regarded it as a clumsy British plant, smuggled to him via America, to muddy the waters of his relations with Hitler. There is reason to believe that he actually resented Oumansky's decision to forward the report and censured the ambassador for his naïveté.

Churchill was, of course, given full access to the Woods reports, but until March, 1941, the Prime Minister, too, refused to accept the momentous information at face value. He probably rejected it for some psychological reason, because it sounded too good to be true; and he certainly rejected it on apparently sound intelligence grounds, because his own Joint Intelligence Committee advised him without qualification not to indulge in any delusions about a life-saving Russo-German war.

By then, the British Secret Service was functioning well on the Continent. Its newly-established agents reported in pinpoint detail the movement of German troops, but nothing much could be made of that scattered tactical intelligence. Hitler's war was extremely fluid. His conflicting ideas necessitated constant redeployments. The conclusions that could be drawn from those disconnected reports, covering usually only small areas with no direct relationship to the whole, were hazy at best.

In addition, the German system of deception was working extremely well. The *Wehrmacht* remained in force all along the Channel, went through all sorts of landing exercises and leaked voluminous information about Sea Lion, as if that dead beast were still robust and kicking. In Moscow, General Koestring, the German Military Attaché, received instructions to befuddle the Soviet General Staff with a plausible tale of his own. Koestring told the Russians that "inasmuch as the operations in the West had been concluded, the Germans intended to replace the older men in the East with younger men so that the former could be employed in German production." Another reason, he said, was that training and supply conditions were better in the East and there was no danger of air attacks. The Soviet General Staff was not wholly inclined to believe his tales, but it was discouraged in its skepticism by Stalin who explicitly forbade any doubts in Hitler's best intentions.

On April 7, 1941, the Joint Intelligence Committee presented Churchill with an estimate of the situation. They conceded that Germany had huge forces in the East, and that the Germans would fight Russia sooner or later, but concluded nevertheless that a war at that time appeared unlikely. And on May 23, they reported that "rumors of impending attack on Russia had died down."

The Prime Minister already knew much better. Late in March, he had instructed Major Morton to procure for him the originals of the more significant raw reports. He came upon a report that suddenly revealed the whole complex story.

It was from one of Britain's most trusted sources, an agent to whom Churchill has paid glowing tribute in his war memoirs without identifying him otherwise. The agent, observing the movement of German troops in Central and South Eastern Europe, located five Panzer divisions in Poland near Cracow, where they were certainly not needed to attack England. Yes, Churchill thought, the Fuehrer must be planning some maneuver in the East. Then unexpectedly, the pro-German Yugoslav government was overturned in a *coup*. Two days later, on March 29, another signal arrived from the same agent reporting that three of those five divisions were being hastily moved to Rumania. This still left two divisions in Cracow. Now what did this mean, the Prime Minister asked himself. The transfer of a single Panzer division is a major operation, necessitating the shuffling of twenty trains. Sixty trains, Churchill figured, are not moved for a whim, however whimsical Herr Hitler might be.

There must be some motivating factor, he thought, for those five Panzer divisions being in Cracow at all, and that reason, he concluded, could only be an impending war against the Soviet Union. The departure of three of the five divisions for Rumania then suggested to the Prime Minister that Hitler had temporarily abandoned his plan to attack the U.S.S.R. and was to mount a punitive expedition against Yugoslavia to retaliate for the *coup*. After its conclusion, Churchill reasoned, the Panzers would rejoin the others at Cracow.

The Prime Minister no longer doubted. Next day he wrote of his discovery to Eden, who was in Athens, working hard to anticipate developments. Churchill sketched in what soon proved to be uncannily accurate details, the actual moves of Hitler, which were yet to come. Seven days before the Yugoslav campaign was unleashed, Churchill told Eden that it was certain to come, adding that Greece would be next. He told him that after Yugoslavia and Greece, Hitler would turn against the Russians.

He was so convinced of the accuracy of his deductions that three days later, on April 3, he instructed Sir Stafford Cripps, his Ambassador in Moscow, to advise Stalin *personally* of his assumptions based on "sure information from a trusted agent." There was no response until April 12, and then only a cable from Cripps that he had not yet delivered the message. Churchill was stung; he cabled Cripps to do as he was told. Still things moved slowly. The message was delivered only on April 19, and then to Andrei Y. Vishinsky, Under Secretary in the Foreign Commissariat, and not to Stalin. At last, on April 22, word came from Cripps that Vishinsky had assured him the message had been handed to Stalin.

If Oumansky's warning from Washington irritated the Soviet dictator, the message from the British Prime Minister made him seethe. Now he was convinced (was not this the proof?) that Churchill was behind the insidious campaign to alienate him from Hitler. "Nothing that any of us could do," Churchill later wrote, "pierced the purblind prejudice and fixed ideas that Stalin had raised between himself and the terrible truth."

By then, even Moscow was buzzing with rumors about the imminence of a Russo-German war, but, in view of Stalin's attitude, it was dangerous to express such fears. The German Naval Attaché signaled to Berlin on April 24, that German visitors in Moscow spoke rather loosely about Barbarossa, and, he added, the British Ambassador predicted that war would break out on June 22 (!), the exact day that was yet to be fixed by Hitler.

Nothing ignited the imagination of the Soviet Ambassador in Berlin. He assured Molotov, and Molotov in turn assured Stalin, that the last thing the Germans intended to do was to attack the Soviet Union. He reported he was so certain that the rumors lacked foundation that he had made arrangements to hold the annual outing of the Embassy—on June 22.

In the face of such reassurances, Stalin ordered an investigation to track down the rumor-mongers and punish them severely. The chief of his secret police reported that the perpetrator was an intelligence officer of the General Staff's Fourth Bureau, serving as technical adviser with the Soviet Embassy in Berlin. Upon Stalin's instructions, the man was to be recalled and sent to Siberia, but he managed to escape at the last moment, and so lived to see his fears come true and to relish Stalin's monumental humiliation.

12

Footloose In "Sicily"

The Soviet Union, traditionally the leading espionage power of the world, had inherited a complex secret service organization from Czarist Russia and had both enlarged and improved it.

The pre-war Soviet espionage organization was brilliantly and purposefully organized and was managed with exceptional skill, despite a frequent change of directors, and in spite of frequent duplications. Altogether, the Kremlin had at its disposal six major intelligence organizations, five of them operational in various fields, one in charge of strategic evaluation. This latter was the so-called Confidential Department of the Secretariat of the Communist Party's Central Committee, a conveyor belt for the transmission of intelligence from the procurement agencies to the Politbureau and the Central Committee.

Among the five operational agencies, the Fourth Bureau of the Red Army General Staff and the Foreign Department of the Commissariat (later Ministry) of the Interior, the notorious NKVD, were equal in importance and influence. A third branch was the political intelligence department of the *Narkomindel* (Foreign Commissariat), with a sub-section in Tass, the official news agency, whose correspondents abroad doubled as spies. The others were the industrial and commercial intelligence department of the Commissariat of Foreign Trade; there was also the intelligence apparatus of the Communist International, which had its headquarters in Moscow and branches throughout the world in the regional Communist Parties, both legal and illegal.

The Soviet combine was able to set up and maintain an unprecedented network of active operatives abroad. These were both professional spies and enthusiastic lay agents, chosen from among local Party members and Soviet sympathizers. There was said to be, at the headquarters of the Comintern in Moscow, a master index card file of some four hundred thousand persons throughout the world who could be counted upon to serve Soviet intelligence at one time or another, in one way or another.

The Soviet secret service was unique for another reason—in the understanding and manipulation of conspiracies. Blending conventional espionage with political conspiracy, the service, for utter ruthlessness and comprehensive coverage, surpassed any of its opposite members in the capitalist countries.

At some time in 1937, the Fourth Bureau of the Red Army General Staff acquired an exceptional agent. On the staff of the German legation in Warsaw was a staid Silesian aristocrat, an aging, impeccable career diplomat of the old school, Rudolf von Scheliha by name. He was apparently the prototype of the striped pants diplomat, very correct and formal, suave and *soigné*, with expensive tastes in food and women. He was married to an elderly lady of considerable means and was drawing a respectable salary, but his substantial revenue still was not enough to cover his expensive love affairs and, especially, his gambling losses.

With the help of a German journalist to whom Scheliha had confided his woes, a Soviet agent made contact and, by holding out money as bait, enticed the old-fashioned gentleman to become an old-fashioned spy. From 1937 on, Scheliha kept the Kremlin well supplied with intelligence about every development in German-Polish relations and was the first to alert the Fourth Bureau when these relations showed signs of deteriorating.

In February, 1938, he was engaged in an especially costly liaison with an exquisite lady of Warsaw's best society, and at an all-night card party in the Polonia Hotel he lost some fifty thousand zloties (about ten thousand dollars). His friends gave him until the end of February to settle the debt—upon his honor.

On a trip to Berlin, he made a frantic search of confidential files for information that would bring a high price and found the evidence of Hitler's impending moves on Austria and Czechoslovakia, with Poland as a more distant target. Back in Warsaw he met his Soviet go-between and the horsetrading began. Scheliha asked for ten thousand dollars, a sum the Fourth Bureau had never before doled out to a single agent. They offered him one thousand dollars in American currency, with the suggestion that he improve upon it by selling the dollars on the black market. The bargaining continued for the better part of February.

At last, on February 26, Scheliha received a circumspect invitation to spend the weekend at Zakopane, a fashionable winter resort. He was instructed to go on skis to an abandoned hunting lodge high in the Tatra Mountains. In the lodge Scheliha found a courier specially sent from Moscow. He had six thousand five hundred dollars with him and offered it on a take-it or leave-it basis. To lend proper emphasis to the offer, he told Scheliha bluntly of instructions to kill him at the lodge if he refused. Scheliha dickered no longer. He handed over his document and took the money. By selling the dollars on the black market as the Russians had suggested, he realized far more than he needed to pay his gambling debt.

After this incident, the Fourth Bureau more or less blackballed Herr von Scheliha, despite the high quality of his information. Even so, he was kept in the fold and continued to work for the Soviets even after his own country was actually at war with them.

In the fall of 1938 a young Englishman arrived in Geneva, Switzerland, looking for a woman carrying a string shopping bag with a green parcel in it and holding an orange in her right hand. He himself wore a white scarf around his neck and held a leather belt in his hand. Anyone familiar with third-rate movies could deduce from this quaint mixture of grocery and haberdashery that these were spies. The foreman of Soviet spies who arranges such *rendezvous* had either a lurid imagination or some marvelously prescient acquaintance with the *Late Late Show.*

The youthful Englishman was a vague adventurer who had graduated *summa cum laude* from the school of hard knocks on the Loyalist side of the Spanish Civil War but was otherwise an innocent abroad. At the central post office the woman came, exactly on time. She was slim and moderately good looking, in her early thirties, with a sexy figure and good legs. Her black hair was combed back and her dress was simple.

Without looking to the right or left, she walked up to the fidgety young man and gave the melodramatic password, a silly question to which she received the required silly answer.

"Excuse me," she said, "but where did you buy that belt?"

"I bought it in an ironmonger's shop in Paris," the youth answered. Then he asked, "Where could I buy an orange like yours?"

"Oh," the woman said, "I could give you mine for an English penny."

The young man was Alexander Foote, a native of Britain, who here was called Jim. The woman was called Sonia, although her real name was Ursula-Maria Hamburger Schultz; she was assigned to "Sicily," which in reality was Switzerland. Jim had just been recruited in London at $300 a week, although he had no qualifications whatever for the spy trade. Jim, Sonia, and their colleagues were puppets manipulated from 19 Znamensky Street in Moscow, where the "Director" of the Fourth Bureau had his headquarters. More immediately they were manipulated from a house in Geneva near the observatory in Bellevue. That was where Albert lived.

Albert was Alexander Rado, a Hungarian cartographer of international reputation and partner in a reputable Swiss firm of map-makers, called Geopress. He was the manager of this particular Swiss "roof," the technical name of a specific espionage ring operating behind a legal front. Rado was a short, rather rotund little man, with a round, gentle, scholarly face. Arthur Koestler knew Rado well, not as a spy, but as a human being and friend in whose house one could eat well and have excellent conversations. Koestler still waxes sentimental when he talks of Rado.

"He was kind and warm-hearted by nature," Koestler recalls, "but very shy and inhibited in personal relations, as true scholars sometimes are, and also rather absent-minded and awkward in his movements, so that he always reminded me of that pathetic character, the Fat Boy, bad in studies, bad at games, and the good-natured target of practical jokes."

Until 1937, Rado lived in Paris, where he operated a minor press agency from two barely furnished rooms in the Rue de Faubourg St. Honoré. He was sent to Switzerland to organize a new network. Until then, the Red Army had depended largely on reports pouring in from Soviet military attachés, like General Putna in London, and from the *Apparat,* the world-wide espionage arm of the Communist International. The Fourth Bureau had its own men in the field, like Colonel Bykov in the United States and General Krivitsky in The Hague, to maintain liaison with the *Apparat's* lay agents, but the coverage was slipshod and produced spotty results. And even this inadequate organization was badly shaken by the great purges of 1937 at home and subsequent defections abroad. Putna was called home and executed. Krivitsky deserted. Agents who worked for them had been liquidated.

So Rado, the little fat man, who would sweat profusely from the brow whenever the most trifling matter went wrong, set out to construct an enormously intricate net, not with any efficiency—of this he was congenitally incapable—but with instinctive purposefulness and shrewd improvisation. If ever there was a comic spy, Rado was that man. He was timid and constantly violated the rules of good espionage. His boners were innumerable. Forever stumbling over security precautions, he handled the ring's funds with bohemian carelessness and observed none of the trade's Spartan rules in his private life. He was a sentimentalist and a soft touch, trusting indiscriminately all who attracted his sympathy. He was loved by his civilian friends, as

Koestler's homage to him shows, but he was intensely disliked by his operatives.

Yet Rado managed to muddle through to greatness in this fantastic business. He performed better, and produced more valuable material than any of his colleagues or opposite numbers in any one of the secret services. Rado tapped the anti-Nazi underground inside Germany and soon had agents inside the *Wehrmacht* High Command itself and in virtually every war-essential agency of the Nazi government. Even today, long after the whole ring has been blown to bits, only a handful of his contacts have been identified. By late 1938, Rado was getting vast quantities of information and was the busiest man in Switzerland. He devoted a full day's work to his Geopress in downtown Geneva and every minute of what was left to the management of his clandestine pastime. The latter required enormous attention to detail with plenty of paper work, because at this stage Rado had no "music boxes," no secret radio transmitters, at his disposal. He was getting so many documents in their original form, or as transcripts, that he could not have encoded them all and put them on the air even if he had wanted to.

He would photograph these documents on 35mm film and send them by courier to the military attaché at the Soviet Embassy in Paris. From there they were either sent on to Moscow by other couriers or radioed to the "Center" over a transmitter operated by the French branch office of the Fourth Bureau.

Until 1939, the pattern which emerged from these documents was not clear. But then suddenly the evidence Rado was waiting for started to pour in. On April 6 or 7, he received on microfilm a German order dated only three or four days earlier. A couple of weeks later, he sent a courier to Paris with another batch of film clips on which was reduced a lengthier document, a variation on the same theme. These two papers were copies of Hitler's orders to start translating "Case White" (the operations plan against Poland) into practice.

What was made of these reports in the Kremlin nobody at

this end can tell. But was it sheer coincidence that on April 17, 1939, a few days after Rado's information had reached Moscow, the Soviet Ambassador to Berlin spoke of the possibility of a Russo-German *rapprochement* during a routine meeting with Baron von Weizsaecker, Under-Secretary in the German Ministry of Foreign Affairs? Was there no connection between Rado's information and Stalin's decision to conclude a pact with Hitler?

Thanks to Rado's scoop, the Kremlin knew exactly in what direction the wind was blowing and set its sails accordingly. The signing of the Russo-German pact in August, 1939, had its grotesque aftermath in Rado's private underworld. On August 26, 1939, he received orders from the "Director" in Moscow to dismantle his German ring and stop spying on Germany. Stalin was taking the pact rather seriously.

Rado must have thought this was a senseless order and that it was a pity to destroy such a well-oiled ring. He disobeyed his instructions, as he had many times before, and kept his German ring going. As we shall see, his insubordination made all the difference between victory and defeat for the Soviet Union. The fat little spy in his landlocked Swiss hideout could see more clearly than the supreme dictator in the Kremlin. It was, therefore, simple for him to return to full operations when in October, 1940, he received instructions from Moscow to resume speed.

Rado had about fifty agents working for him, going by all sorts of cover names, living all kinds of double lives. Two of them—Sissy and Taylor—loomed up at this critical moment. Sissy was Rachel Duebendorfer, a woman of obscure Balkan origin but Swiss by a marriage of convenience; she was working in the International Labor Office, an agency of the League of Nations. Taylor was Christian Schneider, a German by birth. He was Rachel's colleague at the I.L.O. until he gave up his legitimate job and became a full-time cut-out for Rado.

Rado was using three aliases: Albert and Kulicher, and then, throughout the war, Dora. He kept in touch with Moscow through three clandestine radio stations. One was operated by

Jim, the wayward British expatriate; the second was managed by a French couple, Edmond (Eduard) and Olga (Maud) Hamel, from the back room of their legitimate radio shop; the third was operated by Rosie, Rado's twenty-one-year-old paramour, a pretty Swiss girl named Margaret Balli.

It was not too difficult to operate such a network in Switzerland. The country was the ideal, traditional locale of wartime espionage, facilitated by Swiss democracy with its scrupulous regard for civil rights; Switzerland's geographical location in the heart of Europe; its role in high finance as the banker of the belligerents; and the fact that the Swiss themselves had a very real stake in espionage, which they regarded as their country's first line of defense. Most anxious to keep a constant check on German intentions insofar as their own country was concerned, the Swiss Army Intelligence Service (the world famous *Nachrichtendienst*) utilized all sources of information, their own as well as the agents of others. The N.D. was frequently willing and even eager to make deals and barters with foreign agents as long as their activities were not directed against Switzerland.

It was from Switzerland that the Fourth Bureau received its most explicit warning, *"from Dora to Director."*

It was June 10, 1941, a cloudless, beautiful near-Summer day in Geneva. Rado was just getting up when his home telephone rang. It was Taylor, violating the most elementary rule of good espionage. Rado himself would violate the rules wholesale, but he disliked it when his cut-outs got in touch with him in this direct manner.

"Yes . . . What do you want?" he barked.

"I have to see you at once," Taylor said. "I'll come to your house right away!"

"That's impossible," Rado replied. "We'll have to meet somewhere," but Taylor broke into his sentence:

"This matter cannot wait," and hung up. Fifteen minutes later, a cab drove up in front of a restaurant and out of it stepped Taylor, making his way in stages to Rado's house. His boss waited for him in his study.

Taylor, a stolid, somewhat slow-witted German of extreme reserve, was almost breathless.

"Sissy has put me in touch with the most phenomenal source we ever had," he blurted. "She refused to tell me who he is and how she got hold of him, but he is as real as life, has direct lines to the German High Command and has his own lines of communications. And he's safe! He's working for the *Nachrichtendienst*. They vouch for him and protect him!"

He gave Rado the first piece of information he had received that morning from the mysterious contact and left. Rado spent an hour, writing a concise message, enciphering it (something he rarely did himself), then pondering whether to send it. It was monumental news, if it was true. But if it was not, he would make a fool of himself and bring down upon his head the wrath of the Director.

At last, when it was almost eleven o'clock, he called Jim from a booth and asked his chief radioman to meet him at a street corner. Rado was still worried when they met, almost shaking with fear, but Jim calmed him down. He simply took the piece of paper with the cipher on it from Rado's trembling hand and left the shaking spymaster at the street corner.

That night, two officers of the German radio monitoring station at Cranz in East Prussia, combing the air waves for other people's secrets, picked up a message. It attracted their attention because it was repeated again and again, on wave lengths 18.9 and 21.3, for hours every half hour, always the same monotonous signals, identical five-figure groups. The Germans had monitored the station before, but they never succeeded in breaking its cipher. It was, of course, Jim in Geneva:

"*From Dora to Director,* source: Taylor. Hitler's attack on Soviet Union definitively scheduled for June 22. This is new date representing postponement from original June 15. Hitler reached decision only two days ago. Report from absolutely reliable new source, received by Swiss General Staff via special diplomatic courier. More to follow."

The message reached Moscow that night, but it was not

deciphered until the next morning. It was immediately sent to General Kuznetsov, the Director, who was in the Kremlin, attending a military discussion in Stalin's office. The general was called out of the meeting and was handed the message. He returned to the conference and read it out loud.

Stalin still remained skeptical, but the others around the table no longer shared his doubts. The conceited dictator who alone could have given the order to meet the onslaught still preferred not to give it.

Who was the source of the message that Stalin so rashly disregarded?

Not far from the discreetly cloaked headquarters of the Swiss Military Intelligence Service in Lucerne was the modest office of a small, esoteric publishing house, Vita Nova by name, the publisher of books with a liberal Catholic philosophical slant. It was run by a short, owlish, ascetic-looking man. He called himself Rudolf Roessler, and it may be that it was his real name.

It happens but rarely that a single individual spy can exert decisive influence on the main course of history, but Rudolf Roessler was such a person. According to Alex Foote, it was mainly his contribution that enabled the Red Army to beat Hitler.

Roessler was born on November 22, 1897, in Kaufbeuren, Germany, the son of a Swabian forestry official. He worked as a journalist in Augsburg and later became the manager of a theatrical association in Berlin. When the Nazis came into power Roessler had to flee. He found a haven in Switzerland, and, from then on, his life was devoted to anti-Nazi activities. He settled in Lucerne with the aid of a young friend, Dr. Xavier Schnieper. Throughout his subsequent espionage activities, Schnieper remained his sole confidant and associate. He became the representative of an enormously powerful German conspiratorial group that extended into the highest echelons of the High Command and the Foreign Office.

Schnieper was friendly with a major of the Swiss Intelligence Service in whose house also lived a certain Uncle Tom, apparently a relative or a friend of the family. In fact, Uncle Tom was Colonel Svoboda, Military Attaché of the Czechoslovak Government-in-exile. Roessler placed his information at the disposal of the Swiss and also gave it to Uncle Tom for the Czech secret service in London. At the same time, he tried to establish a working relationship with General West, the British Military Attaché in Berne, ex officio resident chief of the Secret Service. But West turned him down, probably because his sources happened to be the same German dissidents with whom the British, after the shock of the Venlo incident, refused to cooperate.

With no other place to go, and realizing that the Swiss and the Czechs could never defeat the Nazis by their own efforts, Roessler groped for a link to the Russians. Schnieper introduced him to Sissy and she brought him to Taylor. Until then, Taylor had never amounted to much as a secret agent, but his association with Roessler was so highly valued in Moscow that he was taken into the Fourth Bureau's fraternity as a charter member with a monthly stipend of eight hundred Swiss francs.

Sissy and Taylor were the only members of Rado's ring who ever met Roessler in person. All the deals were made through Taylor. They were substantial even financially because Roessler insisted that he be paid well for his services. It was Taylor who picked up Roessler's information and forwarded it to Rado; and it was he again who took the money back to Roessler. Roessler agreed to work for Rado, but only on his own terms. He was never to reveal the sources of his information, and, in all those years of co-operation, he merely hinted that his chief contact in Germany was a senior officer in Hitler's High Command for whom he coined the name Werther. Even today, it is not known who Werther was.

When Roessler's first message arrived in Moscow, the one heralding the imminent outbreak of the Russo-German war, this new source of information was received with skepticism. Kuznetsov asked Rado to tell him more about his new contact, but there was little Rado could tell. Kuznetsov was amazed by the quality of Roessler's information and impressed by the promptness with which it was obtained and transmitted, but he suspected a plant and for some time refused to accept the material as genuine. The suspicion was not to last long. According to Foote, this was the only time Moscow was willing to cooperate with an "unvetted source," a man who remained as mysterious to his employers as he was to the Germans against whom he worked.

To the end, Roessler remained outside the Rado ring. Foote was assigned to transmit most of his information, but the two never met and even years later the Englishman thought Roessler was a certain Czech named Selzinger.

Roessler was to be paid seven thousand Swiss francs a month and special bonuses for scoops. He made it clear from the outset that he would not accept orders from the Center in Moscow or from Rado in Geneva. Roessler subsequently earned what is regarded as an astronomical sum in espionage. Between the summer of 1941 and the spring of 1944, he was paid a total of three hundred and thirty-six thousand francs in monthly stipends and about two hundred and fifty thousand francs in bonuses. He was given a cover name, Lucy, after the city of Lucerne, where he lived; and Taylor resigned his job at the I.L.O. to be available as a full-time go-between.

Roessler was a gusher. He furnished to the Fourth Bureau the order of battle of the *Wehrmacht* on a day-to-day basis, including the exact location and mission even of single battalions; operations plans and orders well in advance of their execution; diplomatic information of the utmost importance.

He supplied the German operation order for what became the decisive Battle of Rostov, where Marshal Timoshenko succeeded for the first time in stemming the tide of the *Wehrmacht's* advance. He delivered the operation order for the Battle of Moscow, which enabled Marshal Zhukov to make his own arrangements. He furnished the operation plan of the Battle of Stalingrad, including the disposition of all German forces, the emergency plans for Goering's aborted air lift and voluminous data about logistics.

"Not only did he," Foote wrote, "provide the day-to-day dispositions in the Eastern front, but also Lucy could, and did, provide answers to specific questions. It frequently happened that Moscow had lost sight of such-and-such a division. An inquiry was put through to Lucy and in a matter of days the answer would be provided, giving the composition, strength and location of the unit in question." Sometimes Lucy's reports followed a unit all the way from its inception to its extinction. He would report that such and such a division was about to leave its sinecure in France for the Eastern front. He would follow with the date of departure, the route of transportation and the destination. He would wind up by reporting the arrival of the unit, its order of battle and its operations order, pinpointing the exact sector where it would be thrown into the struggle—and when.

"As far as Moscow was concerned," Foote remarked, "this was obviously the most important function Lucy could perform. Russia, fighting with her back to the wall and scraping up her last resources, was obviously vitally interested in trustworthy information regarding the armed forces ranged against her—and this Lucy supplied."

Roessler was not a spy in the usual sense of the word, for he had no direct access to the secret information he was peddling. He performed the function of a conveyor belt. He received his information from his mysterious source in Germany, and, to this day, nobody knows for certain how he obtained it, especially so swiftly. Some say he had access to the diplomatic pouch of the Swiss; others say he was on the Europe-wide clandestine radio network of the Red Orchestra, the other enormous espionage ring that flooded the Fourth Bureau with material straight from the safes and files of Hitler's diplomatic and military apparatus.

The Fourth Bureau is usually stingy with monetary rewards and it is even stingier with praise, but Lucy received the highest accolades from the Director. Among the intercepted communications of Rado's Dora period, there are scores that contain nothing but thanks which Rado was to convey to Roessler. It is generally agreed today that Lucy's contribution to the Russian victory was of the greatest significance and "the effect of the information [he supplied] on the strategy of the Red Army and the ultimate defeat of the Wehrmacht [was] incalculable."

Roessler continued to work for the Russians until June, 1944, but shrewdly covered his rear by also working for Swiss Intelligence.

At one point during the war, Hitler toyed with the idea of invading and occupying Switzerland. During those weeks and months, Roessler's importance to the *Nachrichtendienst* became crucial. He procured all the pertinent data, including private conversations Hitler had about Switzerland, and placed them at the disposal of the *Nachrichtendienst*. He received no remuneration whatever from Swiss Intelligence, except that he was allowed to function unmolested for others.

The chief of the Swiss Intelligence Service, Colonel Roger, insisted that Roessler's information of those critical weeks enabled the Swiss Federal authorities to forestall the projected German invasion by staging a timely counter-offensive of their own in the military and diplomatic fields. Colonel Roger gives Roessler full credit for averting war from Switzerland in 1939-45.

With Roessler's help and by their own remarkable efforts, Rado and his fifty agents managed something that was unprecedented in the whole history of espionage. No comparable network has ever succeeded in staying in business with such an elaborate apparatus for so long and with such feverish activity. By 1942, the total of outgoing messages averaged eight hundred per month. Rado had to use daily all three of his radio transmitters and he had to drive his operators as hard as he could. This was almost too good to be true or too good to last forever. An end was inevitable and when it came at last, in stages in 1943 and 1944, it was due to a combination of the carelessness that forever characterized Rado's operations, of the chaos that goes even with the best-managed war, and of the jealousies that are rampant in the secret service.

Rado persistently violated many rules of good espionage, but none of his trespasses was as serious as his amorous involvement with "Rosie," the pretty Swiss demoiselle, Margaret Bolli. She was a native of Geneva, what the Germans call *ein Maedchen aus gutem Hause*, a young lady of good family. But behind her philistine façade, she was a Communist activist, member of the inner circle of Léon Nicole, the bigtime Swiss Comintern agent, whose hatchery supplied the fish for the Soviet espionage nets in Switzerland.

Nicole introduced Mlle. Bolli to Rado, and the aging master spy, never before seized by this kind of passion, completely forgetful of his wife at home, was promptly smitten by the young woman's charm. As a prospective spy, the Bolli girl was a very rough little diamond at best, but Rado in his amorous bias saw in her a great operative and he had her learn radio telegraphy and cipher work from Foote.

Rado's love for Margaret never slackened, but she gradually cooled to the elderly man. Before long, she found herself yearning for the companionship of younger men and became involved with a handsome barber in Geneva, Hans Peters by name. Now she had to live still a third secret life, for she was anxious to conceal her faithlessness from Rado.

Young Peters had more than just romantic interest in Margaret. He was a German by birth and was in secret communication with the German consul in Geneva. The German counterespionage organization, operating out of the consul's office, was fully aware of the existence of a Soviet network in Switzerland, but it was frustrated by its inability to locate its transmitters, break its ciphers or to find out anything concrete about it. All they had were a few scattered clues that showed Miss Bolli was a member of the ring and operated one of its radios.

Her private life was investigated and it became quickly evident that she was restive and frustrated in love. Young Peters was put to work and it did not take long for Gretel to fall head over heels in love with her Hansel. In her infatuation she could keep no secrets from him. In the end, she even delivered to him the book on which her code was based, a German volume entitled *Es geschah in September—It Happened in September.*

In October, 1943, Margaret was arrested, on evidence the Germans had slipped to the Swiss. She was trapped in Peters' arms during a tryst in his apartment, to which the ungallant suitor had also invited the police. From then on, the decline and fall was only a matter of time and before long, the phenomenal ring of Alexander Rado was smashed.

Rado went into hiding, but he was hunted, and not only by the police. His own associates, who somehow never liked him, now supplied voluminous information about him to the Swiss and the Germans, but also to the Russians, charging that he had embezzled some of the funds of the network for some stock speculations in New York. A lot of money was involved in this gargantuan espionage operation and the sum that allegedly vanished into Rado's pocket was said to be in excess of one hundred thousand dollars.

Pursued from so many quarters, Rado embarked on a pathetic odyssey that led, through treacheries and disillusionments, most probably to death from a bullet fired by a Soviet secret policeman. After Margaret's defection, shattered both romantically and professionally, he tried to quit—something no spy master is ever permitted to do. He pleaded with the Director in Moscow to grant him leave and then to permit him to retire gracefully. The answer was no. In his plight Rado sought salvation from a new association, the British. He approached a key British agent in Geneva known to him as John Salter, and the Briton took him to Colonel Cartwright, a British Military Attaché in Berne. A vague deal was made, binding on neither, but fatal to Rado. The Russians found out about it and put a price on his head.

In the meantime, France was liberated and Rado escaped with his wife to Paris. But every one of his successive hideouts was discovered by the Russians. Paris became too hot and he slipped away to Cairo. He placed himself at the disposal of the British secret service there, but someone denounced him and the British refused to have any dealings with the man. Those were the days of the Grand Alliance; the British were still complying with Russian demands, and now these demands included the extradition of Rado. A trigger man of the Soviet secret police was sent especially to Cairo to collect him, and the British delivered the fallen spy.

What happened after the Russian colonel left Cairo with Rado nobody knows for sure. According to one version, which I was told by the source apparently best qualified to speak, Rado was first taken to Prague on his way to Moscow. There, according to this story, he managed to escape and reached the extraterritorial haven of the British diplomatic mission. But the Prague chief of the British secret service had orders from London and, for a second time, they handed him over to the Russians.

In Moscow, it is claimed, he was tried by a special tribunal of the secret police. According to some, Rado was sentenced to a long term and was shipped off to an Arctic prison camp. According to others, he was shot in a basement cell of the Lubyanka. Whatever happened, Rado is dead, for even if he still lives, a fallen spy is but a breathing corpse.

13

Rhapsody in Red

Thou that cometh from on high,
 Stilling suffering and pain,
When despair is doubly nigh,
 Doubly quickening like rain;

Ah, I long for pain to cease
 And for joy to give me rest!
Lovely peace,
 Come, ah come, into my breast!

This English translation of Goethe's melancholy *Wanderers Nachtlied* was written by an American woman in a German prison on a dismal March night in 1943, only a few hours before her execution. She was Mildred Harnack-Fish, a handsome New Yorker who had married Arvid Harnack, scion of a great German family of statesmen, poets and thinkers. A school marm by profession, a genteel and genial, high-spirited, self-effacing, dedicated person, she could have lived life out to a serene conclusion under different stars. But the violent challenge of Nazism turned the schoolteacher into a rebel and a spy. She perished with her husband and a small band of fellow conspirators who had set themselves up in opposition to Hitler.

If, despite their martyrdom, the names of Mildred Harnack and her fellow conspirators are rarely honored and little known, it is because they were humble members of an ill-starred movement. They failed, and they paid a bloody price.

Aside from the Red terror in Russia, this underground
German war was the bloodiest of its kind in history. Its fatal
casualties far exceeded those of the United States in the liberation
of Europe. In the state of Saxony alone, sixteen thousand and
sixty-nine persons were executed for treasonable activities against
the Hitler regime. The city of Hamburg had four hundred and
fifty-eight such dead. The Gestapo blotter of a single month on
the eve of the Second World War showed that only six hundred
and three persons were arrested for ordinary crimes, but one thousand and thirty-six for political crimes. According to the roster
of the post-war organization, Victims of Fascism, which carefully examined every claim, more than a quarter of a million
Germans participated in one or another underground group
which actively opposed the Nazis.

Some of the anti-Nazi plotters formed themselves into informal intelligence groups and placed their services at the disposal
of foreign governments. The survivors today resent being called
spies, but their activity was, in fact, espionage. The material they
smuggled out of Germany was specific and detailed, disclosing
the contents of top secret documents, the verbatim text of operation orders, the battle order of the *Wehrmacht,* the movement
of troops, timetables, logistic material and, above all, evidence of
Hitler's intentions.

These operations were unprecedented. Never before had
there existed, on such a scale, a secret service composed of lone
wolves and free lancers performing voluntarily the intricate
function on which governments spend so much money and
effort.

The group supported itself from the private resources of
its own members. It operated on its own technical facilities. No
official secret service aided or maintained it; on the contrary,
innumerable monkey wrenches were thrown into the works by
the bureaucratic intelligence services of the Allies for whom these
lone wolves were doing a job.

Some of the intelligence was shipped West, especially to
London; some of it went East, especially to Moscow. Mildred

Harnack was a member of a group that banked on the Soviet Union. The group to which she belonged came to be known as *Rote Kapelle* or the Red Orchestra, because it worked like a company of instrumentalists, trained and led by a conductor.

The *maestro* was a shadowy figure deep underground, known as Agis. He was a remarkable young man, Harro Schulze-Boysen by name, a first lieutenant in Goering's *Luftwaffe*, son of a naval officer, a lineal descendant of Grand Admiral Tirpitz. He was dedicated body and soul to the struggle against Hitler. In 1939, Schulze-Boysen expressed the personal philosophy that motivated him: "This war will bury the old Europe, together with its civilization as it existed to date," he wrote, "and then, when the air is cleansed, the atmosphere will be healthier. Our own lives, it seems to me, are no longer important. *Vivere non est necessere.* At any rate, I propose we should all show we are worthy human beings."

Lieutenant Schulze-Boysen was a devout Communist, but he succeeded in concealing his political orientation and was able to hold down a post inside one of the *Luftwaffe's* intelligence organizations. There he had access to some of Germany's most closely-guarded secrets.

His group was as remarkable as he was. The Red Orchestra operated in cells that in turn combined to form two separate rings—a small, inner ring of the organization's one hundred and eighteen leaders and sub-leaders; and a large, outer ring of rank-and-file secret agents and propagandists. It was an enormous organization; it had branches as far away as Brussels and Marseilles. Although the Red Orchestra was avowedly Communist, it had only a handful of proletarians among its members. Most of them were middle-class intellectuals, professionals and artists.

The group maintained its own elaborate communications network, and constantly changed the location of its transmitters. One night they would be sending messages from the X-ray room of a woman physician's office in Berlin's best residential district. On another night, in the guise of repairmen, they would drive up in a van to a manhole on Moritzplatz, a drab working-class neighborhood, open the manhole and place a tent over it. While passers-by thought a cable was being repaired or the sewer cleaned, radio specialists of the Red Orchestra were putting Schulze-Boysen's latest messages on the air.

In the summer of 1939, the Red Orchestra merged with a newer group, led by a man known as Caro. He was Mildred Harnack's husband, Arvid, a high-ranking government official. Like Schulze-Boysen, Arvid Harnack was a dedicated man. Up to the date of the merger, his organization had confined its activities to propaganda, plastering the walls of Berlin with little posters printed on their concealed hand-presses, but under Schulze-Boysen's impatient, energetic leadership, the new, enlarged organization began to broaden its activities. While Hitler was at war only with the West, their efforts were half-hearted and groping, not because their pro-Soviet orientation had dampened their anti-Nazi ardor, but because they could not establish a working liaison with Western intelligence organs. But when Hitler's honeymoon with Stalin was drawing to a close, the group undertook a series of groping free-lance operations even before Moscow's emissaries called for their services. That happened in June, 1941.

On a balmy morning of that month, a short, broad-shouldered man went for a stroll in the Tiergarten. At a secluded spot off the beaten path, he sat down on a bench, took out the morning's *Voelkische Beobachter* and read.

A few minutes later, a solemn-faced, hard-eyed man walked by. The little man got up, followed the passerby and then, behind a cluster of low trees, he joined him. For several hours, they strolled together.

This was an emergency conference of the utmost importance, one Soviet spy winding up his business and handing over his affairs to another. Even in the murky underworld of spies, the little bullet-headed fellow was a mystery man. He was known only as Alexander Erdberg, his *nom d'espion*, but he was a highly-trained, full-time professional operative of the Fourth Bureau.

Erdberg belonged to a relatively small ring of resident agents operating behind the Soviet Embassy in Berlin, actually out of the private apartment of Counselor Bogdan Kobulov. Kobulov's ring, and another directed by the more orthodox official spy, General Tupikov, the Military Attaché, was well-nigh all that the Soviet Union had in Germany, except the organization of Erdberg's staid companion on this morning's stroll. He was Arvid Harnack, Caro of the *Rote Kapelle*.

In spite of Stalin's blind complacency, Kobulov saw the war approaching and knew that his diplomatic group could not stay long in Germany. Kobulov searched far and wide for a band of trustworthy native Germans in whose hands he could entrust the conspiracy. He picked the Red Orchestra.

Harnack accepted the invitation with alacrity. In subsequent meetings he introduced Erdberg to Schulze-Boysen and others he had selected to act as his radio operators. One was a metal worker named Hans Coppi, a member of the underground Communist Party in Germany; the other was a prominent author and theatrical producer, probably not a Communist at all, Adam Kluckhoff by name. At 56, he was one of the oldest members of the group.

In Kobulov's apartment Harnack and Schulze-Boysen received their instructions from Kobulov and the two military attachés, Tupikov and Skornyakov. Erdberg taught Schulze-Boysen, Coppi and Kluckhoff the operation of clandestine radio sets. Harnack was handed the code books and given lessons in the difficult art of cryptography. He was also appointed treasurer and received thirteen thousand five hundred marks from Kobulov.

The glaring shortcomings of this network of amateurs became evident at once. Harnack and his associates were not short on enthusiasm, and they did not lack excellent intelligence material. One of the very first dispatches they sent to the Fourth Bureau was a comprehensive report on the *Luftwaffe*. They followed it up with a warning of an imminent German offensive along the Dnieper. But because of Harnack's inexperience as a

cryptographer, these important reports were so badly enciphered
that the Fourth Bureau could not make head nor tail of them.
Coppi and Kluckhoff constantly neglected even to call Moscow
on their radios and remained silent most of the time while the
Fourth Bureau's operators tried frantically to raise them. Something had to be done at once.

In August, therefore, Erdberg ordered his best agent in the
West, Captain Victor Sukulov, to go to Berlin. Sukulov was
stationed in Brussels where he was the *Petit Chef* of a Soviet
network covering the Low Countries and France. His importance
was attested by his string of code and cover names: Dupuis,
Lebrun, Fritz, Cirin, Arthur, Alamo, Charles, and, most frequently, Kent. In Brussels, he was Vincente Antonio Sierra, a
wealthy merchant from Uruguay, who lived in an elegant villa
on Avenue Sieghers with his mistress, Margarete Barcza, the
widow of a Hungarian.

His group had its headquarters in a villa on rue des Attrebates, rented from an elderly Belgian lady who thought her
tenants were important international businessmen. In actual fact,
they were. Señor Sierra did business with the Nazis on an impressive scale and even recruited labor for German factories.

Following his instructions from Moscow, Sierra went to
Germany on an official permit issued to him through his influential German contacts, on a train that also carried a contingent
of his slave laborers. He met Harnack and Schulze-Boysen in
the Tiergarten, following the pattern established by Erdberg;
and Harnack took him to Coppi and Kluckhoff.

The Señor was now Kent again, and he went to work at
once. He built new radios and repaired old ones; he gave post-
graduate courses in operative technique to Coppi and Kluckhoff;
he brushed up Harnack on his cryptography; and he tightened
the administration of the group. He recruited a number of other
agents, whose names were supplied to him by the Fourth Bureau
from the roster of trustworthy Communists. He also looked up
Herr von Scheliha, the old-fashioned gentleman in the Foreign

Ministry, who was still doing some spotty espionage work, although it was much inferior to his previous contributions.

His presence in Berlin, brief as it was, fulfilled Erdberg's fondest expectations. After that, the Caro group functioned with clock-like precision, the value of its messages second only to the intelligence from Roessler via Rado. Among the *Rote Kapelle's* material were the strategic plans of the German High Command in the fall of 1941; the times and places of scheduled German parachute raids and planned attacks on British convoys en route to Murmansk; and an enormous amount of information enabling the Fourth Bureau to keep the order of battle of the *Wehrmacht* always up to date. Once, the *Rote Kapelle* even saved the Russians from the disastrous consequences of a lost Russian code. The book was captured by the Germans at Petsamo in Finland and was used in the familiar carillon game. Schulze-Boysen discovered the trick and warned the Russians who could then turn the carillon against the bell ringers.

In this formidable network, even Sukulov represented only the second echelon. Sukulov was called the *Petit Chef*—the Little Boss. Over him, conducting the whole complex orchestra, was the Maestro, the *Grand Chef*—the Big Boss, forming, with Sorge in Tokyo, and Rado in Geneva, the legendary *troika,* or Big Three of Soviet espionage in World War II. He was also known as the General, an elusive master of espionage, who had appeared virtually everywhere between Moscow and Shanghai, Madrid and Buenos Aires.

He was a Pole. Leopold (Poldi) Trepper was his real name; he was born in 1904 in the ghetto of Cracow. Poldi used his real name for the last time in 1932 when, after a frantic chase of rainbows, he arrived in Moscow to throw in his lot with the Bolsheviks. He was twenty-eight years old, a married man, and a total failure in life. He thought he might try his hand at espionage.

The Polish branch of the Comintern obtained for him an appointment with a talent scout of the Fourth Bureau, who recognized in Poldi an exceptional talent. His new bosses put him through a five-year-long educational training period that took him through Moscow University, the Moscow College of Diplomacy, and the Fourth Bureau School.

When Poldi emerged from this wringer, he was a different man: a suave operator who spoke Polish, Russian, Yiddish, Hebrew, German, French, English, and Spanish with equal fluency. He was sent to Paris as Monsieur Jean Gilbert to establish himself behind a front: the Simex Corporation of exporters and importers, with plush offices on the Champs Elysées and a Hollywood-type executive suite for Monsieur Gilbert.

In the back of Gilbert's swank office was a hidden room, where he became Poldi Trepper again. It housed his radio, the safe with the codes and ciphers, his little black books with innumerable useful addresses, the roster of his sub-agents. A hidden door led from his big office into this small one and a staircase went from the hidden office into the backyard of another building.

The hidden room was secured with a special radio transmitter attached to a clock that had to be wound once a day. When all was well, the little transmitter emitted signals at regular intervals to the security guard in the front office. When the signals stopped, something was wrong. In an acute emergency, a warning could be sent out without waiting for the clock to do the job.

From that office in Paris, Gilbert's tentacles reached to every German government office, not only in Berlin and Paris, but also in Brussels, The Hague, Copenhagen, everywhere in occupied Western Europe. Working for him were the outstanding agents of the Fourth Bureau. Contact with Moscow was chiefly by radio. Trepper had transmitting and receiving sets in Brussels and The Hague, three in Switzerland, the new stations in Berlin, and two in France: one in Paris operated by a Polish refugee, another in Pecq near Paris, in the hands of Robert and Lucie, a French Communist couple.

The net's chief signal officer was the Professor, so called because his knowledge of radio techniques and transmissions was unique in the underground. He was also called Hans, Hermann, and Bergmann. His real name was Johann Wenzel and he hailed from somewhere in East Prussia. An aging man who spent his life in the Comintern, the Professor was getting tired, terribly tired of it all.

Until June, 1941, his station in the villa in Brussels was well oiled, ready for instant use, but silent.

Then the Professor suddenly became operational, as did his scattered colleagues in France and Holland, and even inside Germany.

The monitors of Canaris' signal corps, the *Funk-Abwehr*, pricked up their ears at their station in Cranz, East Prussia. The monitors jotted down the signals and rushed them to Berlin, but no matter how the *Abwehr's* best cryptoanalysts tried, they could not break the code.

The *Funk-Abwehr* was under the command of Major Werner F. Flicke, a wizard at locating transmitters. Slowly and gradually, through innumerable trials and errors, Flicke's men groped their way from Norway through Germany proper, via Holland to Belgium at last, and then to Brussels, to the suburb of Erbettes and, finally, to a villa on the rue des Attrebates.

The groping lasted almost six months. It ended on the fatal December 13, 1941. That night, the villa was encircled by agents of the Abwehr and the Secret Field Police. At 11:30 p.m. sharp, the agents slipped thick cotton socks over their boots, sneaked into the villa and made their way to the second floor so quietly that none of the three Soviet operatives who happened to be in attendance heard their coming. The Germans pounced upon them and seized the scattered paraphernalia of their work, but in the commotion one of the spies, a stalwart man named Mikhail Makarov, still managed to destroy the code books. And the Professor was not in the building.

The *Grand Chef* happened to be in Brussels on that day and while the raid was on, he appeared at the villa to deliver some urgent intelligence for transmission. He ran into the arms of the German agents and was seized at once, but in that pinch the *Grand Chef* put on an act of fantastic audacity. He pretended to be a peddler of rabbits, of all things, and impersonated a rabbit peddler (whatever that may be) so convincingly that the Germans, amused and fooled by his antics, let him go. He immediately alerted his *apparat*. Most of them fled, escaping the German noose.

Trepper returned to Paris and Sukulov went to Marseilles. The *apparat* was left in the hands of young Colonel Yemerov, going by the code name Bordo. The Professor took over all transmissions, operating from his home in Brussels. It took the Germans another six months to locate him. On June 30, 1942, they finally nabbed the Professor in front of his set, transmitting his last message to Moscow.

He was the first really big fish in the *Abwehr's* net and they went to work on him. Under the pounding, the old Bolshevik broke and betrayed the whole intricate *apparat:* his associates, the codes, the rules, the entire system of Soviet espionage. He opened the floodgates.

In the *Abwehr's* files reposed hundreds of messages that had been sent between Moscow and its spies and that had been intercepted. Among them was the order sent a year earlier to Sukulov telling him to go to Berlin and tighten up the Harnack operation. Confident of their code and pressed by urgency, the Russians had been indiscreet enough to include in the message even the names and addresses of the spies Sukulov was to see.

Now that message came out of the files and, with the Professor's help, the Germans were able to understand it for the first time. It read:

"KLS de RTX. 1010. 1725. 99wds. qbt. From Director to Kent, personal. Proceed at once to three addresses listed below in Berlin and ascertain why wireless connection consistently fails. In the event of further interruptions, take over transmission. Work of three Berlin groups and transmission of intelligence of the utmost importance. Addresses: Neuwestend, Altenburger Alley 3, third floor right. Caro.— Charlottenburg, Fredericia Street 26a, second floor left. Coppi.—Friedenau, Kaiser Street 18, fourth floor left. Adam and Greta Kluckhoff. Remember 'Ulenspiegel'.— Password everywhere: Director. Advise until October 20. At all three places, resume (I repeat) resume radio plan the morning of the fifteenth. qbt. 50385. ar. KLS de RTX."

A year and twelve days after the message was sent, on August 30, 1942, the Gestapo picked up Schulze-Boysen as he was leaving the Air Ministry. Three days later, they got Harnack at a summer resort. One by one, the scattered musicians of the Red Orchestra ended in the net, until only Sukulov and Trepper were missing. Sukulov was trailed to Marseilles and was arrested on a train in November, trying to evade his pursuers by going north. Now the last manhunt began—for the Big Boss, Poldi Trepper himself. His cover, the Simex Company, was raided by German *Kommando* but Monsieur Gilbert was gone. On his desk, however, the Germans found an appointment calendar. It listed Trepper's periodic visits to his dentist. The *Abwehr* nabbed him as he was under the drill.

14

War in the Wings

Italy entered the war on June 10, 1940, not to hasten, but to benefit from France's collapse. Mussolini came in with Hitler's reluctant permission. The Fuehrer was confident that, whatever mischief Il Duce could perpetrate, it would not materially affect the outcome. He recalled an impudent quip of World War I attributed to General von Falkenhayn. When, in 1915, the Kaiser was told that Italy planned to switch sides, von Falkenhayn assured the sovereign that it would not make any difference. "You see, your Majesty," he said, "if they're against us, we need ten divisions to beat them. If they're on our side, we'll still need ten divisions to help them."

Sure enough, by the following spring Mussolini came to regard every day, when nothing unpleasant befell his forces, as a day won. May 24, 1941, appeared to be such a day. On the Pincio, the trees abandoned themselves to the balmy caresses of a glorious Roman spring. On the elegant Via Condotti, the smart ladies of Roman society paraded; nothing in their finery betrayed the austerity of a country at war. But on that day a seemingly insignificant event occurred which was destined to have a special impact on the future of Mussolini's Italy. Admiral Franco Maugeri became director of the S.I.S., the Italian Office of Naval Intelligence.

Not yet 46 years old, Maugeri was a slight, slender figure with prematurely gray hair and keen gray eyes; he had an informal manner and was innately modest. He was an intellectual, well bred, well read, and had a preference for desk jobs, because he was inordinately susceptible to seasickness and sunburn. He had previously served in S.I.S. between 1927 and 1929. At that time, S.I.S. was an extremely small agency; its entire staff consisted of ten officers and twenty enlisted men. It maintained not a single secret agent, either at home or abroad. Its job was to collate the periodic reports of the Italian Naval Attachés and to perform the other routine duties of desk-bound intelligence.

During those years, there was an extremely intimate relationship between the Italian and British navies. When the Italian Navy was originally built up before the First World War, it was designed to fight alongside the British Navy as an auxiliary force. Many Italian naval officers became imbued with this tradition and continued to regard themselves, even when their country had drifted apart from Britain, as honorary officers of the Royal Navy. Admiral Maugeri, a determined anti-Fascist, was a member of this pro-British group. When he became director of S.I.S., it became a clandestine British agency at the very heart of the Italian military establishment, for all practical purposes functioning as the Italian branch of the British Naval Intelligence. This clandestine function was never regarded as improper or treasonable, either by Maugeri or his subordinates. On the contrary, they were firmly convinced that by aiding Britain in their own way they were saving Italy from total extinction.

When Maugeri returned to S.I.S. in 1941, it had changed radically. It consisted of three major regional organizations, with headquarters in Madrid, Istanbul and Shanghai (each under the respective Italian Naval Attachés); and four functional sections bearing the letters B, C, D and E. Section B was the efficient "black chamber," monitoring foreign radio traffic and translating the codes and ciphers of others. Section D was the intelligence service proper. The material that B and D procured was fed to Section C which collated and evaluated it. Section E was exclusively counter-intelligence and counter-espionage.

Heading Section D was Commander Max Ponzo. He was short, squat and sturdy, built like a miniature bull. He had a swarthy complexion and nervous, darting eyes which gave him a shifty, sinister expression. He was brilliant and resourceful, courageous and aggressive. By the strength of his personality, Ponzo dominated the whole S.I.S.

Before Maugeri's arrival, Ponzo had set up an intelligence and espionage network such as S.I.S. had never before possessed. He established several tight rings in neutral countries like Switzerland, Spain, Turkey and Portugal. He even established a minor ring in the United States. One of the room service waiters in the Wardman-Park Hotel in Washington, D.C., where Mrs. Dwight D. Eisenhower and Secretary of State Cordell Hull lived, was a Ponzo spy.

While considerable information flowed from his networks abroad, the best material was procured right at home. Ponzo concentrated his efforts in Rome on the American Naval Attaché, probably on the assumption that Americans, being very much like Italians, outgoing and trusting, loquacious and boastful, would make easy targets for his snoopers.

Between 1939 and 1941, Captain Thomas C. Kinkaid, USN, was American Naval Attaché in Rome. He was a gallant officer of the line, who was destined to make a great name for himself in later years. There was, however, a serious loophole in his office. The department was badly understaffed and because Washington could not send him United States personnel, Kinkaid was compelled to hire a few Italians.

At least one of those employees worked for Ponzo. He was a fairly highly-placed clerk and had occasional access to the safe. He managed to make a duplicate key to it and from then on, until the United States entered the war, S.I.S. knew the exact contents of that American safe.

Early in 1941, Kinkaid was recalled and Captain Lester N. McNair, USN, replaced him. McNair decided, undoubtedly upon instructions from Washington, to hire a few spies. Free-lance espionage was a favorite pastime of certain Italian ladies, and among them McNair found an attractive and charming young woman who appeared to be a splendid candidate.

She was Signorina Elena (her last name is covered by charitable anonymity). She was sufficiently well situated in Roman society to develop some useful sources and was of a romantic disposition, generous with her affections when the occasion required.

Elena found herself in something of a dilemma; she really did not know how and where to pick up the information Captain McNair expected. She solved the problem in the traditional manner by becoming a double agent. She called Ponzo, exposed herself as an American spy and volunteered to keep Ponzo posted about the affairs of the Americans and to pass on to McNair whatever information Ponzo wanted to slip into American files. The arrangement satisfied all concerned, including Captain McNair, who never found out about Elena's double deal.

On December 11, 1941, Italy declared war on the United States and this made Elena vastly more valuable since she was virtually the only spy the U.S. Navy had left in Rome.

Before his departure, McNair arranged that the young lady was to send her material to Colonel Barwell R. Legge, the American Military Attaché at Berne, Switzerland. With Ponzo continuing to manage this minor but stimulating phase of American espionage, arrangements were made for a courier from Legge to call at Elena's apartment on Lungotevere to pick up her information. Ponzo made his own arrangements to observe the visitor; he was anxious to find out who else was working for Legge in Rome.

Agents of S.I.S. were posted around the building and Elena was instructed to signal the arrival of her visitor by displaying a quaint assortment of laundry. If the courier was a man, she was to put a bathing suit in her window; if the visitor turned out to be a woman, she was to hang out a towel.

Ponzo's agents did not have to wait long. In due course, a dainty bathing suit appeared in the window. An hour later a man came out of the building and Ponzo's agents followed him along the broad, tree-lined avenue on the left bank of the Tiber, until they saw him meet a warrant officer they knew was working for Major Pontini's Section E in S.I.S., the counter-espionage branch. They saw the two shake hands, enter a waiting car and drive away in apparently the most cordial manner.

The Ponzo agents, sent to trap a single American spy, had encountered two! And—*horribile dictu*—one of them was a trusted *carabinieri* of Major Pontini. They reported the discovery to Ponzo and Ponzo in turn tipped off the major. Pontini received the news with a burst of laughter.

"My dear Max," he said, "that enemy agent whom you've been following so cleverly—he's no more an enemy agent than you are. He's one of my own officers. The Americans in Switzerland hired him to work for them and at a good, fat price, too! Ah," he sighed with mild contempt, *"che stupidità americana!"*

Such are the vagaries of espionage when it ambles into war from haphazard peacetime beginnings.

It took some time for American Intelligence to get adjusted to the challenge of war. It was different with British Intelligence.

Ponzo was sending a steady flow of excellent intelligence to the Italian Navy about the movements of British ships in the Mediterranean. As soon as a British vessel passed through the Straits of Gibraltar, either entering or leaving the Mediterranean, a signal advised the fleet of it. In Algeciras, the Spanish city bordering on Gibraltar, the Italian Consul was a member of Ponzo's espionage ring. He lived in the Hotel Reina Cristina, whose owner was in sympathy with Italy and allowed him to build an observatory on the roof. It had powerful telescopes, long-range binoculars on firm tripods, chronometers, and cameras with telescopic lenses. In a room of the hotel, the consul had a clandestine transmitter on which he reported his observations to Rome every few hours. In this manner, Ponzo was told almost immediately when a British ship passed through the Straits.

That dazzling espionage coup at Algeciras was what could be called elaborate eyewash, the way S.I.S. had of giving the impression that it was in the war against the British up to its neck. Nobody seemed to notice that virtually the entire S.I.S. effort vis-à-vis the British was confined to this operation. It escaped attention that Ponzo was as conspicuous for his absence in London, for example, as he was conspicuous for his presence in Algeciras. During a visit to Rome, Admiral Canaris boasted to Count Ciano about his splendid spy net in Britain, claiming that one of his spies was sending to Hamburg up to ten signals a day. (It was actually the British carillon.) Ciano had to concede that Italy had nothing comparable to that. The S.I.S. had nothing at all in Britain. Still more remarkable was the fact that Commander Ponzo had not done to the British what he had so brilliantly done to the Americans. He neither ensnarled them with double agents nor relieved them of their secrets with aggressive espionage.

Admiral Maugeri made a startling statement after the war. "Actually," he wrote, "I doubt that there were many British spies in Italy. There really was no need for them. The British Admiralty had plenty of friends among our high-ranking admirals and in the Ministry of Marine itself. I suspect the English were able to get authentic information straight from the source." What he omitted to say was that his own S.I.S. did much of the necessary spadework for British Intelligence.

On a colorful old Roman street named after the dark little stores which lined it, the via delle Botteghe Oscure, dwelt a remarkable individual, and Max Ponzo lived under his spell. He was one of Italy's most prominent barristers, Giovanni Serao, a man of dizzying brilliance. He was short and heavy set, but an extremely agile man, with a luxuriant beard. His eloquence was unique even for Italy. His clients included some of the country's noblest houses and greatest corporations and a string of big foreign firms such as Paramount Pictures and the Canadian Pacific Railway as well. For many years, Signor Serao served as the legal adviser of the British Embassy in Rome and performed so effectively in that capacity that he was knighted for his services to the Crown. He was the only Roman entitled to hear himself addressed as *Sir* Giovanni, and he relished the title.

Serao was Ponzo's father-in-law, and more than that, the idol of his son-in-law. Serao himself gave the British all sorts of confidential information, which he procured in the course of his practice; thanks to his intimacy with Ponzo, he could also supply military and naval intelligence of the highest order. For all practical purposes, Giovanni Serao was the clandestine chief of the British Secret Service in Rome.

Before Franco Maugeri's arrival in S.I.S., Ponzo's contribution had to be limited by sheer necessity. His superiors were no parties to the plot. He had to operate on his own. Serao's Embassy connections were broken at the outbreak of the war. Serao and Ponzo had to confine their services to limited intelligence which they slipped to the British as best they could, mainly through a surreptitious contact with the British Legation that remained at the Vatican. Even this was of great value.

The British had an accurate appreciation of the Italian fleet and refused to regard it as a mortal threat to Britain's control of the sea, but its nuisance value was recognized. There was some apprehension, in particular, about the forty-odd submarines owned by the Italians, which could have wrought havoc with British shipping in the Mediterranean if properly employed. Naval Intelligence succeeded in acquiring the special code used by the Italian submariners.

An ingenious officer on Admiral Sir Andrew Cunningham's staff hit upon a fantastic idea. Devising signals in the Italian code, and impersonating the Italian command, he would dispatch an Italian submarine to a certain spot in the Mediterranean to attack supposed Allied merchantmen. When the hapless submarine arrived at the spot, it was met by British destroyers waiting to send it to its doom.

In this manner, the British decimated Mussolini's submarine arm. The operation would have continued most probably to its inevitable conclusion had it not been for an accident. The

British ordered a certain Italian submarine to one of those spots where the destroyers were waiting, but that particular sub happened at the time to be in drydock at La Spezia.

The blunder alerted the Italians and ended the game, but severe damage had already been done.

Rommel was hammering the British mercilessly in Africa, and he was being supplied by shipping across the Mediterranean. The conspiracy inside the S.I.S. became of essential importance. On March 25, 1941, mysterious information alerted Admiral Cunningham to an ominous stirring of the Italian Fleet. Some of its major elements, led by the battleship *Vittorio Veneto*, were supposed to move in the direction of the Aegean to draw off elements of the British Fleet from the route of those Italo-German convoys. That obscure message resulted in a great British naval victory on March 28, in the memorable Battle of Cape Matapan. In Churchill's words, "This timely and welcome victory off Cape Matapan disposed of all challenge to British naval mastery in the Eastern Mediterranean at this critical time."

By the beginning of April, the steady flow of intelligence enabled the British to intensify attacks on the shipping which had to feed Rommel's forces in Libya on a substantial scale. So effective was this surreptitious co-operation that Commander Malcolm Wanklyn in the submarine *Upholder* could win the Victoria Cross for his apparently uncanny ability to track down and sink German supply ships. An outstanding victory was scored in April, when a task force of four destroyers was guided to a large convoy. In this one action, fourteen thousand tons of enemy shipping, fully loaded with war materials for Rommel, was destroyed.

As time passed, Ponzo developed better communications with the British. A sympathetic S.I.S. agent in Berne became a pipeline to British Intelligence there. And still later the British managed to plant a clandestine radio transmitter in Rome. Now Ponzo needed a go-between to take information to the operator.

His eye fell on the Countess Montarini, an Englishwoman by birth, married to an Italian nobleman, the mother-in-law of a gallant young lieutenant of the Italian Navy. She worked as the *direttrice* of Elizabeth Arden's beauty salon.

Each morning, on her way to the shop, the Countess stopped at the church of the Trinità dei Monti for a brief prayer. Leaving, she would stop in front of the church to look down to the elongated Piazza di Spagna below, at the bottom of a flight of steps, inhaling the beauty of the sight.

At this famous Piazza, Rome is at its best. In the center of the square stands Bernini's fountain, *La Barcaccia*. It was made in the shape of a barque of war, spouting water from its marble cannons. Leading down to it is the Scala di Spagna, a flight of one hundred and thirty-eight steps.

When the Countess Montarini descended the grand staircase, she might pass a young man who stood on one of the steps. There would be nothing unusual, apparently, in this chance encounter, but, in fact, it was an ingeniously devised means of communication. The step on which the young man waited for the passing of the signora had a special significance. Each of the one hundred and thirty-eight steps meant a specific, separate message according to an elaborate system of codes. Each step had a different meaning when counted from the top or the bottom. Additional messages were passed on by having members of the ring do something specific on individual steps, such as lighting a cigarette, blowing a nose or cupping a hand over an eye.

The Countess was not only a transmission belt; she also gathered much useful information on her own. The Arden Beauty Salon was patronized by many of the most influential women of Rome, including the wives, daughters, and mistresses of Axis diplomats and officers. They gossiped freely while having their hair done, their faces mudpacked, and their nails manicured.

The Countess hired operators who could be trusted and taught them how to listen to the conversations of their celebrated

clients and how to pose loaded questions without making them
even slightly suspicious. Frequently the mention of a name would
start the ball rolling. An operator once reported to the Countess
that one of her clients had told her she wanted to be especially
attractive since she was to have a reunion with her husband she
had not seen for more than a year. She was the wife of a general
assigned to the African front. From this pebble of information
it was possible to develop the intelligence that the general's
recall had ushered in a complete reorganization of the Italian
command structure in Libya.

Meanwhile, in Africa, Rommel went on to his greatest
triumphs. He reached his peak in the summer of 1942 when he
defeated the Eighth Army between Gazala and Tobruk, and
then chased what was left of it almost to Cairo.

The British managed to halt his advance at El Alamein. In
August, however, Rommel returned to the offensive, only to be
finally checked this time. He could not go beyond El Alamein
and saw his chances of conquering Egypt go up in the sand dust
of the Western Desert.

There were several factors that robbed him of ultimate
glory: the British utilized the interval he had granted them to
shake up their high command, to send General Sir Bernard
Montgomery to lead the Eighth Army, and to give him adequate
reinforcements. But fully as important as what Monty received
was what Rommel did not get: reinforcements and supplies via
Italy and especially that confounded "shprit"—his word for
gasoline.

Marshal Kesselring was sending all the fuel that Rommel
was asking for, but somehow only a fraction of what left Italy
ever arrived in Africa. As Liddell Hart put it, the Desert Fox was
"vitally crippled by the submarine sinkings of the petrol tankers
crossing the Mediterranean."

The Germans were sure there was a leak. A special detachment of the usually infallible *Funkabwehr,* the *Abwehr's* radio
monitoring service, was brought to Italy to search for outgoing

messages. They failed to find a single suspicious signal. Another special detachment, this one from *Abwehr* III (counterespionage) was sent into Italy, and, in close co-operation with the brave *carabinieri* of Section E of the S.I.S., they instituted a manhunt for the presumed spies. The source of the leak was never found. The leak itself was never plugged.

What actually happened was simplicity itself. Since wars cannot be conducted in silence, the Italians had to advise their African command about these convoys. Their routing was radioed to Africa in a naval code that nobody expected the enemy to break. But someone at the Italian end had slipped the key of that sacrosanct code to the British and also advised them promptly whenever the code was changed.

Rommel was effectively deprived of his "shprit." In the words of Captain Liddell Hart: "That decided the issue, and once the enemy began to collapse at their extreme forward point they were not capable of any serious stand until they had reached the western end of Libya, more than a thousand miles back."

Ponzo's operation continued until the Italian Armistice in September, 1943. When the Germans occupied Rome, the city became too hot for him; and he was needed in Taranto, to the south, where the Italian Navy was being resurrected to a new life in a new war, this time to do exactly what most of its flag officers wanted, to fight against the Germans.

On October 10th, Max Ponzo sneaked out of Rome. Disguised as a straggler, he succeeded in making his way to Taranto where he was received with open arms. The morning after his arrival, he was named chief of the reconstituted Italian Naval Intelligence, with the wholehearted approval of the Allies.

The situation in Rome remained in excellent hands. Admiral Maugeri disappeared underground and became one of the chiefs of the resistance organization inside the Eternal City.

Countess Montarini's position became untenable. She could no longer maintain her masquerade. Her son-in-law, the naval lieutenant who was himself on the periphery of the ring, escaped to the Allies at the first opportunity, and that tipped off the Germans to the mother-in-law's true sentiments. With the help of friends, she vanished from sight, although she never left Rome. She disappeared into the vast palace complex of Prince Colonna, where she remained in hiding until that June day of 1944, when at long last Rome was liberated by the Allies.

15

A Man Called "Ramsey"

In the spring of 1935, a tourist arrived in New York en route to Berlin from Tokyo. He registered at the Hotel Lincoln on West 44th Street as Dr. Richard Sorge, a foreign correspondent for the *Frankfurter Zeitung*, one of Germany's major newspapers.

The intelligence services of various countries had tried to keep up-to-date biographical cards on this fascinating man, but it proved somewhat difficult to follow him on his erratic course. His "suspect card" in the files of American counter-intelligence dated back to 1929 and contained a number of melodramatic entries. It put down Sorge as a very important member of the great Soviet espionage apparatus.

This Sorge was a melancholy intellectual who had been born in Baku, in Southern Russia, in 1895. His grandfather was Adolph Sorge, secretary to Karl Marx at the time of the First International; his father was a German engineer working for an oil firm in the Caucasus; his mother was more obscure, said to be a Russian. He was a sensitive, good-natured, studious boy, somewhat spoiled by his parents who called him "Ika."

When, as a youngster, he moved with his family to Germany and found out more about his grandfather's association with Marx, he became deeply interested in Socialism. The First World War (in which he fought at Ypern and Langemark) supplied the ferment for his ideas and, when it came to an end, young Richard groped his way to the Bolsheviks. A strange woman played an important part in Sorge's conversion. She was the wife of a professor under whom he studied at Kiel University, the familiar neglected faculty wife who lures a student into a campus romance. She was considerably older than Sorge and she turned him into a fanatical idealist and took him to the Soviet Union. The Bolsheviks received him with open arms and gave him odd conspiratorial jobs in various parts of Europe. Eventually he was absorbed by the Fourth Bureau of the Red Army General Staff and became a full-time Soviet espionage agent. Inside the apparatus he was known by the cover name "Ramsey."

He was a key operative in the "Shanghai Conspiracy," a major espionage operation of the late Twenties and early Thirties, when Soviet interest was focused on China. From Shanghai he returned to Moscow, but in May, 1933, he went to Germany where he joined the Nazi Party. He developed contacts with the new German intelligence agencies mushrooming under Hitler and joined General Karl Haushofer's geopolitical study group, the quasi-scientific propagandists of the *Lebensraum* idea. He joined the editorial department of the *Frankfurter Zeitung*, which sent him to Japan toward the end of that same year.

In Tokyo, Sorge lived in a big house in an excellent residential district. He joined the German Club, became a confidant of the German Ambassador and an informant of the German Military Attaché. The Germans regarded Sorge as one of their own and trusted him implicitly. The only objection the Embassy men had to him was that he was prone to start affairs with their wives. They did not know that Nazism was only a cover for his real mission.

This was the situation in 1935, when Richard Sorge suddenly showed up in the United States. He traveled under his own name, on his own genuine German passport, with papers to show that he was en route to Frankfurt for conferences with the newspaper he represented. He carried no incriminating documents. Except for one visitor, he was alone all the time.

His sole visitor was also a stranger among strangers, travel-

ing on a foolproof "legend." He was a captain of the Fourth
Bureau, sent especially from Moscow to deliver into Sorge's
hands a fake passport for a clandestine detour to Moscow.

For a few weeks Sorge vanished from sight. His editors in
Germany were left with the impression that he was still in New
York, but the letters and postcards they received from Sorge
during this period had been written by him in advance and were
mailed at proper intervals by the courier.

Sorge reached Moscow unobserved and found a new man,
General Uritsky, at the head of the Fourth Bureau; and he also
found a whole set of new policies based on an uncanny estimate
of the situation.

As seen through a Kremlin window, the Europe of 1935 was
unsettled and turbulent. France was as usual in the throes of
grave domestic controversies. Britain seemed firmer, but its
stability was deceptive. The Kremlin was looking through Hitler
rather than at him. Germany was a problem, Uritsky told Sorge,
but subsidiary in importance, and well under control. The
problem of the Third Reich would resolve itself, either when
Hitler collapsed under the weight of his own blunders, or when
he was destroyed by war.

Soviet intelligence was mainly interested, Uritsky said, in
what would happen *after* Hitler's collapse. The United States
was certain to have a hand in his destruction and would, therefore, emerge as the dominant world power. Consequently, he
said, Soviet intelligence was moving fast to cover the United
States. It was moving even faster to provide coverage for the
countries that Uritsky expected to become stepping stones in the
ascendancy of the United States. Foremost among these was
Japan, with whom a showdown seemed inescapable. Sorge was
to probe for the signs of that showdown and to find out in what
direction the Japanese expected to move: whether against the
Soviet Union or against Britain and the United States. He was
to discover Japanese aspirations and intentions, its war potential
and the secrets of its war machine, and especially to survey on a

month-to-month basis Japanese relations with the United States as they deteriorated toward war.

Uritsky gave Sorge a generous budget, considerable independence and a new radio operator, a heavy-set, stolid German named Max Klausen, whom Sorge knew from his Shanghai days.

Sorge returned to New York, then went on to Germany, and finally back to Tokyo. Klausen followed him in a roundabout route: in Tokyo he found a primitive radio set built by a predecessor and made a new one with a maximum range of two thousand five hundred miles. He was set to operate his "music box" from behind the façade of an export-import business, selling German presses for blueprints and fluorescent plates, an excellent front to attract such customers as the Japanese Army and Navy, the big Tokyo banks and Japanese industrial plants.

When Klausen arrived in Tokyo in November, 1935, he found plenty of work awaiting him. Sorge was already receiving invaluable information daily on the policies and plans of the Japanese Government from a certain Hozumi Ozaki. He was a confidant of Prime Minister Prince Konoye, a highly respected publicist who was a charter member of the Breakfast Club, a cabal of the highest political and diplomatic echelons where much of Japan's secret diplomacy was openly discussed.

Within the spy ring, the Soviet Union was called "Wiesbaden," after the famous German spa. It was to "Wiesbaden" that Klausen sent his signals via a Soviet relay station that was located near Vladivostok. The traffic was in a numerical code keyed to the pages of a German statistical year book. Klausen used the call letters AC to which he added a number and two letters, changing the latter frequently. "Wiesbaden's" call signals began with XU and followed the same arrangement. To the radio operators in "Wiesbaden" Klausen was known as "Fritz."

For six years, Klausen operated his station without interruption and his was a busy transmitter, indeed. Sorge managed to procure an incredible amount of information. In 1939,

"Fritz" made a total of sixty transmissions, totaling twenty-three thousand one hundred and thirty-nine words. The peak was reached in 1940, when almost thirty thousand words were sent.

Ozaki remained Sorge's most important supplier of information, but there were other informants. Altogether his ring totaled thirty-six members, from a fifty-seven-year-old dressmaker to a twenty-one-year-old clerk at the China Research Institute, the cover-name of a Japanese intelligence agency. Among Sorge's employees were government officials, journalists, artists, students, two brokers and a physician. Some of them had access to the files of the Japanese secret service. Additional intelligence was acquired from the files of the German Embassy which were open to Sorge.

Included in the mass of intelligence were innumerable original documents, many of them given to Ozaki by high-ranking government officials who sought his advice. Ozaki was able to pass on to Sorge certain top secret state papers which Prince Konoye had given him. The documents were photographed on microfilm and taken out of Japan, mostly by couriers who came especially from Moscow to collect them, but occasionally by Klausen or by Sorge himself. Within a few months, Max carried to Shanghai a score of microfilm rolls of a thousand frames each. This was followed by another shipment of thirty rolls, then many more, until a regular shuttle service was operating between Tokyo at one end and Shanghai, Hong Kong, and Manila at the other. Sorge himself once went to Manila as an official courier of the German Embassy, carrying confidential documents in the diplomatic pouch. He also had microfilm copies of those same documents under his shirt. The pouch was consigned to Berlin; his microfilms were for Moscow.

Sorge's material was of extreme importance in shaping Soviet policies. Although Japan was regarded as the Soviet Union's perennial competitor in the Far East and its most likely enemy in war, Sorge steadfastly assured Moscow that Japan would *not* attack the U.S.S.R., but in the end would wage war against the United States.

These reassuring dispatches culminated in a message which Sorge had Klausen put on the air very early in October, 1941. By then, the Soviet Union was reeling under the savage onslaught of the Nazis. In 1941, during the first few months of the Russo-German war, the Red Army lost millions of men; reinforcements were desperately needed to stave off defeat. If only the Far Eastern divisions of the Red Army could be moved to Europe!

In his last dispatch, Sorge advised the Fourth Bureau without equivocation that the Japanese Government and High Command had definitely made up their minds *not* to move in a northerly direction against the Soviet Union, but they would strike south against British possessions, against the Netherlands East Indies and the Philippines, and across the Pacific against the United States. That last message advised Moscow that Japan would definitely launch an attack on the United States "probably in December [1941] but certainly not later than January, 1942."

The Kremlin was relieved and moved enormous contingents of their Far Eastern army to Europe, using these reinforcements to stem the German advance in the last moment. Sorge's intelligence saved the day for Stalin; probably it saved the Soviet Union itself; it certainly saved Moscow. The Germans were at the outskirts of the city. They could see the onion-topped churches and the tall building of the Moskva Hotel. The Red Army had suffered all the anticipated losses, but miraculously it was still in the field, and, more than that, putting in fresh divisions. Hitler asked General Franz Halder, the chief of his General Staff, how the Russians managed to conjure up those fresh divisions, but Halder could not explain the mystery.

The veil has now been lifted. "The Sorge spy ring in Tokyo," wrote Brigadier Dixon and Dr. Heilbrunn, "could inform Russia in 1941 that Japan would not attack her, and this intelligence enabled the Russians to transfer their reserves from the Far East to the European theatre where they arrived in time for the battle of Moscow. Russia was then assured of a one-front

war, while Germany had to keep a considerable part of her
forces in the West in defense of a second front. Germany fought
from then on with one arm tied behind her back, while Russia
could use both fists."

Sorge was not allowed to enjoy the fruits of his triumph.
On October 18, 1941, he was arrested at his home by officers
of the *Tokkoka*. His downfall must have struck him as an ironic
anticlimax. Three days before his arrest, he gave Klausen a
dispatch for Moscow, telling the "Center" that he saw no further
reason to continue operations in Japan. He suggested that he be
transferred with new instructions.

Klausen thought the message was premature. He told Sorge
nothing about his opposition to the suggestion, but never put
that message on the air.

Sorge was kept in a cell at the headquarters of the Tokyo
Metropolitan Police Board, more or less unmolested, left to stew
in his own juice while damning evidence was being extracted
by the most cruel means from his fellow conspirators. He and
Ozaki were finally hanged on November 7, 1944. Klausen was
sentenced to life imprisonment, but was released by the American
Occupation authorities in 1945.

Sorge remained a wayward intellectual to the bitter end,
a fanatic and an idealist with a poetic turn of mind. Whenever
in his double life he was seized by doubts and scruples, he
escaped into poetry, a pastime he bashfully concealed even from
his few friends. Only a handful of his poems survive, but they
afford an insight into the soul of this very strange man. One
of them began:

"... eternally a stranger who condemns himself—never
to know real peace ..."

16

Target: United States

During the decade before Pearl Harbor, the world of espionage acquired a new figure who could not help being conspicuous. He was the secret agent of Japan who attained a comic prestige with an oddly sinister overtone. The "spy of the Rising Sun" became a favorite cartoon character, a familiar little man bowing deeply and hissing, "So solly, please," with a toothy smile, his hands fumbling busily in someone's pocket.

The Japanese themselves saw nothing funny in their spies. They regarded espionage as a deadly serious business, an important instrument of national policy. Fundamentally oriental in character, Japanese espionage was distinctly schizophrenic. In Asia, it operated with unbridled savagery, but in the United States, for instance, it could be civil and courteous. In Asia the Japanese manipulated narcotic drugs, prostitution, pornography, gambling. Its basic aim was to gain its ends by corruption. Rape, murder, kidnaping, arson, and counterfeiting were primary weapons in the arsenal of Japanese secret agents. Their victims were handled with medieval cruelty and even their own agents, if they happened to be Chinese or Caucasians, were treated with contempt.

This system triumphed in Manchuria, whose conquest was largely the handiwork of the secret service, but it failed in China. The lords of Tokyo had to bring in their armies after all; no amount of Japanese-inspired corruption could bring about China's collapse.

Their espionage effort against the Western world was more subtle. It was a large-scale and smooth maneuver in which spies were used along conventional lines with an organization patterned after Western intelligence services.

In the lore of espionage, the Japanese who attained the greatest fame was General Kenji Doihara, sometimes called the Lawrence of Manchuria. The epithet thus gave him major credit for the cheap conquest of Manchuria, which he captured, according to legend, with a pocketful of espionage tricks and a handful of spies.

In actual fact, Doihara was no master spy. His prominence was due chiefly to the fact that, being the brother of the concubine of an Imperial prince, he was given credit for other people's achievements. There was, indeed, a major espionage *coup* behind the lightning conquest of Manchuria, and there were fantastic secret maneuvers in China and elsewhere in Asia, but they were thought up and managed by faceless, nameless specialists who loathed Doihara for hugging the limelight.

The Japanese spy system was not spectacular at all, nothing like Canaris' "Fox Lair" in Berlin or the Fourth Bureau on Znamensky Street in Moscow. It was bureaucratic and pseudo-Prussian in its stolidity and humdrum efficiency.

The structure of the Japanese secret service is difficult to blueprint because it was vague and widely dispersed. It consisted of four major agencies operating as equals, although the semblance of a central intelligence agency existed within the Foreign Office.

This secret service arm operated under the nominal direction of the Foreign Ministers. The instructions issued to agents in the field were frequently signed by the ministers themselves. The Foreign Office supplied resident directors for networks abroad. It provided quarters in its various embassies and legations. It took care of the technical services, supplied the documents of authentication (including the customary forgeries), made necessary disbursements and handled the lines of communications.

The anchoring of the secret service in Japan's diplomatic machinery proved cumbersome even in peacetime, and disastrous in war. Rupture of diplomatic relations inevitably disrupted the espionage system of Japan when and where it was most urgently needed. This happened in the United States on December 7, 1941, when the Japanese Embassy had to close down. With its departure, the entire apparatus of Japanese espionage in the United States had to be dismantled. The espionage effort was shifted to the Embassy in Rio de Janeiro, then to Argentina and Chile, where it was too far removed from the United States to be effective.

The Department of Naval Intelligence was another senior branch of the service and it naturally played a very great part in the preparations for Pearl Harbor. It was a somewhat bizarre coincidence that Kichisaburo Nomura, who was the Japanese Ambassador in Washington at the time of Pearl Harbor, was once director of Naval Intelligence. It operated along more or less traditional lines, under a captain of the Imperial Navy.

Military Intelligence was handled by the Third Section of the Imperial General Staff as a headquarters organization. Its importance was reflected in the fact that its chief was usually a lieutenant general or at least a major general. The service was decentralized and the various armies stationed abroad, like the Kwantung Army in Manchuria, maintained their own, autonomous intelligence organizations.

The fourth echelon, counter-intelligence, was a two-pronged organization: the *Kempetai,* which was the secret police of the army, and the *Tokkoka,* the Metropolitan Police of Tokyo, whose Special (Political) Branch was mainly responsible for counter-espionage. It was the *Tokkoka* that, in the fall of 1941, succeeded in demolishing the Sorge ring. Prior to that, it had smashed a British network allegedly headed by the Reuters correspondent in Tokyo, James M. Cox.

These two secret police organizations shared the guilt for Japan's unsavory reputation. Their methods of interrogation were ruthless and cruel. The torture to which they subjected

Cox drove him to suicide. They were equally brutal with others they pulled in on whimsical charges of espionage, like Otto Tolischus, Tokyo correspondent of *The New York Times* at the time of Pearl Harbor. He presented a shocking picture of the Japanese spy-busters in the book he wrote after his release and return to the United States.

Japanese espionage against the United States had begun spasmodically as early as 1920; the Naval Attaché in Washington directed the operations. He was followed by a motley cavalcade of lazy spies, some in uniform, others behind elaborate covers. It is possible that some of Japan's better spies operated in the United States during this leisurely era of peace, but there could not have been too many of them. Prior to the Pearl Harbor operation, Japanese espionage in the United States had its halcyon days during the regime of Captain Tamon Yamaguchi as Naval Attaché in Washington in the middle 1930's. This was the only period when the Japanese succeeded in enlisting native Americans (and ex-members of the U.S. Navy at that) to work for them. A Yamaguchi aide, Commander Toshio Miyazaki, persuaded a dismissed chief petty officer, William Thompson by name, to steal several classified manuals for him and to procure some tactical information. Yamaguchi went to work on a cashiered commander, a certain John S. Farnsworth, trying to obtain similar information from him. Both men were caught before they could do appreciable damage.

A third man Yamaguchi tried to enlist was a civilian, who worked in the Naval Gun Factory in Washington. He reported the contact to Naval Intelligence, was told to cultivate this relationship and was given the doctored blueprint of a new eight-inch projectile. Yamaguchi was delighted with the loot and gave the man five hundred dollars in brand new, crisp American banknotes. The operation compromised him and he had to leave Washington shortly afterwards, leaving a gap that Japan took some time to fill.

After Yamaguchi came a swarm of Japanese spies. There

was at Calle 10a in Colon, Panama, a little haberdashery shop owned by an attractive, sexy, elegantly dressed woman in her early thirties, Lola Osawa by name. That name was an alias and her shop was a blind. She was in reality Chiyo Morasawa, wife of a Japanese naval officer with whom she formed a husband and wife espionage team, specializing in the secrets of the Panama Canal. Her shop was local headquarters for one of several Japanese spy rings scattered throughout Panama, with fifty-five branch offices in as many barber shops.

The Caribbean was swarming with Japanese fishing craft, fishing for information under the eagle eyes of a certain Ketarino Kabayama, a gentle, soft-voiced, middle-aged businessman, actually Captain Kabayama of the Imperial Navy. The catch of Kabayama's fishing fleet was taken to Japan by a certain Shoichi Yokoi, an exporter, who was Commander Masakazu Yokoi. More such fishing craft crowded the waters all along the Pacific Coast from Alaska to Mexico, and every one carried a trained operative of the secret service. In Vancouver, British Columbia, residents of Japanese ancestry bought into filling stations and fuel firms. These people were Japanese agents gaining quasi-legitimate access to gasoline and fuel oil, which they siphoned off and stored surreptitiously in hidden tanks in secluded inlets of the rugged coast for a rainy day.

There were few spots along the sensitive perimeter of the United States without at least one representative of the Japanese secret service in attendance.

Within the country, the Japanese had hundreds of operatives at important and seemingly unimportant posts. The Japanese secret service controlled banks and purchasing agencies. It had so-called Army and Navy Inspectorates, a Silk Intelligence Bureau, tourist agencies, a cotton intelligence office, and several other quasi-commercial organizations. Most bizarre among its outposts was the mysterious "Tokyo Club," a narcotic and gambling ring which had branches in many West Coast cities. The clubs not only collected information, but also supplied much of the money needed for the operation and provided occasional trigger men for direct action.

The Domei News Agency was another front. Consular offices were the regional headquarters of the network. On the eve of Pearl Harbor, Japan had consulates in San Francisco, Los Angeles, Seattle, New York, Philadelphia, Houston, Chicago, Honolulu and Manila. This formidable apparatus was directed by a single man, Nobutake Terasaki, who sat in an office in the handsome white Japanese Embassy building on Massachusetts Avenue in Washington, D.C. He hardly ever attracted attention because he appeared to be small fry, holding down the minor job of Second Secretary. He was a quiet, precise, uncommunicative man, the prototype of the studious intellectual, punctilious, modest, with an almost exaggerated passion for anonymity. He mixed little in the flamboyant society of Embassy Row. He had no friends. Yet this shy little man was the supreme chief of the whole Japanese network, not merely in the United States, but in the entire Western Hemisphere. The modest Second Secretary gave orders to the counselor in Buenos Aires, the Consul General in New York and even the Ambassador in Washington. He had at his disposal a small army of aides, including a brilliant communication technician named Kosaka, who operated his radio. Kosaka was sent to the United States in the late summer of 1941, when traffic became heavy, and he arrived with a new set of codes and ciphers.

Out in the field, the most important of all outlets was, of course, Hawaii, where an estimated four hundred secret agents were working for the Japanese secret service. The operation was directed by Consul General Nagao Kita, next to Terasaki the most important Japanese spy chief in the United States. His chief assistant was Consul Atojiro Okuda. Liaison with agents in the field was in the hands of Consulate Secretary Tadasi Morimura. He also took care of disbursements to spies and occasionally served as courier.

In actual fact, Morimura was Ensign Takeo Yoshikawa of

the Imperial Navy. He had been transferred from his desk at
the Intelligence Division where he specialized in the U.S. Pacific
Fleet and its main bases, to the biggest base earmarked for
attack.

It was in the winter of 1940 that his preparation for this
secret mission began in earnest. He was instructed to take the
Foreign Ministry's English language examination and was then
appointed vice-consul. As his cover, also, he was given his new
name and his new identity. In August, the Director of Naval
Intelligence told him: "Yoshikawa, you are going to Honolulu
as vice-consul. Tension is building up in Hawaii, as you know,
and short-wave transmitters can too easily be spotted by radio
direction finders. So you will go as a diplomat and report on
the daily readiness of the American fleet and bases by diplomatic
code. This is the only secure channel of communication left and
you will be our only agent. I do not have to tell you the importance of the mission."

"*Hai*," Yoshikawa replied, the unquestioning "aye, aye,
sir" of the Naval service.

"We have arranged," the director continued, "for a new
consul-general to be your chief for this operation. Nagao Kita,
a diplomat now at Canton, has been dealing closely with the
Imperial Navy on intelligence and other matters incident to our
occupation of China. He can be trusted to cooperate with you
fully. Kita goes to Honolulu first and you follow. Prepare
yourself."

Ensign Yoshikawa arrived in Honolulu in April 1941, and
went to work at once to carry out his mission. The freedom
with which he was permitted to move about amazed him. "For
instance," he later recalled, "I habitually rented aircraft at the
John Rodgers airport in Honolulu for my surveillance of the
military airfields, and walked nearly every day through Pearl
City to the end of the peninsula where I could readily survey
the air strip on Ford Island and battleship row in Pearl Harbor."

He swam about in the harbor as he pleased, looking for

data about underwater obstructions, tides, beach gradients; and strolled through the hills overlooking Honolulu, "magnificent vantage points," he said, "to observe the sorties of the fleet's units." His favorite vantage point was a pleasant Japanese restaurant called *Shanchu-ro,* just below Aiea. Sitting on a straw mat and sipping sake, he was entertained by a geisha while he himself observed the fleet below through a high window with a breathtaking view of the harbor. "I gained," he recalled, "much useful information on ships present and deployment patterns. From the geisha too, who would have entertained U.S. personnel earlier in the evening, I occasionally gleaned small bits of information."

As X-day drew closer, the Japanese secret service sent to Hawaii another authentic genius of espionage. He had an enormously important job, yet little if anything is known beyond his name. He was Ichiro Fuji, if that, indeed, was his real name. He arrived in Honolulu in September, 1941, with specific instructions from Admiral Yamamoto in person, and promptly superseded Consul Kita at the head of the hierarchy, but only inside the organization. To outsiders, he remained non-existent. There is reason to believe that his identity and his presence in Honolulu was not known even to the American counter-intelligence agencies, despite the fact that, by then, they had a good coverage of the Consulate General.

The information gathered by these spies ended ultimately on the desk of Admiral Isoroku Yamamoto, commander in chief of the Combined Imperial Fleet. It was he who hatched the monumental plan to attack the United States Fleet at Pearl Harbor.

A Naval Attaché in Washington in 1926, Yamamoto knew the United States well, and that knowledge helped him shape the plan. In 1941, when he appeared before the Cabinet Council, he promised a quick and decisive victory because, he warned, a protracted war would end, inevitably, in the defeat of Japan. "If you tell me," he said at the secret meeting, "that it is necessary that we fight, then in the first six months to a year of war against the United States and England I will run wild, and I will show you an uninterrupted succession of victories. I must tell you that, should the war be prolonged for two or three years, I have no confidence in our ultimate victory."

For his surprise attack on the U.S. Fleet, Yamamoto needed but limited intelligence, largely information of a tactical nature. Much of the material was already on file in Tokyo. It came mostly from published American sources, which described the composition and employment schedules of the U.S. Pacific Fleet with amazing candor. His intelligence service advised him that the American planes in Hawaii were distributed among the Hoiler Air Base, Hickam Field, and the naval air base on Ford Island. Every single anti-aircraft position was pinpointed for him from espionage reports. On the basis of this information, Yamamoto assigned one hundred and ninety-nine planes to deal with the airfields, and one hundred and fifty-four planes to take care of the fleet. From then on, all he needed from Intelligence was information about basic changes in the American organization and the movements of the ships.

The secret service was promptly mobilized to supply this data on a day-to-day basis. On January 6, 1941, the Consul General in Honolulu was told via Terasaki that he was to send continuous reports on the movement of U.S. vessels in Pearl Harbor; he was to report even when there were no such movements; and he was to tighten up his espionage clusters.

On February 15, Tokyo cabled a "Ministerial Instruction" to Terasaki in Washington for immediate distribution to his network. The agents were instructed to drop everything, discontinue their propaganda operations and concentrate exclusively on intelligence work. The dispatch included a voluminous "shopping list" of diverse items in twelve major categories.

On September 24, Tokyo asked Honolulu to divide the waters of Pearl Harbor into five separate sub-areas and to report the ships present in each of them separately, evidently to make possible the assignment of individual targets to the attacking squadrons. The message specified, "With regard to warships and aircraft carriers, we would like to have you report on those at anchor (these are not so important), tied up at wharves, buoys, and in docks. (Designate types and classes briefly. If possible, we would like to have mention made of the fact, when there are two or more vessels alongside the same wharf.)"

On December 1, in Tokyo, the Cabinet Council formally approved the commencement of hostilities on the day proposed by Yamamoto—December 7. Tokyo also moved to wind up Terasaki's apparatus which, Yamamoto apparently thought, would not be needed after the deadly blow. On December 2, Terasaki and his four chief lieutenants were ordered to leave by plane at once. This was a blow to the Ambassador who depended on Terasaki's continuous intelligence to guide him in his negotiations with the White House and the State Department. He sent an urgent plea to Tokyo to let Terasaki stay, but back came the answer turning down his request. The modest Second Secretary was more important than the hapless Ambassador.

In Honolulu, the activities of Japan's last ditch spies were taking a new and melodramatic turn. The mysterious master spy Ichiro Fuji was making his last-minute dispositions. His scattered operatives were to communicate their final messages, no longer to him or to Kita at the Consulate, but directly to the approaching striking force via clandestine relay ships lying off shore. They were given a code of signals to indicate the preparedness of Pearl Harbor and to report any last-minute movements of American ships.

The chief field agent of the Japanese, on whom they depended most, was functioning admirably. He had just told the Consulate that things looked promising down at the harbor: he had succeeded in identifying seven battleships, six cruisers, two aircraft carriers, forty destroyers, and twenty-seven submarines, the vast bulk of the Pacific Fleet.

This formidable spy was not a Japanese at all. He was Jimmy, owner of Post Office Box 1476 at Honolulu, a source

Tokyo had developed in 1936. Jimmy was sometimes referred to as Friedell, and he was in fact a German named Bernard Julius Otto Kuehn, an apparently well-heeled individual, with a house at Lanikai, another at Kalama, and a pleasure boat with a star on the sail. The pseudonym Friedell was derived from the first name of his wife Elfriede, whose nickname it was, spelled with one *l*.

Kuehn must have performed well because he was able to deposit seventy thousand dollars in a Honolulu bank between 1936 and 1939. He told friends that the money had come from an inheritance in Germany, which was transferred to him by a Tokyo bank. In reality, of course, it came from the Japanese secret service. Kuehn bought his two houses and the boat from the money supplied by the Japanese. In 1940-41, Kuehn intensified his activities and was paid an additional sixteen thousand dollars. The last payment of fourteen thousand dollars more was delivered to him by Morimura virtually on the eve of Pearl Harbor.

The Japanese spymasters usually communicated with Kuehn by mail, sending him postcards to P.O. Box 1476. On December 2, such a postcard alerted Kuehn to a rendezvous with Morimura. When they met the next day, they exchanged a system of codes and signals that was most ingeniously devised. It was based on Kuehn's two houses and his star-studded sailboat. The house in Lanikai Beach was on the east coast of Oahu; the other was in a beach village one mile northwest of Lanikai. The houses were to show hourly lights, each light at each hour signifying a different prearranged message. For instance, one light in a certain window in the house at Lanikai turned on between midnight and 1 a.m. was to mean, "All carriers have departed." A light in the attic window at Kalama between 7 p.m. and 8 p.m. was meant to say, "All battleship divisions have now departed."

They also arranged for still other methods of communications, just in case the light signals could not be made. Fuji sent agents to Maui Island to signal with bonfires visible far out at

sea. Even this was topped with still another arrangement. Camouflaged want ads, placed on radio station KGMG in Honolulu,
were to serve as coded signals.

The Japanese were leaving nothing to chance.

On December 4, the Japanese armada was closing in, receiving hourly intelligence. Fuji received the final query: "Please
report comprehensively on the American fleet." He sent reassuring words: "The fleet is in. Three additional battleships have
just arrived."

Nothing escaped the attention of his anonymous little spies.
A British gunboat sailed into the harbor with the diplomatic
bag for the Consul. A Japanese spy followed the courier from
the berth of the boat to the Consulate General, then back to the
gunboat, and he watched from shore as she was leaving. Within
the hour, his report was encoded and on its way to Tokyo. It
was a bit of useless incidental intelligence, but it showed Tokyo
that its coverage of the target was uncannily complete.

On December 6, Kita put a last coded cable on the air,
the complete list of all American warships present in Pearl
Harbor, divided into the five strategic sub-areas. He identified
eight battleships, three light cruisers, sixteen destroyers. The
spies missed a few. In actual fact there were two heavy cruisers,
six light cruisers, twenty-six destroyers and five submarines in
the harbor, in addition to the eight battleships. But it did not
matter. What the spies had missed, Yamamoto's planes would
find.

Out at sea that night, the Japanese armada moved to its
target. Its radios were silent. Its ships showed no light. Then
came a message from Tokyo. It read (in English translation):
"Climb Mount Niitaka."

It was the signal to attack.

As the planes roared off into the dawn, there was in the
cockpit of each a strange little map. The maps showed an aerial
view of Pearl Harbor, divided into little numbered squares. Each
bomber knew which square was his target and what ships he
was likely to find there.

The maps had been taken from an ordinary picture post-card, one of a so-called Laporello set. The cards show a panoramic view of the whole harbor from the air. One of Kita's agents had bought them a few months earlier in a Honolulu gift shop.

The price? One dollar, the set.

17

The Magic of the Black Chamber

To many people, Pearl Harbor is not only a synonym for infamy, but also for the failure of American intelligence and the monumental triumph of Japanese espionage. This is by no means an accurate picture. On the eve of Pearl Harbor, the Japanese Intelligence set-up was enormous, to be sure, but, like Porgy, it had plenty of nothing. They knew minute details of the American and British order of battle, of the disposition and movements of the fleets, the *tactical* data a prudent commander must have on the eve of attack. At that point their wisdom ended. They gave Pearl Harbor their Sunday punch and expended on it all the intelligence they possessed.

So deficient, indeed, was the vaunted Japanese secret service that on the morning after Pearl Harbor, it could not tell its High Command the full measure of the Japanese success. On the night of December 7, an American admiral was asked at Oahu, "Do you think they could come back with troops, land here and take the islands?"

"Yes, damn it," he answered, "but if they let us hold on for the next couple of weeks, we can make it."

The Japanese did not come back, because they did not have the *strategic* information to take advantage of their historic opportunity.

The United States, on the other hand, was extremely poor in tactical intelligence about the Japanese. But on the *strategic* level it had a single secret service arm that was ingenious, technically competent, and reached into the very heart of the Japanese government. It was the world's best cryptographic secret service; thanks to it the United States could read some, though by no means all, of Japan's most confidential communications and acquire a general picture of her intentions and dispositions. Yet even this superb intelligence weapon could not overcome a mountain of deficiencies elsewhere.

Cryptographic analysis had demonstrated its usefulness as far back as the Washington Naval Conference of 1922. The Japanese came to the conference with great expectations, but returned home sorely disappointed. Japan had to agree to a ten-year naval holiday, and to limit her naval strength to three hundred and fifteen thousand tons as against an aggregate of one million two hundred and fifty thousand tons of American, British and French warships. Japanese acquiescence in this arrangement was largely the result of the uncanny skill with which the American delegation had maneuvered the negotiations. Throughout the conference, the Americans appeared to be anticipating every move of the Japanese, defeating them at every step. How was that possible?

The mystery was unexpectedly resolved in 1930 with the publication of a strange book. It was *The American Black Chamber*, by Major Herbert O. Yardley, a former crypto-analyst of the U.S. War and State Department. Yardley borrowed the phrase for the title of his book from the French *cabinet noir*, the name of a secret bureau that opened and read the mail of the king's enemies. Yardley revealed that in 1922-23 the United States had had a Black Chamber of its own, conducting cryptographic espionage from an inconspicuous brownstone house in midtown New York. By this means, he said, American diplomats could read in advance the secret instructions which the Tokyo Foreign Office cabled to the Japanese delegation, giving them minimum and maximum terms for their difficult bargaining.

When Yardley came out with his disclosures, his Black Chamber was dead. In 1929, Secretary of State Henry L. Stimson had closed it down, with the scandalized remark, "Gentlemen don't read each other's mail." Stimson's decision riled

Yardley and, in his pique, he published his unauthorized exposé. His revelations enraged the Japanese. They moved promptly and virulently to denounce the treaty and began to prepare behind the scenes measures to pay back the loss of face.

Countering the efforts of the Japanese secret service was an American set-up in the Department of State. In 1941, the Department had no specialized agency for diplomatic intelligence; rather, this was a collateral function of the Foreign Service as a whole. In Washington, the Department's Far Eastern Division (headed by Maxwell M. Hamilton) had a Japanese Desk manned by brilliant experts, and the United States was equally fortunate in its diplomats at the Embassy in Tokyo. Those men, under Ambassador Joseph C. Grew, procured intelligence of the highest quality and significance.

Other agencies not directly connected with the State Department also supplied it with material. They included:

(1) *Army General Staff, G-2 Intelligence,* under Major General Sherman Miles, collected, evaluated and disseminated information pertaining to the war potential, topography, military forces and military activities of foreign countries, and the strategic vulnerability of the United States and its possessions. G-2 also performed some counter-intelligence functions, conducted military mapping and performed cryptographic duties.

(2) *Chief of Naval Operations,* The Office of Naval Intelligence under Rear Admiral Theodore S. Wilkinson operated in two major branches. The foreign branch (headed by Captain William A. Heard) received, collated, analyzed and disseminated information. The domestic branch (under Rear Admiral Howard F. Kingman) dealt with internal subversion, espionage, and similar activities.

(3) *Military and Naval Attachés,* with quasi-diplomatic assignments, actually represented G-2 or ONI respectively. In Japan, Lieutenant Colonel Harry I. Creswell served as Military Attaché after 1938. Until 1939, Captain Harold Bemis was Naval Attaché; he was then succeeded by Lieutenant Commander Henry H. Smith-Hutton.

(4) *The Federal Bureau of Investigation,* directed by J. Edgar Hoover, with Robert L. Shivers as Agent-in-Charge in Hawaii, performed certain collateral intelligence functions of its own. It was primarily responsible for counter-intelligence and counter-espionage, but from time to time it also supplied positive intelligence obtained in the course of its own regular activities.

Both the Military and Naval Intelligence units, of course, had their subsidiary combat intelligence organs in the field. Both also had their cryptographic arms. Army Signal Intelligence enjoyed the services as chief cryptographer of Mr. (later Colonel) W. F. Friedman, regarded as the world's foremost expert in the field.

The Office of Naval Communications, headed by Rear Admiral Leigh Noyes (Captain Joseph R. Redmond was Assistant Director), was organized in several sections. Captain L. F. Safford was in charge of Communications Security; the Translation Section was headed by Captain A. D. Kramer; and the Cryptographic Research Section was headed by Lieutenant Commander George W. Lynn, Senior Watch Officer. There were also Communication Intelligence Units attached to the scattered Naval Districts. In Hawaii, Commander Joseph J. Rochefort served as Officer in Charge. He also had jurisdiction over radio intercept stations at Oahu, Midway, Samoa and Dutch Harbor. Other direction finder and interception stations were located in Washington, Corregidor, and on the West Coast.

In addition to all of these, the Federal Communications Commission also maintained a radio monitoring service.

This, in bare outline, was the American organization on January 3, 1941. On that day, Admiral Yamamoto conceived the plan for Pearl Harbor. Although he communicated the plan only to a very small group of individuals, it spread nevertheless from the *Nagato,* his flagship, to Tokyo. Then, on January 27, 1941, Edward S. Crocker, First Secretary of the U.S. Embassy, was given an ominous bit of diplomatic gossip by his friend, Dr. Ricardo Rivera Schrieber, the Peruvian Minister, who had an exceptional circle of friends among influential Japanese. Crocker

rushed the information to Ambassador Grew who at once sent
the following message to the State Department:

"The Peruvian Minister has informed a member of my
staff that he has heard from many sources, including a Japanese
source, that in the event of trouble breaking out between the
United States and Japan, the Japanese intend to make a surprise attack against Pearl Harbor with all of their strength and
employing all of their equipment. The Peruvian Minister considered the rumors fantastic. Nevertheless, he considered them of
sufficient importance to convey this information to a member of
my staff." That same night, Grew also entered this strange
rumor in his personal diary.

The dispatch was routed from the State Department to
the Office of Naval Intelligence for evaluation and comment.
There a majority of the experts insisted that Japan would think
twice before moving against the United States. O.N.I.'s evaluation carried this unequivocal comment: "The Division of Naval
Intelligence places no credence in these rumors. Furthermore,
based on known data regarding the present disposition and employment of Japanese Naval and Army forces, no move against
Pearl Harbor appears imminent or planned for in the foreseeable
future." This note was dated February 1, 1941.

The theory seemed to be supported by at least circumstantial
evidence. The flower of Japan's land forces, the much-vaunted
Kwantung Army, was stationed in Manchuria, and its highly
independent military politicians were said to be itching to take
on the Russians in the Far East.

However, by June, 1941, Russia as a possible or probable
target for Japan should have been ruled out. The United States
had come into the possession of some astonishing hard intelligence. It was a report the director of the Japanese secret service
in Manchukuo (like Terasaki, himself a mere Second Secretary
at the Hsinkiang Embassy) had sent to his chief in the Foreign
Ministry. Reflecting the consensus of the Kwantung Army's
commanding generals, the man in Hsinkiang advised Tokyo to

take German claims about an imminent collapse of the Soviet Union with a grain of salt. "Geographical vastness," he wrote, "abundance of human material resources, and the approach of winter all require careful consideration when predicting the outcome. Since Russia is now thoroughly communistic, the possibility of a counter-revolution to overthrow Stalin is very slight."

He counseled that "Japan's viewpoint regarding war should be cautious watchful waiting"; and bluntly advised against "joining the offensive against Russia." On the contrary, he suggested, Japan should concentrate on a definitive settlement of the "China affair" so that she might turn with her total resources against the United States.

How was it possible for such a delicate communication from one Japanese intelligence authority to another to fall into American hands? The answer lies in cryptoanalysis. The United States was again reading many of the diplomatic messages of Japan. Although hundreds of persons were involved in this activity, nothing about it leaked out that enlightened the Japanese. This was a remarkable feat of security, and completely misled the Japanese, despite the fact that in the cryptographic war nothing is taken for granted except that every country tries to break codes and ciphers.

With the progress of radio, wars had become, as Fletcher Pratt remarked, conflicts of cryptographers. "From the day in August of 1914 when German-controlled radio stations all over the world flashed out the message 'A SON IS BORN,' the Imperial Army's code-phrase for 'War,'" he wrote, "there was no great event that was not preceded by feverish activity in the code-rooms of the nations; and in many cases victory or defeat was underwritten in those code-rooms before it took place on the battlefield or across the seas."

Cryptoanalysts, by the nature of their highly secretive work, form a mystic little band and live in almost complete seclusion. Describing his own time spent in Room 2646 of the Navy De-

partment, Admiral Zacharias wrote: "Hours went by without
any of us saying a word, just sitting in front of piles of indexed
sheets on which a mumbo jumbo of figures and letters was displayed in chaotic disorder, trying to solve the puzzle bit by bit
like fitting together the pieces of a jigsaw puzzle."

The raw material from which these men worked was, of
course, supplied by the radio interception stations. Everything
that was intercepted on an odd date of the month was handled
by the Navy; on the even dates the Army received all the material. Each service would then decrypt the material (this work
was often done by men who could not speak Japanese!), trans-
late it, and prepare fourteen copies, which were shared with the
other service, the White House, and the State Department.

By this means, an extraordinary flow of information of the
highest quality was streaming upwards from the intelligence men
to the policy makers. Once again it must be emphasized that
intelligence officers can only supply information; they have not
the power to act upon it. Moreover, I must repeat that the men
who evaluate information are often puzzled by seemingly contradictory bits and pieces and, in their bureaucratic desire never
to be wrong, will often make evasive and vague recommendations.

Finally, the man at the very top, President Roosevelt, was
no Churchill with a burning interest in, and understanding of,
intelligence. Could a Churchill in the White House have averted
—or at least mitigated—the Pearl Harbor disaster? We can
only speculate. . . .

At all events, on December 2, 1941, what should have been
an iron-clad tipoff was intercepted. A message from Tokyo instructed the Embassy in Washington to begin the destruction of
codes, a certain indication that Japan was preparing for war.

The message read: "No. 867. *Strictly Secret*. 1. Among the
telegraphic codes with which your office is equipped burn all
but those now used with the machine and one copy each of 'O'
code (Oite) and abbreviating code (L). (Burn also the various
other codes that you have in your custody.)

"2. Stop at once using one code machine unit and destroy it completely.

"3. When you have finished this, wire me back the one word 'Haruna.'

"4. At the time and in the manner you deem most proper dispose of all files of messages coming and going and all other secret documents.

"5. Burn all the codes that Telegraphic Official Kosaka brought you. (Hence the necessity of getting in contact with Mexico mentioned in my No. 860 is no longer recognized.)"

The message went up the ladder of the U.S. government. There is no indication that anything was done about it.

Aside from the information obtained from such direct sources in which Japanese intentions were actually spelled out, crucial tactical and operational information was obtained by the various Radio Intelligence Units which monitored the traffic of the Japanese Navy. Up to that time, all attacks on the Japanese naval codes had been in vain, but even though American cryptographers could not read the verbatim contents of the Japanese naval messages, they could still make significant deductions from them. These were inferences drawn from analysis of Japanese radio traffic and from changes in its regular procedure, from deviations from norm.

The most important Unit was the one attached to Admiral Claude C. Bloch's 14th Naval District in Hawaii, headed by Commander Joseph J. Rochefort, one of the most remarkable personalities of the secret war. He was virtually unknown, even within the Navy, beyond a small circle of superiors and co-workers, although he was undoubtedly the Navy's foremost cryptographic expert. In addition, he was also a student of the Japanese language, thus able to make his own translations and evaluate for himself the various intercepts. He was stationed in Pearl Harbor.

At the time of Pearl Harbor, the high quality of Rochefort's work was especially remarkable, in view of the fact that his equipment was obsolescent, that he was short on qualified personnel, and that his electronic snooping had to be done over enormous distances. Energetic efforts to obtain more modern equipment failed, but this did not discourage Rochefort. In the summer of 1941, with the support of Admiral Bloch, he overhauled his equipment at Pearl Harbor and put up additional direction finder sets in the Midway and Palmyra Islands, using material which he had to swipe from the Pearl Harbor pool.

Much of the tactical and operational intelligence which Lieutenant Commander Edwin T. Layton, the Fleet Intelligence Officer, handed up to Admiral Husband E. Kimmel, the commander-in-chief of the Pacific Fleet, was based on the output of Rochefort's unit. It was both voluminous and persuasive, and became increasingly so as Pearl Harbor day approached.

Throughout November, Rochefort kept in touch with the striking force of the Japanese by monitoring its traffic and drawing his conclusions from its hectic, erratic, and spasmodic nature. Frequent changes in call signals and other signs hinted at an elaborate maneuver and persuaded Rochefort that something big was in the air. His daily verbal reports to Bloch and his daily written summaries to Kimmel mirrored this conviction.

Around November 1, Rochefort first observed unusual, feverish, and ominous Japanese activities. Early in November, the Japanese introduced an entirely new set of calls for their units afloat. A series of high priority signals, sent from the main Yokosuka naval base to fleet commanders, was also discovered. On November 3, Communication Intelligence summarized its observations in these significant words: "General messages continue to emanate from Tokyo communications. Such an amount is unprecedented and the import of it is not understood. A mere call change does not account for activities of this nature. The impression is strong that these messages are periodic reports of a certain nature to the major commander."

On December 1, Communication Intelligence indicated that the Japanese were to commence some kind of operation on a large scale. It was definitely established that a striking force was on the move. "Summing up all reports," Communication Intelligence concluded, "it is believed that the large fleet made up of Second, Third and First Fleet units has left Empire waters."

Most ominous of all was the complete radio silence of Japan's aircraft carriers; consequently, they were listed as missing. It was this apparent disappearance of the carriers that made Kimmel most apprehensive. When his Fleet Intelligence Officer failed day after day to account for them, the admiral asked: "What, you don't know where the carriers are? Do you mean to say that they could be rounding Diamond Head [the southeast corner of Oahu on which Pearl Harbor is situated] and you wouldn't know it?"

"I hoped they would be sighted before now," was all the Fleet Intelligence Officer could answer. Nothing was found out about those missing carriers, nothing, that is, until the morning of December 7.

Much has been made of the military and naval unpreparedness that made that day so disastrous. However, this unreadiness was by no means confined to the military establishment and the policy makers. During those days, the Department of Justice was as much a part of America's first line of defense as was the Pacific Fleet. In a sense it *was* America's first line of defense. The armies and the navies were not in action as yet, but the spies were.

Before the war the responsibility to defend the United States from foreign espionage was widely scattered; no central counter-espionage agency existed to deal with the problem. It was mainly the job of the F.B.I., but both the Navy and the Army maintained their own counter-intelligence organizations. Though they had no power of arrest, they regarded themselves nevertheless as the senior guardians of military, naval, and industrial secrets.

After the outbreak of the war in Europe, on September 6, 1939, President Roosevelt issued a directive in which he designated the F.B.I. as the central Federal agency in "charge of investigative work in matters relating to espionage, sabotage, and violations of the neutrality regulations." Under his limited powers, Roosevelt could do no more. He could not give orders to law enforcement agencies maintained by the states, counties or municipalities, or by private industry. He could merely request them to pass on to the F.B.I. any information they dug up about subversion.

Despite the Presidential directive, confusion and conflict remained, enabling foreign agents to operate with something approaching impunity. Nowhere was the situation more deplorable than in Hawaii. In December, 1941, when the F.B.I. had a total of two thousand six hundred and two agents, Hoover assigned only nine of them to its field office in Honolulu. The Navy's District Intelligence Office, which functioned mainly as a counter-intelligence agency, had about a hundred officers, interpreters and translators. The Army was also engaged in counter-intelligence, but the number of people assigned to the function was negligible.

There was superficial co-operation between the various agencies, but under the surface bickering was rampant. Important operations were conducted at cross purposes. Surveillances had to be abandoned when agents of the various American security organs ran into one another. Promising projects were discontinued when rival agencies fought each other on petty jurisdictional matters.

In November, 1941, for instance, the F.B.I. tapped the telephone of the Japanese Consulate General in Honolulu, which was rightly suspected of being the general headquarters of Japanese espionage in Hawaii. That single tap was yielding substantial results when the F.B.I. was forced to discontinue it. Competitive agencies, Naval Intelligence and the Federal Communications Commission, found out about the tap and chased the Bureau away from it. Then a jurisdictional quarrel sprang up between the F.C.C. and Naval Intelligence. The dispute was finally settled by the withdrawal of both agencies from the scene, leaving the Consul General's hot wire uncovered on the very eve of Pearl Harbor.

Discouraged by this fratricidal war and unable to run the show as he wanted to, Hoover retired from energetic prosecution of the espionage war with Japan in Hawaii. In December, 1940, he told Robert L. Shivers, the Special Agent in charge of his Honolulu field office, that "the Bureau does not consider it advisable or desirable at this particular time for your office to assume the responsibility for the supervision of all Japanese espionage investigations in the Territory of Hawaii."

The list of Japanese suspects which the Bureau kept up-to-date included seven hundred and seventy individuals, a formidable force in aggressive espionage. The F.B.I. knew who they were and what they were doing, but was able to do little, if anything, to render them harmless.

Among those suspects was a certain Tachibana, a commander in the Japanese Navy, sent to the United States on a semi-official detail as a language officer. In May, 1941, the Bureau came into the possession of conclusive evidence that Tachibana was an espionage agent. Hoover advised the State Department of the facts and inquired whether the Department would approve his arrest. On May 27, the Department notified the F.B.I. that there was no objection. The commander was taken into custody in Los Angeles.

On June 14, Ambassador Nomura called on Secretary Hull and besought him "in the interests of promoting friendly relations between our two Governments" to let Tachibana go home without a trial. "I went carefully into this case," Hull wrote, "and decided to grant Nomura's request."

It was not easy to develop a major espionage case like that of Tachibana. The F.B.I. was understandably chagrined when it thus saw its trapped bird fleeing the cage with the approval of the State Department. Under the circumstances, it is apparent that Pearl Harbor was not exclusively a military and naval disaster for which only generals and admirals must bear the responsibility. It was also a disaster of America's internal security establishment.

During the post mortems, it became a popular pastime to

ask high-ranking army and navy officers where they were when
the bombs began to fall. Much was made of the fact that General George C. Marshall could not recall exactly what he was
doing at that exact moment and said he thought he was out on
a constitutional. But if the Army and the Navy were thus off
guard, expecting nothing in particular to happen on that fateful
Sunday, so was the Department of Justice.

Attorney General Francis Biddle was away in Detroit.
Hoover was in New York. His ranking aides, including Assistant
to the Director Edward A. Tamm, filled a box in Griffith Sta-
dium watching the pro football game between the Washington
Redskins and the Philadelphia Eagles.

America's internal security organs had a Pearl Harbor of
their own. They were so preoccupied with fratricidal strife that
they had too little energy or interest left for an effective campaign
against alien foes on American soil.

Once the war had begun there was no reason to question
the FBI's ability to deal energetically with foreign espionage
agents and saboteurs. The efficiency at this end was somewhat
aided by a strange inefficiency in the enemies' camp. After the
war, General von Lahousen, one of the surviving executives of
the *Abwehr,* told me that this was so because his organization
never really had their hearts in planting spies and saboteurs on
Uncle Sam's back. However, the astonishingly clumsy German
effort was not substantially different from the general pattern
and quality of the *Abwehr's* activities elsewhere. They were good
only in countries where domestic dissension existed, where Nazism was popular with key segments of the population and where
the *Abwehr* or the Kaltenbrunner-Schellenberg organization
could subvert the natives.

As early as 1941, the FBI managed to break up what appeared
to be the major ring of Nazi spies in the United States, headed
by one Kurt Frederick Ludwig, a native of Ohio, presiding over
a quaint assortment of Sad Sacks. The Ludwig ring of second-
raters was set up here by an itinerant German *Abwehr*-man mov-

ing about on a forged passport made out to Julio Lopez Lido. He was actually Ulrich von der Osten, an old-timer in German espionage, a sort of traveling sales manager covering an enormous territory from Shanghai to New York. His sudden death in a traffic accident on Times Square in New York led the FBI to Ludwig and from him to the other members of the ring.

In 1940, the FBI scored a tremendous victory of lasting significance, when it succeeded in penetrating, through exceptionally smart detective work, one of the *Abwehr's* greatest secrets, the microdot system used in the transmission of secret messages. In the early summer of 1942, the FBI arrested a group of German would-be saboteurs Canaris had sent to this country in two U-boats. This was the pathetic *Pastorius Operation,* arrogantly code-named after the first German ever to immigrate to the United States. The idea behind the ill-fated mission was to sabotage the American aluminum industry. Had it succeeded, it could have seriously slowed down aircraft production.

With the aid of a double agent still known only as ND98 (a mercenary spy who sold his services to the U.S. Legation as soon as he arrived at his overseas outpost in Montevideo), the FBI also participated in a carillon concert of its own. ND98 was supposed to forward information collected by three German agents in the United States from a clandestine radio somewhere in Uruguay. When he was safely in FBI hands, he asked the *Abwehr's* permission to transfer his activities to New York. There the FBI established him at a cozy hideout on Long Island with a radio transmitter. He began to send his baited messages on December 4, 1941, and kept at it until May 2, 1945, when the British captured the *Abwehr's* radio center near Hamburg. A total of two thousand eight hundred and twenty-nine doctored messages were thus sent to the *Abwehr* and eight hundred and twenty-four were received from the Germans. ND98 reached the height of arrogance, and maybe also absurdity, on June 1, 1944, when he advised his employers that D-Day had to be delayed "by a breakdown in the production of invasion barges" and that the troops in England, which *Luftwaffe* reconnaissance could not fail to detect, were being rerouted to the Mediterranean.

The FBI covered the whole waterfront, North as well as Central and South America. It succeeded in thwarting several major resident directors of the *Abwehr*, Major Ludwig von Bohlen in Chile, and also his successor, Bernardo Timmerman; Josef Jacob Johannes Starziczny and Otto Uebele in Brazil; and a number of lesser fry in other Latin lands. It also broke up a large-scale smuggling operation, which supplied the eager Germans with such rare strategic materials as platinum from Colombia and industrial diamonds from Venezuela, by catching the head of the operation, a bogus British banker named Harold Ebury, at his palatial California home on Monterey Peninsula.

An interesting sideline of the FBI's big manhunt on spies and saboteurs was its campaign to recapture German prisoners of war who managed to escape from prison camps maintained in this country by the U.S. Army. At the height of the season, there were some four hundred thousand such prisoners in the United States, and they kept escaping at a rate of about seventy-five a month. All told, such escapes totaled two thousand eight hundred and three during the war years and the FBI managed to bring all of the Germans back alive, except three: Kurt Rossmeisl, Georg Gaertner and Curt Westphal. They are still at large.

J. Edgar Hoover directed the huge spy hunt with unprecedented finesse. Far from promoting it, he vigorously resisted the spy hysteria that was rampant in the early stages of the war. He was firmly, even bitterly, opposed to the mass evacuation of one hundred and twenty thousand Japanese-Americans on the West Coast to so-called "relocation centers." He was appalled, not only by the inhumanity of this mass deportation, but also by motives that had little, if anything, in common with the needs of national defense. The sour taste that the "relocation" left in Hoover's mouth was reflected in a passage in Don Whitehead's authoritative book, *The FBI Story.* He wrote: "With the hysteria, there were the cold calculations of men who wanted the Japanese moved for economic reasons and because of racial prejudices. The decisions for the movement were made in the upper reaches of the Administration. And so it was that tens of thousands of loyal Japanese-American citizens made the sad journey from their homes after a directive was issued giving the Army authority for the roundup."

Hoover knew that those one hundred and twenty thousand Japanese-Americans represented no clear and present espionage danger. His own pre-war efforts had already located the seven hundred and thirty-three Japanese aliens he suspected as actual or potential spies. He had every one of them safely in custody.

The absence of large-scale German, Italian, and Japanese espionage and sabotage efforts in the United States was one of the miracles of the war. Aside from the FBI's energetic measures to plug every loophole, two major events aided in foiling any such enemy effort. The first occurred in June, 1941, five months before Pearl Harbor, when the Treasury Department moved to freeze all German and Japanese assets in this country and in most Central and South American countries. The lifeblood of espionage and sabotage is money. Not even the best secret service can operate without it.

The other event could not be surpassed in its ingenuity and melodrama. The center of German espionage in the United States was the Consulate General in downtown New York. When the Consulate was closed down months before Pearl Harbor, in another smart measure of prophylaxis, the *Abwehr*-men posing as consuls had to burn their papers. They called in the janitor of the building, a man named Dick Holland, and asked him to make a fire in the furnace, for this was summer and the furnace was cold. Holland (who almost certainly was an agent of the FBI) made the fire so that it burned in only one side of the furnace. When the Germans came down with their papers and gave them to Holland for burning, the ingenious janitor dumped them into that side of the furnace where there was no fire. In this manner, the papers, only slightly seared, came into the possession of the Bureau.

Among the papers was the complete roster of German spies and informants active in the United States.

18

Donovan's Brain

On a January afternoon in 1942, President Roosevelt called William J. Donovan to the White House and told him bluntly, almost bitterly: "We have no Intelligence Service!"

What the President thus compressed into just five words, General Dwight D. Eisenhower spelled out in detail after the war. He wrote:

"Europe had been at war for a full year before America became alarmed over its pitifully inadequate defenses . . . the greatest obstacle was psychological: complacency still persisted! Even the fall of France in May, 1940, failed to awaken us— and by 'us' I mean every professional soldier, as well as others —to a full realization of danger.

"Within the War Department a shocking deficiency that impeded all constructive planning existed in the field of Intelligence. Between the two World Wars no funds were provided with which to establish the basic requirement of an Intelligence system, a far-flung organization of fact finders. Our one feeble gesture in this direction was the maintenance of military attachés in most foreign capitals, and, since public funds were not available to meet the unusual expenses of this type of duty, only officers with independent means could normally be detailed to these posts. Usually they were estimable, socially acceptable gentlemen; few knew the essentials of intelligence work. Results were almost completely negative, and the situation was not helped by the custom of making long service as a military attaché, rather than ability, the essential qualification for appointment as head of the Intelligence Division in the War Department.

"The stepchild position of G-2 in our General Staff system was emphasized in many ways. For example, the number of general officers within the War Department was so limited by peacetime law that one of the principal divisions had to be headed by a colonel. Almost without exception the G-2 Division got the colonel. This in itself would not necessarily have been serious, since it would have been far preferable to assign to the post a highly qualified colonel than a mediocre general, but the practice clearly indicated the Army's failure to emphasize the intelligence function. This was reflected also in our schools, where, despite some technical training in battlefield reconnaissance and intelligence, the broader phases of the work were almost completely ignored. We had few men capable of analyzing intelligently such information as did come to the notice of the War Department, and this applied particularly to what has become the very core of Intelligence research and analysis— namely, industry.

"In the first winter of the war these accumulated and glaring deficiencies were serious handicaps. Initially the Intelligence Division could not even develop a clear plan for its own organization nor could it classify the type of information it deemed essential in determining the purposes and capabilities of our enemies. The chief of the division could do little more than come to the planning and operating sections of the staff and in a rather pitiful way ask if there was anything he could do for us."

This brutally frank appraisal by Eisenhower was presented six years after the events he described took place and three years after the war he helped to win. His scathing criticism was confined to G-2, and rightly so, because, even during the period he described, the over-all intelligence picture was not so bad as the one he painted. Neither was President Roosevelt apparently well informed, nor was he quite fair, when he told Donovan that the United States had "no intelligence service."

For one thing, the amazing cryptographic espionage organization of the Army and Navy was functioning better than ever, reading the enemies' most confidential dispatches almost at will. It was during this period that the Navy's cryptoanalysts began to collect the data which enabled Admiral Chester W. Nimitz to repay the debt of Pearl Harbor astonishingly early in the war, and which actually turned the tide in the Pacific. Perhaps this is the place to tell that story so that the reader will have a balanced picture—both the good and the bad—of the state of U.S. intelligence at the time.

In the immediate wake of Pearl Harbor, Nimitz had to figure out what the enemy's next move would be. Nimitz allowed full scope to his intuition and assumed that the Japanese would next move against Midway, a lonely atoll one thousand one hundred sea miles west-northwest of Oahu, covered with a lush blanket of dwarf magnolia and inhabited by the gooney bird, a comic member of the albatross family.

Nimitz's intuition was inspired. In Tokyo, the move he suspected had, in fact, been decided upon by Yamamoto. He hoped to capture Midway and to destroy whatever was left afloat of the U.S. Pacific Fleet.

Nimitz's intelligence officers had very little hard intelligence and even what they had was deficient in the estimate of the Japanese strength. Where Yamamoto had eleven battleships, Nimitz was told he had only two to four. No light cruisers were identified in the Japanese force, although it contained six. The Americans counted sixteen to twenty-four Japanese destroyers, but Yamamoto had forty-nine; and he had sixteen submarines as against the American estimate of eight to twelve. Only our estimates of his carrier and heavy cruiser strength were approximately accurate.

In one sense, this underestimation of Yamamoto's fleet was fortunate for the U.S. Nimitz would have thought twice before devising his bold and brilliant plan to meet Yamamoto in a head-on clash had he known how prodigious his adversary's power really was. But Nimitz had a powerful weapon of his own—cryptoanalysis.

After the commencement of hostilities, each Japanese fleet was assigned several coding systems and each code was changed at intervals. Even so, the American cryptoanalysts found enough clues in this wireless traffic to obtain a fair idea of Japanese intentions and arrangements. The clues included the volume of traffic, the repetition of call letters, the length of the messages, the types of the codes used. All these telltale clues were catalogued by Commander Rochefort and his staff, until they presented a clear pattern: Yamamoto *was* getting ready for another major move. But the target of their preparations, referred to in Japanese messages as "AF" and "AF," could mean any of several places—Midway, to be sure, but also perhaps Hawaii or the Aleutians or New Caledonia or even Sydney, Australia.

At this point, in the spring of 1942, it became imperative to find out. Nimitz hit upon an idea. He instructed Commander Cyril T. Simard, his man on Midway, to report to Pearl Harbor by radio that the atoll's water system had broken down. The signal was sent in plain language that the Japanese (who, of course, were just as busy monitoring our traffic as we were intercepting theirs) could pick up and read. For two days Rochefort and his staff were glued to their sets, waiting for the Japanese to fall into the trap. On the third day it happened. One of the intercepted messages about "AF" included a passing reference that the place was having difficulties with its fresh-water supply.

Now Nimitz could make his plans in the definitive knowledge that Midway was the target. Now cryptoanalysis had no dark areas left; virtually everything could be intercepted with pinpoint accuracy. The plan that Nimitz devised was exceptional for its ingenuity and daring. It will remain forever a classic blueprint of the war at sea. The description of the great battle of June 4, 1942, is beyond the scope of this book, but Nimitz knew that it was won when, early in the morning of June 5, Commander Rochefort handed him an intercepted signal from Yamamoto's flagship. In translation it consisted of but five words: *"Occupation of Midway is canceled."*

After Midway, Admiral Yamamoto went to bed for a week with a stomach ailment for which his doctor could find no physical cause. It was clearly a psychosomatic attack, for Yamamoto realized, sooner and more clearly than anybody else at his level, that in essence Japan had lost the war when he lost the Battle of Midway. "Yamamoto's failure to take Midway was bad enough," wrote Thaddeus Tuleja. "What made it worse was the fact that this failure resulted in the loss of four fleet carriers with all their planes and most of their pilots. For a nation like Japan, with limited industrial capacities, this was an insupportable loss."

Yamamoto had been defeated by American cryptography. In the end, he was to perish by it. In the late spring of 1943, almost exactly on the anniversary of the great battle, Yamamoto went on an inspection trip to the embattled Solomons. The exact itinerary of his trip was intercepted by American cryptoanalysts. Naval Intelligence prepared a lethal ambush for Yamamoto. He flew into it on schedule, his plane was shot down, and he was killed.

Cryptoanalysis continued to play a decisive role through the Pacific War. The system was jeopardized once when the *Chicago Tribune* triumphantly revealed the decisive part it had played in winning the Midway battle. It was compromised again when an overzealous team of O.S.S. agents raided the office of the Japanese military attaché in Lisbon, Portugal, cracked his safe and went off with his code books. Both events caused the Japanese to change their codes. The system was endangered a third time when certain intercepts based on monitored Japanese communications were removed from the Office of Naval Intelligence in Washington. Some of their contents later showed up in articles in *Collier's* magazine, thus tipping off the enemy, if only by inference, that his code was not as safe as it might be.

After each indiscretion, the cryptoanalysts had to start again from scratch, but they always succeeded in penetrating the enemy's system anew.

But if these men were the bright stars of American intelligence at the beginning of the war, they were not quite the only useful group; the United States also had by then a quasi-intelligence organization. This was the department known as the Co-ordinator of Information, set up before Pearl Harbor at the prodding and under the leadership of Donovan. It was a somewhat nebulous agency with a strictly civilian status, consisting largely, as John Chamberlain put it, "of the so-called 'One Hundred professors'—a group of middle-aged specialists in anthropology, economics and a dozen other fields, plus a few young instructors who had had Ph.D. training in applying the seat of the pants to the seat of the chair in libraries."

Ridiculed, sniped at and ignored by the professionals, these newcomers were far better than their reputation. Those one hundred professors and their young assistants were fact-grubbing researchers who understood how to cull significant intelligence from library books and between the lines of newspapers. Most important was the New York outpost, headed by William Vanderbilt, former Governor of Rhode Island. Left to its own resources, it began the collection of intelligence from sources the professionals neglected, tapping individuals who had specific knowledge of certain areas of installations, collecting so-called "Aunt Minnies"—photographs taken on peacetime trips in what now were enemy countries, and buttonholing arriving travelers from abroad.

Much later, during the bombing of Germany, a certain factory in the Reich could be pinpointed for the raiders from a blown-up picture that was originally acquired by someone in the Co-ordinator's office. He remembered that big firms frequently printed pictures of their plants on their stationery and made it his specialty to collect such foreign letterheads. The picture of that key factory was such a collector's item.

Another outstanding contribution of the Co-ordinator's office was vital information needed for the capture of the city of Bône in North Africa. It was procured in the New York office by the multi-lingual wife of a prominent psychoanalyst during the routine interrogation of a French refugee engineer from Bône.

Even so, in the first half of 1942, Roosevelt was fundamentally correct; the United States did not have the intelligence apparatus that a major power needed for the prosecution of a major war. In the first line of the intelligence establishment still stood, as Eisenhower pointed out, the military and naval attachés. In both the Army and the Navy, the service attachés first formed an elite, then became a clique. Much of their time was spent upon asinine social amenities. They were prone to adapt their own thinking to prevailing trends in the countries in which they served, instead of maintaining an open mind. President Roosevelt, exasperated, not so much by their frequent ignorance as by their notorious bias, could be heard frequently complaining on this score.

There is nothing on the record to indicate, for instance, that Captain Henry H. Smith-Hutton, the Naval Attaché in Tokyo, was able to give the Navy Department any clear warning of the impending Japanese attack in December, 1941, although it is known that he had on his own burned his codes on the 5th. In his final evaluation of the imminent future, he was misled by outward appearances, the true meaning of which he could not fathom. During the days immediately preceding the attack, a large number of Japanese sailors showed up in the streets of Tokyo and Yokohama, apparently crews of the ships that were supposed to be at Yokosuka. In fact, the sailors were soldiers. They had been sent out in naval uniforms as dress-extras to mislead observers.

Colonel Ivan Yates was an American Military Attaché in Moscow at the time of Hitler's invasion of the Soviet Union and he flew back to Washington in the summer of 1941, to advise General Marshall, giving a totally erroneous evaluation of the situation. In this connection, Eisenhower had another characteristic little incident to relate:

"An example of the eagerness," he wrote, "with which we

seized upon every bit of seemingly authentic information was provided by the arrival in Washington of Colonel John P. Ratay, who, at the beginning of the war, had been our military attaché in Rumania. The colonel was an extremely energetic officer, one of our better attachés. After Rumania joined the Axis in November, 1940, he had been interned and eventually transferred through a neutral port to the United States.

"The Operations Division learned of his arrival and immediately called upon him for such information as he could provide. He was thoroughly convinced that the German military power had not yet been fully exerted and was so great that Russia and Great Britain would most certainly be defeated before the United States could intervene effectively. He believed that the Germans had then forty thousand combat airplanes in reserve, ready with trained crews to operate at any moment. . . .

"In the Operations Division we refused to give credence to Ratay's information concerning the forty thousand operational planes. The German Army had just been halted in front of Moscow, and we were convinced that no army possessing a weapon of this overwhelming strength would have withheld it merely because of a future plan for its use, particularly when its employment would have insured the destruction of such an important objective as Moscow."

The situation in O.N.I. was pungently described in a letter a frustrated intelligence officer, Colonel John W. Thomason, Jr., of the Marine Corps, felt compelled to write during those early war days in 1942 to a friend at sea:

"Our department resembles more than anything the outside fringe of a cyclonic or whirling storm. Everything being tossed about. [Admiral Ernest J.] King is superimposed on [Admiral Harold C. 'Betty'] Stark, having absorbed most of the latter's functions: simply another planet of the first magnitude added to our galaxy; both shine, perplexing the navigator.

"[Admiral Theodore S.] Wilkinson has O.N.I., the third chief in a year and a half. Bill [Captain William] Heard has the Foreign Branch; [Captain J. B. W.] Waller, Domestic. Your old

[Far Eastern] desk is in the entirely capable hands of [Captain Arthur H.] McCollum. We are swollen enormously: never was there such a haven for the ignorant and well connected. As a matter of fact, O.N.I. isn't bad, so far as collecting information goes. But what good is information if it isn't used? Here the museum idea seems to prevail."

Aside from the museum spirit, the situation was aggravated by the fact that O.N.I. also had its peculiar philosophy and quota of prejudices. The officer personnel of O.N.I. was traditionally anti-Communistic and, therefore, their assessment of Stalin's chances could have been somewhat colored by their prejudices and desires.

There was only one exception to this point of view, represented by the officer-in-charge of O.N.I.'s Soviet desk, the one man who should have known best and who actually knew. He was the scion of a great naval family, himself a major in the Marine Corps, Andrew C. Wiley by name. The entire Russian branch consisted of the major and his yeoman.

They had a single room in the Navy Department Building in Washington. Major Wiley turned it into a small Russian oasis. He was as opposed to Communism as any man on that deck—probably even more so because he actually knew what he was opposing—but he had a weakness for the Russians as a people. In his enthusiasm for their splendid showing, he decorated the walls of his office with Soviet posters which the Soviet Naval Attaché had given him. He had a phonograph in his room and kept a collection of recorded Red Army songs on tap.

The major was very much ostracized for his views about the war in the Soviet Union. This ostracism went so far as to exclude him as a reporter of the war in Russia in the plot room during the daily situation conferences. His fellow O.N.I. officers were not inclined to listen to him and imported a colonel from G-2 to give them a more pessimistic presentation.

President Roosevelt was given the benefit of G-2's doubts every morning in the White House map room. He rarely liked what he was told, partly because the news was so bad, and partly because some of the familiar G-2 bias usually managed to seep into these Presidential briefings. Roosevelt developed a bias of his own—against intelligence in general and G-2 in particular.

The situation became so bad that when later a much improved intelligence apparatus tried to persuade the President to develop crucial policies that could have shortened the war, Roosevelt refused to accept them, chiefly because of his small faith in intelligence. Thus he persisted in his low opinion of the potentialities of the European underground; refused to accept reports about acute dissidence within the German High Command; and rejected all recommendations for a change in the unconditional surrender formula, though hard intelligence data strongly supported such change.

Roosevelt was a great war leader, but unlike Churchill, he was not sold on intelligence. It was remarkable that in the face of such a crippling handicap, American intelligence nevertheless developed into the brilliant and efficient system that it became when it was freed of the spell of the oldtimers.

The great change for the better began on May 5, 1942, when Major General George V. Strong was appointed head of G-2. It continued in June with two major developments: Captain Ellis M. Zacharias was ordered to Washington to become Assistant Director of Naval Intelligence; and Colonel William J. Donovan was named chief of a brand new organization under the Joint Chiefs of Staff, the Office of Strategic Services.

Strong was picked by General George C. Marshall, not because he was an outstanding expert in intelligence matters, but because he was known to be possessed of a driving energy and ruthless determination. G-2 needed a housecleaning badly and only a man who had initiative, daring, independence, and integrity could do the job. Marshall thought Strong was such a man.

Strong more than confirmed Marshall's expectations. As his first act, he went to London to see how the British were handling intelligence activity and he established the closest possible co-operation with them.

Upon his return he set up virtually an entirely new organization. He did not do the job by stepping on sensitive toes or chopping off heads indiscriminately. He not only left the old-timers at their posts, to utilize their experience and unquestion-able knowledge, but ended their dominant influence by bringing in new men and giving them wide latitude.

In O.N.I. "Captain Zack" did not have the power of a Marshall behind him, so considerable department politics ensued, but, in the end, that agency also attained its majority. For one thing, within a couple of years, O.N.I. had had four directors. The new one was Harold Train, an officer, as Zacharias himself later put it, "who had been passed over in the regular selection process for rear admiral and who had never had one day's experience in intelligence work." For his new job, however, Train was advanced to the rank of rear admiral.

"A few weeks in O.N.I.," Zacharias wrote, "convinced me that we had to start from scratch and do a complete job of overhauling if we were to make O.N.I. an efficient wartime intelligence organization; and I was often reminded of Thomason's prophetic words that the museum idea still prevailed. My assignment as assistant director was, therefore, the greater dis-appointment, since I knew that the traditional system of the chain-of-command would slow down the realization of my pre-pared plans, but I hoped I would receive complete support from Admiral Train, who was a newcomer to intelligence and not familiar with any of its peculiar problems and their solutions. But the months ahead of me proved extremely difficult. I was compelled to wage an uphill fight. . . . Here, then, in 1942, I was confronted with the second war that we were waging: the never-ending battle of Washington, in which memoranda clashed with memoranda, and draft proposals were the usual casualties."

Zacharias first turned his attention to the training of a brand new crop of intelligence officers, virtually all of them recent civilians, many of them "ninety day wonders." He established the Basic Intelligence School in Frederick, Maryland, and the Advanced Intelligence School in a row of rented rooms in the Henry Hudson Hotel in New York.

"What we needed was operational intelligence," Zacharias

recalled, "an activity between strategy and tactics providing in intelligence everything a commander might need to take his ships into combat or to conduct amphibious warfare." He planned to train hundreds of operational intelligence officers. He actually trained a thousand.

Zacharias also played midwife at the birth of new branches of O.N.I. to deal specifically with such tasks as prisoner interrogation, the study and exploitation of captured enemy documents, psychological warfare, and with the collateral problems of intelligence about chemical and bacterial warfare. He introduced secret intelligence (an activity between intelligence proper and espionage improper) and developed projects for action behind enemy lines, especially in China, but also in Italy. He established intimate liaison with his opposite numbers in the British Admiralty and he organized the Japanese language schools where young Americans by the hundreds learned the difficult tongue virtually overnight.

When he left Washington on September 5, 1943, to take command of the battleship *New Mexico,* he could look back on the job with justified satisfaction and say, as he did: "This baby of mine has certainly come of age!" Zacharias' departure, at a time when he was Deputy Director of Naval Intelligence, was abrupt. "Even now," he wrote after the war, "I do not know what caused that action or whether it was justified. It will have to be credited to the fact that I was moving too rapidly, and was becoming too strong for the good of more ambitious individuals and agencies."

His departure was not only regrettable, it was damaging to the war effort. It did to intelligence what the unfortunate departure of Sumner Welles did to diplomacy: it slowed it down and petrified it along conventional lines. Had Zacharias been permitted to remain and carry his plans and dreams to their logical conclusion, the United States would have produced in him a towering figure. He could have become the American Reginald Hall. No greater tribute than that could be made.

The third man responsible for the great change was a sport

in the history of espionage, "Wild Bill" Donovan. Donovan appeared from nowhere to conjure a motley army of spies and saboteurs out of the ground; he trained them and equipped them; sent them on missions of deceit, arson and murder. Then, when they were no longer needed, he sent them back to their humdrum lives, and he himself retired with them to the quiet and dignified practice of corporation law. His was the incredible triumph of the blessed amateur at the head of a band of gifted dilettantes.

It is still a mystery, and a delightful one to contemplate, why Donovan, of all people, was chosen to do such a job. He was ebullient and dynamic, as so many Irishmen are. He had nothing sinister or sordid about him. If anything, he was rather gentle and equable, even somewhat naive.

William Joseph Donovan was born on New Year's Day in 1883, in Buffalo, New York, the son of a railroad yardmaster who dabbled in county politics. At Columbia he earned the sobriquet "Wild Bill" for quarterbacking a fondly-remembered football team. After that, he practiced law and carved out a military career as a pastime. In 1912, he organized a cavalry unit for the New York National Guard and served with it at the Mexican Border. In 1917, he went to war in earnest and was a full colonel by October 14, 1918, when he won the Congressional Medal of Honor for his fantastic courage in the Meuse-Argonne operation.

Afterwards, he took up intelligence as a hobby. Just as a big game hunter goes all the way to India or the Sudan, Donovan started chasing wars all over the world. It was an expensive hobby, because he went as a semi-official observer, at best, often as a private citizen, and he always had to foot the cost. In his capacity as a martial sidewalk superintendent, he attended Admiral Kolchak's rear-guard action against the Soviets in Siberia; the so-called Manchurian incident of 1931; Mussolini's Ethiopian adventure in 1935; and the Spanish Civil War the year after it. When Colonel Frank Knox became Roosevelt's Secretary of the Navy, he gave Donovan a quasi-official status and sent him to England to study British military strength and intelligence. He brought back a detailed account of British secret intelligence and special operations, which highly impressed Roosevelt. Hence, in January, 1942, Roosevelt sent for Donovan and told him to draft a plan for a new intelligence service cut to fit a global war. "You will have to begin with nothing," the President told him. We have seen that this was too sweeping a statement, but it was true in an urgent and grave sense.

"If you wanted a Michelin road map of the Vosges or Haute Savoie," John Chamberlain wrote, "in the Washington of early 1941, it was a hundred to one that you could not find one. Nor could you successfully apply to any governmental agency for the gauge of an Algerian railroad track, the kilowatt hour supply of the Japanese power grid, the number of wharf-side cranes in Casablanca, the quality of drinking water in Tunis, the tilt of the beaches off Kyushu or the texture of the Iwo Jima soil."

This was the kind of minute information Donovan was to procure, whether from the Congressional Library or straight from the secret files of the enemy. A few months later he returned to Roosevelt with a plan. The President liked it and on June 13, 1942, the Office of Strategic Services was set up with Donovan as Director.

The O.S.S. was organized in three parallel echelons. One was "R.&A." for *Research and Analysis,* by far the biggest. It was to continue and vastly expand the work of the one hundred professors, culling all sorts of vital intelligence from normally accessible sources.

Second was "M.O.," for *Morale Operations,* to conduct black propaganda and related maneuvers, to undermine the resistance of the enemy and to soften him up by any means, fair or foul.

The third was "S.I." for *Secret Intelligence,* the clandestine core of the organization, the band of spies and saboteurs, guerrilla fighters, weapon instructors, guides, *femmes fatales* and operators of clandestine radios. The activities of this division gave O.S.S.

its nicknames, "Oh, Shush, Shush" and "Oh, So Secret." Its exploits frequently came to little or nothing, but they were always highly romantic, whether it meant the surreptitious entry of a neutral embassy in Washington (to obtain some compromising information about Germany), or the climbing of the Himalaya to persuade the Dalai Lama to join the Allies.

The O.S.S. was called by still another nickname: "Oh, So Social." In the beginning, when O.S.S. was still small, Donovan populated it almost exclusively with his own friends, associates and acquaintances. Ned Buxton, his first tutor in espionage, became his chief assistant; from his New York law firm came "Oley" Doering and Ned Putzell. Others in the top echelon included financiers Charles Cheston and Russel Forgan; David Bruce, a Mellon son-in-law; Atherton Richards, heir to the Hawaiian pineapple millions; Bill Vanderbilt, of the Rhode Island Vanderbilts; controversial international lawyer Allen W. Dulles; Louis Ream of U.S. Steel; polo-playing Winston Guest; a former Czarist colonel named Serge Obolensky, who was also a Russian prince; scions of the Armour packing dynasty; and others from such unusual breeding grounds of espionage and sabotage as the Social Register, the Stork Club and El Morocco.

In the course of the war, O.S.S. employed a total of twenty-two thousand people on a staff that leveled off at about twelve thousand, or something like the numerical strength of a combat division. The personnel ranged from emeritus professors who had won the Nobel Prize to playboys and screwballs; from world-famous movie personalities (like George Skouras, John Ford and Garson Kanin) to card-carrying Communists and ex-members of the Abraham Lincoln Brigade; from pious missionaries to drunks and drug addicts; from Americans to virtually every nationality on the globe.

The personnel policy of Colonel Donovan was another demonstration of that man's remarkable mind. In December, 1942, I met him on a train going to Washington and we talked about the big mistake France had made when it interned without discrimination the bulk of German refugees, instead of utilizing the cream of the crop for the war against the Nazis. He mentioned a book he had read recently on the subject and that stirred him to considerable thinking. It was Arthur Koestler's *Scum of the Earth*. "I will never make that mistake," he said. "Every man or woman who can hurt the Hun is okay with me." He was backed up in this to the hilt by President Roosevelt. His faith in and loyalty to these pariahs was amply repaid. Not a single enemy alien employed by O.S.S. betrayed the trust. The handful of traitors within the O.S.S., like Carlo Marzini, were native Americans and their treachery favored the Russians.

In the course of its activities, O.S.S. scored brilliant victories and suffered grave disappointments. The mortality rate of its agents sent to Tunisia was astonishingly high, due to misplaced faith in local contacts. A big contingent of O.S.S. men smuggled into Slovakia to exploit an incipient rebellion was caught and eventually died in a concentration camp because intelligence about events in Slovakia was faulty: by the time the O.S.S. delegation arrived, the Germans had already quelled the rebellion. Even when no human lives were sacrificed because of inadequate preparations, some of the one hundred and thirty-five million dollars O.S.S. spent must have gone down the drain. But Donovan liked to say that as a team his organization batted at least .260 and that, he adds, is a good team figure in any league.

Donovan was an inveterate gadgeteer, forever devising gimmicks for a business that has enough of them anyway. He had a number of guns that came in the shape of pipes. You could shoot well with these pipes, but you could not smoke them. So, whenever a fellow turned up behind the Nazi lines with a pipe in his mouth that would not smoke, he was promptly assumed to be a Donovan man.

Donovan inspired a small mechanism that made briefcases explode when unauthorized persons tried to open them. Several such explosions enlivened cocktail parties in Washington to which O.S.S. staffers went straight from their offices. Then there was the secret compass, which was concealed inside a false tooth.

But one of the requirements to be employed by O.S.S. was that an agent must possess all his teeth. Where to put the compass? The problem was solved by pulling a tooth of any agent who was given the compass.

The O.S.S., of course, was cloaked in elaborate secrecy and yet . . . There was the case of a professor who arrived in Washington in answer to an urgent summons. When he showed up, nobody seemed to know anything about the summons, the professor or the job that was supposedly awaiting him.

Quite disturbed, the poor fellow went from pillar to post, shuttling about headquarters on innumerable passes and with grim-faced escorts to assure ironclad security, but he could not clarify the situation. At last it became 5 p.m. and most of the O.S.S. closed down for the day. As a desperate last resort, he decided to call Donovan himself, and tried to obtain his private telephone number. The watch officer in charge of security indignantly refused to divulge such a grave secret. The man tried to obtain the phone number with ruses and subterfuges, but all in vain.

He returned to his hotel, exhausted and desperate, and decided to call a friend to whom he could unload his plight. As he leafed through the phone book, he stumbled upon the secret: the listing of Donovan's number and address.

19

The Misery and Grandeur of the Secret War

Hitler's metallic and orderly war was getting into trouble. The stunning precision with which the Germans had begun was seeping out like air from a punctured bag. The Axis appeared to be winning everywhere, but there was something happening that was conspicuous by its absence from the communiqués, something so vague and obscure that it was not yet apparent to the naked eye. A second front was opening in the darkest recesses of the global conflict, in the nocturnal streets and the deadly forests of the occupied lands.

Looking back on those uncertain days, General Sir Colin Gubbins, director of the British S.O.E., thought that the Germans hoped to enslave the conquered peoples and the industries to the full support of their war efforts. "In the end," he said, "though this strategy may have helped them initially, they were to pay a terrible price for their violation of all the laws of man, their unprovoked aggression of defenseless peoples, for their unimaginable cruelties, practiced on men, women, and children alike. They could not prevent sabotage for all their efforts. They could not prevent the organization of secret armies, though they well knew it was going on." The overwhelming fact was that the Germans lost control of an important phase of the war—the *secret* phase.

It began in the country which had been first to fall, Czechoslovakia, whose people have a heroic legend. They say there is a ghostly army encamped on the slopes of the Blanik Mountain, watching with eternal vigilance over their land. These are the

Knights of Blanik. When all is going well, they rest in peace; in times of misfortune they come to life and ride out in force to aid their beleaguered country. And in 1940, ghostly knights began to appear.

One was Joseph Skalda, editor of a clandestine newspaper, printed on secret presses in Prague and distributed by volunteers, some of them mere boys, throughout Bohemia and Moravia. Under Skalda's prodding, and the leadership of a few faceless men, who appeared stealthily in the wings, anti-German acts began to occur. By March, 1941, they were sufficiently numerous to induce the Turkish Minister in Prague to send a report about them to his government.

On July 19, Britain recognized the Czechoslovak Government in Exile. That belated favor, grudgingly granted, excited the imagination of the patriots at home. The BBC broadcasts to Czechoslovakia became somewhat bolder and even incendiary. In August, an advance guard of Soviet agents arrived in Czechoslovakia to start an underground based on the Communists and also to organize a network of spies for the Fourth Bureau. Passive resistance became intensified. Listening to the BBC became more widespread. Sabotage multiplied. There were demonstrations against German troops in Prague and Bratislava.

The Nazis instituted a manhunt for Skalda. They arrested him on September 23, and also apprehended fifteen of his aides. Someone broke under the stress of interrogation and talked, probably in exaggerated terms, of a widespread underground movement. The weak-kneed Baron Konstantin von Neurath was replaced as Protector by the ruthless Reinhard Heydrich.

He arrived in the Hradcin, Prague's ancient castle on the hill, on September 27, and went to work at once, hitting right and left, very much in the dark but determined to do too much rather than too little. Premier Elias was arrested, as were three famous generals of the defunct Czechoslovak Army—Bily, Votja, and Horacek—and hundreds of others, some on actual evidence, others on the flimsiest grounds. In the next four days Heydrich had twenty-two Czech patriots executed, including Skalda and the three generals. In October, he pulled in three hundred and fourteen additional suspects, fifty-eight of whom were either shot or hanged.

The Czechs' answer to Heydrich's sanguine orgy was defiance. The underground now went into action on an impressive scale. Help came also from London. Mysterious planes flew in leaders to take the places of those whom Heydrich had murdered. They also dropped supplies.

The Heydrich terror continued. On a single day in January, 1942, twenty-three workers were shot on suspicion of sabotage. In April, there was an increase of sabotage in Bohemia and Moravia, with tragic consequences at Tetchen and Bohumin: Heydrich hanged twenty-five patriots in the former city, and had six shot in the latter.

May came with the tidings of spring to find the underground better organized than ever, and emboldened by Heydrich's failure to stamp out resistance despite his savage campaign. The aid received from abroad also helped tremendously. On May 5, during an RAF raid on the Skoda Works in Pilsen, an especially important group of men was dropped, with containers in which were concealed super-secret pieces of special equipment. The BBC broke in with an unusually strong attack on Heydrich, and from then on, it made the Protector the sole target of its barbs.

The situation was getting worse by the day and Heydrich decided to start an all-out campaign this time, to liquidate the last vestiges of the underground once and for all. He had the plans drawn and then arranged for a trip to Berlin to lay them before Hitler and Himmler for their approval. He was full of excitement and talked confidently of the future, of the great plans he had for Czechoslovakia after it had regained its sense, as he put it.

But by then, Reinhard Heydrich was himself living on borrowed time. He was to die violently before the month was out, killed by a bomb from the Resistance he could not conquer.

If the secret war began in Czechoslovakia, Russia was not far behind.

On July 25, 1941, the Russian campaign was just thirty-three days old; the communiqués of the German High Command were coming in batches, announcing new victories. Yet one cryptic communiqué spoke of some haphazard guerrilla activity in the combat zones, aimed mainly, and not very effectively, at the German supply lines. It was the first mention of a phantom force, which the Soviets were pitting against the invaders.

It was a glorious summer and the Germans enjoyed the scenic beauty of the land. They were especially enchanted by the virgin forests, as a poetic German correspondent then wrote, "broad green walls into which the rugged roads seemed to penetrate vertically like bright gleaming shafts." That same idyllic forest was soon to lose its enchantment when the Germans found it swarming with the dark soldiers of that phantom force. It "no longer inspired us with such dreams," the correspondent wrote after a two-hour encounter with those men, "as we had had during the first stage of the journey. There it stood, silent, dark, and menacing, on either side of the road. The shadows of the night and the fogs of the marshes crept up in thin veils between tree trunks. An oppressive, nervous feeling began increasingly to possess us."

On September 12, a brief communiqué mentioned a German patrol "in action against bandits in no-man's land." On November 5, bandits were mentioned as doing demolition work after the retreat of a Red Army contingent. Nine days later, the intelligence officer of the German 11th Army was sufficiently impressed to write a memorandum about those bandits.

"According to available reports," he wrote, "a well-organized, centrally-directed partisan organization is operating in the southern part of Crimea. It has at its disposal large and small bases in the Jaila mountains, which are well provided with arms, food, herds of cattle and other supplies." Their task seemed to be, he added, the destruction of signal and traffic installations, and raids on the rear services of the German army, especially its supply columns. A few of them were spies.

By then, several of the bandits had fallen into the hands of the enemy, and the Germans had a chance to size them up. They scandalized their captors for more reasons than one. "Already their outward appearance and their garments mark them as bandits," wrote a Major Schaefer. "Generally speaking, they do not wear uniform with insignia of rank, but plain clothes of all sorts, or in other words, bandit's civvies. They masquerade as innocent peasants. Some wear civilian clothes and an odd piece of uniform, so that they can swiftly change, like a chameleon, in accordance with requirements. We met bands in German uniforms, complete with insignia, and others with two uniforms, a German and a Russian, one over the other."

The partisans came from all walks of life. A band of three men consisted of a young Red Army straggler, a sixty-year-old engineer from Feodosia, and a Tartar. A two-man team was made up of a twenty-three-year-old Russian cobbler and a thirty-four-year-old school teacher from Kerch. By March, 1942, the front no longer was confined to those neat lines drawn on General Staff maps. It was everywhere. On March 6, even Dr. Goebbels wrote in his diary: "An SD report informed me about the situation in occupied Russia. It is, after all, more unstable than was generally assumed. The partisan danger is increasing week after week. The partisans are in control of large areas in occupied Russia and are conducting a regime of terror there." On April 29 he added: "The danger of the partisans in the occupied areas continues to exist in unmitigated intensity. They have caused us very great difficulties during the winter, and these by no means ceased with the beginning of spring."

Partisan warfare was no accidental response of the Russians. As early as 1934, speaking of a possible future war against the Soviet Union, Stalin said, "It would be the most dangerous war for the bourgeoisie, because such a war will be waged not only at the fronts but also at the rear of the enemy." And on the twelfth day of the war, Stalin issued a special order to all men, women and even children, throughout the Soviet Union, to go into action as partisans.

"In areas occupied by the enemy," his decree read, "guerrilla units, on foot and horseback, must be formed and diversion groups created to combat enemy troops, to foment guerrilla warfare everywhere, to blow up bridges and roads, to destroy telephone and telegraph communications, to set fire to forests, depots and trains. In occupied territories conditions must be made unbearable for the enemy and all his collaborators; they must be pursued and annihilated wherever they are, and all their measures must be brought to naught."

Within a week, Stalin's general order was made specific in a directive by the Central Committee of the Communist Party (as distinct from the General Staff of the Red Army, for this was a "patriotic" matter which the Party proposed to handle). Partisan headquarters were set up in Moscow. Its chief of staff was a promising young Communist Party functionary, Ponomarenko. He was given the rank of lieutenant general, a staff, and the equipment. The rest was left to him and he made the most of it.

According to General Sir Reginald F. S. Denning, a British expert on guerrilla warfare, Ponomarenko's army-in-rags made a "considerable contribution to the defeat of the German armies." After the war, Stalin went so far as to assert that had it not been for the partisans, the Soviet Union would never have succeeded in defeating the Germans.

Ponomarenko cited examples of partisan achievements in 1945 when he prepared a report: "The destruction by Ukrainian guerrillas of troops guarding Sarny railway junction; the blowing up of large bridges on the rivers Ptich and Drissa; the rout by the Byelorussian guerrillas of the Germans at Slavnoye station; the rout of the garrison and the destruction of military objectives at Slutks; the blowing up by Orel troops of big Navlya and Vygonits bridges, when the whole of the German guards there were wiped out; the rout by Smolensk guerrillas of the garrison at Prigorye station and the destruction of trains in it; the operations of the Leningrad guerrillas, which ended in the killing of General von Wirtz and his bodyguard; the complete rout of four garrisons by Karelo-Finnish guerrillas on the island of Bolshoi Kremenets; the blowing up of the Savkin bridge and the extermination of the Sutok garrison by Kalinin guerrillas; the rout of an army corps headquarters at Ugodsk Zavod by Moscow guerrillas; the Sdatsk operation, which ended in the annihilation of one thousand two hundred officers and men of the Third German Jaeger Infantry Division, carried out by Crimean guerrillas."

According to Ponomarenko, in just two years of partisan warfare behind the lines, his guerrillas killed thirty generals, three hundred thousand German soldiers and hundreds of Soviet collaborators. A chambermaid blew up Friedrich Kube, the German governor general of Byelo-Russia; another woman partisan killed Fabian Akinchitz, chief of the German secret service in Minsk; and still another killed Friedrich Vench, commandant of the town of Baranovichi.

During the same period (between 1941 and 1943), Ponomarenko's ragamuffins derailed three thousand trains, blew up three thousand two hundred and sixty-three bridges, destroyed one thousand one hundred and ninety-one tanks and four hundred seventy-six planes. Germany had a total of six million six hundred thousand dead from all causes on all fronts. Of these, Ponomarenko claimed his partisans had killed more than a million officers and men. At the peak of their activities, in 1944 in the Crimea, partisans mounted a thousand raids on roads and railways in the German rear *within a period of only seven hours.* "And these raids," Field Marshall von Manstein added, "happened every single day."

Like any other army, this guerrilla force had an insatiable appetite for information. It was supplied by thousands of spies. Vladimir Morosov was a small cog in this service. His importance lay in the fact that he was typical, the average Soviet spy of

World War II. He was thirty-three years old when the Germans came, an accountant by profession, who went to the commandant of the Red Army garrison in his town and volunteered. They sent him to a school in Krasnodar, in the Caucasus, to learn the ropes, and he was graduated with twenty-eight other students in his class after only twenty days. His was one of the extended courses. In the pressure of those days, some spies were sent into the field with as little as a three-day education.

On February 18, 1942, he was taken to Kerch and delivered to the partisans with whom he was to work. Hardly was he settled when he was ordered to go behind the German lines and find out the number of Germans in the Islam-Terek area and the location of a certain ammunition and fuel dump at Itchky. The partisans smuggled him across the Sivash and then, on his own, he made his way to the German rear.

The average spy met an average end. His name and mission are today known because the Germans caught him and shot him, leaving a brief memento of his memory in a two-page document. Thousands like Morosov lost their lives in missions like this; but thousands managed to go and return, bringing back the vital intelligence they were supposed to procure.

Fully half of the partisan spies were women, some pretty girls who performed in the world's oldest profession, both catering to the German soldiers and coaxing information from them; others, elderly matrons doing various manual jobs. They came in all forms and shapes, and in all age groups.

On February 14, 1942, at Kush, a young man was seen slipping a scrap of paper to an older man on a street corner. A member of the German Field Secret Police happened to be passing by and stopped to inquire. When the Russians tried to run away, the German shot them both. Papers found on the man showed he was a fifty-four-year-old Russian railroad worker who served as a courier for the Kush partisans. The young man was a spy whose information the courier came to collect. He turned out to be a girl. She was fourteen years old.

In the spy business, youth was regarded as an advantage.

One of Ponomarenko's directives required that "children must play an important part as scouts and secret agents." An intelligence officer who believed in the directive was Lieutenant Ivan Brusenko, billeted in the house of a certain Derechenko in Poltava. The lieutenant became very friendly with the family, especially with Pavel, Comrade Derechenko's twelve-year-old son. Brusenko's room became an improvised spy school where he taught the boy the tricks of the trade.

Brusenko thought up a plausible cover for Pavel. The boy was to go to Lichovka, on the right bank of the Dnieper, pretending to be a war orphan, begging for something to eat and engage German soldiers in purposeful conversations. He was to return to a rendezvous on the left bank of the river every two to four days to deliver his intelligence and to receive new instructions.

Brusenko impressed on the boy that he was not to make any notes, but had to keep everything he found out in his mind. Furthermore, he was to operate as a lone wolf, taking care of his own needs and maintaining his own lines of communications. It was quite a job for a child, but Pavel was up to it.

A few weeks later, Pavel vanished from home and made his way alone to a prearranged spot on the river where one of Brusenko's assistants was awaiting him. It was a cold night and the barefoot boy, appropriately dressed for the mission, was shivering, as the Red Army sergeant ferried him across the river in a small boat.

Next morning he approached his first German soldier, asked for some bread, and found that the soldier talked freely to the timid questions he posed, camouflaged as the innocent curiosity of an urchin, and so did others. Two nights later Pavel made his way back to the river. Lieutenant Brusenko was waiting for him. He was well satisfied with the information Pavel brought back and ordered the boy to return at once.

Returning from this mission, Pavel ran into a German patrol whose leader refused to accept the little beggar at face value. He took the boy back to Lichovka and handed him over to the Secret Field Police. Under the strain of the interrogation, the lad started to contradict himself. He was turned over to the tough guy of the unit, and, within an hour, Pavel talked. His adventures were over.

I reconstructed Pavel Derechenko's story from a report of Group 626 of the Secret Field Police. It was a relatively short report, written in awkward official German. It concluded with the three words:

"Derechenko was shot."

There was hardly a teen-ager in the Soviet Union who kept aloof from the war. The official account of the partisans abounds with their stories and shows that they distinguished themselves in all phases of the guerrilla war.

"A group of children," the account related, "under the leadership of two twelve-year-old boys, recently carried a charge of dynamite to a bridge and placed it in position, taking advantage of the dark night and of a dozing sentry. They then lit the fuse and made off into the woods. The bridge was blown to atoms."

While this immense partisan effort was run almost exclusively from inside Russia, the underground armies elsewhere in Europe had outside assistance, from the British S.O.E., the American O.S.S. and the various governments-in-exile in London. The agents of the S.O.E. came from many countries and all walks of life. A man named Chastellaine had been a director of an oil company in Rumania, but during the war he plotted the sabotage of some of his own old firm's installations. Denis J. Rake was a famous circus artist who lived in Belgium and became one of the British heroes of the Belgian underground. Yeo-Thomas—the famous White Rabbit—was manager of a celebrated Parisian fashion house and became a leader of the Maquis. Odette Sansom was the pretty French wife of an Englishman and the mother of three beautiful daughters, but she became one of the most effective spies of all, and survived to receive the coveted George Cross, the only one among the ladies of the underground to do so.

Among the shadowy figures of S.O.E. was a little, raven-haired French woman remembered only by her wartime nick-name, *La Souris,* The Mouse. There was nothing really mousy about her except the recognition signal she used on her missions. It was a delicate scratching on a window pane, like the sound of a mouse. She furnished Britain with the first information about the absolute weapon with which the Germans hoped to win the war, the famous guided missile called V-1.

In order to describe the manner in which these agents worked, I will tell a composite story woven around *La Souris.*

The Mouse was a school teacher in Paris and a native of Normandy. When the Germans reached the capital in June, 1940, she returned to her relatives in Lyons-la-Forêt, to sit out the occupation. She could not endure the idleness, however, and she inquired for someone who would take her to England. One night a delivery truck drove up to the farmhouse where she was staying and a man came in, asking for her. She asked no questions, but took her old-fashioned, school-marmish hat and her coat, and followed the man to the truck. He instructed her to climb in and lie down behind some sacks of potatoes. He drove her to a hut near an open field where three men squatted, talking in low tones. She sat down and kept quiet.

Half an hour later she heard a buzzing sound in the air. The three men ran out to the field, lighted torches and attached them to sticks which formed the shape of an L. A small aircraft landed and taxied to the shorter branch of the L. It was a black-painted plane without any insignia on it, one of the little Lysanders of the S.O.E.'s air ferry service.

She climbed in. One of the men followed her into the plane. It taxied and took off, circled the field once, and, when she looked down, she saw only darkness beneath. The torches were gone.

Next morning she was in London, sitting before the desk of Colonel Kenwick who headed the Western Europe Directorate of the S.O.E. in Norgeby House on Baker Street. The colonel had her file; she had been screened while she was still in France.

A short while later, she was interviewed further by a captain named Piquet-Wicks and then driven to 10 Duke Street to meet Colonel Passy, the head of General de Gaulle's secret service.

After her training, she returned to Duke Street and was told what she was supposed to do, and she was asked to memorize the symbols by which members of her small team were known. Then she was given her papers; a *carte d'identité*, a *permis de conduire* and current ration cards, all forged by the S.O.E. That same evening she was taken to a camouflaged airfield somewhere in the Midlands, and given a cup of hot tea, a little box of benzedrine to keep her awake if necessary and a cyanide tablet to put her to sleep quickly and lethally should the necessity arise. There was a special garment waiting for her, a suit, rubber helmet and spine pad, all somewhat oversized, but useful in cushioning her landing by parachute. She was given a revolver, a knife and a compass, and then escorted to the field and put aboard a Lancaster bomber.

At 3 a.m., she dropped into France. When she hit the ground, a man came over to help her up. "Is that you, Marie?" he asked. She said, "Yes," although nobody had bothered to tell her that she would be called Marie. The man drove her to Lyons-la-Forêt and next morning she took the morning train to Paris and went to an address where others were waiting for her. The Mouse had arrived.

The man she had come to see was an engineer who worked in an aircraft factory in Paris, but who lived in a suburb called Vaucresson. He had just returned from Germany, where he worked in a place called Peenemuende and where he had seen some strange experiments with flying bombs that were guided to their targets from the ground. He needed someone to whom he could relay the information. The Mouse went to Vaucresson that same night, found the man's apartment and stepped up to a window on the ground floor behind which a light was burning. She scratched out her signal on the pane and then walked into a dark kitchen through the unlocked back door. She groped her way to a table and picked up an envelope. A man's voice whis-

pered an invitation to come into another room. She followed the
sound of the voice into the dark room and heard the man say,
"I'm not ready for you yet. That is only part of your information.
We will have to meet again next Wednesday."

"Where?" the Mouse asked.

"In a *bistro* called the *Floridore*. It's on Quai Voltaire.
At six o'clock?"

"The plans," the man continued, talking about the contents of the envelope she held in her hand, "they are dangerous.
If they catch you with them, we will all be in trouble."

"They won't," she said, but she wasn't certain. "Are they
making spot checks on the train to Paris?"

"Not as a rule," the man said, "but you can never tell. The
Boche is inscrutable."

"*Adieu*, then," she said. "Till next Wednesday."

"The Mouse, are you the Mouse?" the man asked, but she
left through the dark kitchen without answering the question.
She heard steps on the cobblestoned street and waited until two
soldiers strolled by, a German patrol. They passed and she
walked out, turned a corner, walked down the hill to the railroad station and caught the last train back to Paris.

The Mouse was worried. Her assignment was to pick up
the papers, return them to Lyons-la-Forêt, and take them back
to England on a Lysander. Now she would have to stay on for
five more perilous days, with some of the plans in her hands.
What to do with the plans in the meantime? Where to go? She
was supposed to spend but a single day at the first address.

She decided to return to Lyons-la-Forêt. She went to Pont
de l'Arche, then on to Fleury-sur-Andelle and asked a courier
of the underground to take her home. That night a Lysander
came and she gave her envelope to the pilot.

Next morning she went back to Paris. She had a second
address and even the key to a flat, but when she called at the
house, the *concierge* rudely refused to let her enter. Later she
learned that the *concierge's* rudeness was calculated to warn her
that the flat was "hot," and was under Gestapo surveillance.

She had to make one of her emergency contacts, a woman named Maud, who had a glove shop on rue de la Boétie. She walked into the shop and asked for a pair of green suede gloves, size 6¼, and was conducted to the back of the shop, to a desk behind which sat a plump woman of about sixty. "The lady is looking for green suede gloves, size 6¼," the salesgirl said, and the plump woman stretched out her hand: "I'm glad to see you," she said.

The Mouse stayed in her flat until Wednesday afternoon, then walked to the *Floridore* on Quai Voltaire and entered the bistro at six o'clock sharp. She was looking for a man who would be reading a copy of the *Journal Officiel*, but the bistro was empty.

Her instructions were never to wait for an appointment, so she left at once, but returned fifteen minutes later, sat down on the terrace and ordered a St. Raphaël with soda water. When the waiter put the *siphon* on her table, she absent-mindedly scratched the bottle and the waiter gave her an evening paper in a thin bamboo holder. On the third page, where the last-minute news was printed, the word *Tronchet* was underscored in an ad. Also underlined were the numbers *8* and *5,* and in another column *2* and *7.* She paid and took a cab to rue Tronchet, got out at the corner and walked to No. eighty-five. She went to the second floor and rang the bell of Apartment seven. A man opened the door and the Mouse stood there absent-mindedly scratching the glass pane of the tall door. The man opened the door wide and allowed her to enter.

"The engineer had to go back to Germany," he said. "We will put you up until he returns." That same evening he drove the Mouse to a house in Neuilly where she was given the job of tutoring a little girl of nine. "We don't know how long it might take the man to return from Germany," he explained. "You will be safer here."

She waited two months, then a man came to drive her to Vaucresson. He deposited her in front of the post office, then drove away, and she walked to the engineer's house on the hill.

She scratched the lighted window, walked to the back door, went into the kitchen and picked up an envelope. At that moment a car drove up in front of the house. A man stepped out of it, while another stayed at the wheel. The man walked up to the main entrance and rang the bell. The Mouse made her way quietly to the end of the garden in the back of the house, scaled the low fence into another garden, then into a third, then a fourth. She walked out into the street and saw the car driving away from the engineer's house. She never found out what its mission was. She never saw the engineer again.

The Mouse was ready to return to England. From Vaucresson she took a train south and then came north again to Fleury-sur-Andelle. Two nights later she was in the familiar field near Lyons-la-Forêt, waiting for the Lysander to pick her up. There was the buzzing sound in the air and two men came to light the torches. An hour later the Mouse was in Tangmere and the British had the blueprints of the V-1.

On her next mission she scratched the window pane of a window in a house in Chartres. It was a Gestapo man who opened the door. Her contact had been picked up an hour before and he talked when they were drowning him in his own bathtub filled with ice cold water. That was the last time the Mouse could scratch her signal on any pane anywhere.

This was the frightful flaw in the S.O.E. setup. The Germans knew far too much about it. Some of the best and most intrepid agents of conquered Europe fell into Nazi hands because, after a while, the Germans had planted their spies in virtually every one of the resistance groups.

In Slovakia, they captured a whole O.S.S. team flown in too late to aid a badly prepared and thoroughly corrupted rebellion actually led by a German *agent provocateur*. The members of the mission were later put to death, in violation of international law, in the Mauthausen concentration camp.

In Hungary, His Serene Highness, the Regent himself, was trapped when he started an anti-German plot with two Yugoslav generals, who were in reality agents of the German secret service operating under a brilliant spy named Wilhelm Hoettl.

In France, the most brilliant leaders of the resistance movement were caught one after another: Jean Moulin, the heroic mayor of Chartres who was slated to become France's first Prime Minister after the liberation; General Delestraint; Larat; Bollaert, leaving the leadership of the movement in mediocre hands until the Communists got hold of it. Diana Hope Rowden, a twenty-eight-year-old beauty, was caught, tortured and killed, her limp body dropped into the incinerator at the Natzweiler concentration camp. Violette Szabo, courageous wife of a Free French officer, was put to death in the Ravensbrueck concentration camp when she refused to confess. Even those who survived had to go through hell before the Allies could liberate them. Christopher Burney, who was dubbed "the king of saboteurs" before he, too, was caught, spent eighteen horrible months in the Gestapo prison in Paris and fifteen months in Buchenwald. Scores of Norwegians were kept in the Nazi dungeons on Oslo's Victoria Terrace, as were Belgians and Poles, Italians and Hungarians elsewhere.

Even the imperishable French Commandant Pierre Brossolette, fell and so did the White Rabbit himself, Wing Commander Yeo-Thomas.

Some of the Allied agents fell because the Germans had scored a scoop of their own, the *Englandspiel,* or the Carillon of England. This carillon began to ring out its misleading theme in September, 1940, after the chance capture of a British agent near Leeuwarden in the Netherlands. The arrest of this pioneer agent was reported at once to Inspector Joseph Schreider, a quiet criminologist not addicted to the perverse methods of Nazi interrogations. It was the first definite proof he had that British agents were coming to Holland and that a Dutch underground war was in the making.

Schreider consulted a Major Giskes, head of the *Abwehr's* counter-espionage in Holland. They decided to check this network by infiltrating it, then turn the tables and gain control of it. They had a couple of "V-men"—informers who posed as Dutch patriots in contact with the budding underground. One was named Anton van der Waals, the other was George Ridderhof, called Sweat Brow because he always perspired profusely, even on the coldest winter nights. Schreider and Giskes used their decoys to bring in genuine members of the underground. Anton and George did their best, but for a full year none of the men they guided in fitted the bill.

At last Sweat Brow reported to Giskes that two agents had just arrived from England. One came as a saboteur, the other as his radioman. He even supplied their real names: the saboteur was Thijs Taconis, a Eurasian born in the Netherlands East Indies; the radioman was Hubertus Lauwers, a young spark of the Dutch merchant marine.

A few weeks later, the German Radio Control Station in Holland reported a clandestine sender going in The Hague and located the very house in which it operated. "Next transmission is scheduled for March 6, 1942," Radio Control announced. That day, a delivery van rolled into the street where the radio operated. In the van was Inspector Schreider and a young lieutenant of Radio Control, listening in on the clandestine radio going full blast only a few yards from them. When it was finished, Schreider saw two men come out of the house. A few minutes later both were in the car, handcuffed, being driven at great speed through the icy streets to the Binnenhof, where Schreider had his office. The Germans searched the house and found the radio and the codes. Nobody in Britain knew anything of this misfortune.

Schreider had a method of his own in handling his prisoners. When Lauwers was brought to his office, Schreider got up and greeted him with a handshake. And when Lauwers revealed to him that he was a lieutenant in the British Army, he addressed his prisoner as Lieutenant Lauwers and seemed to be respecting his rank. But in the midst of this kindness, he turned suddenly to the agent:

"How about working for us?"

"What do you mean?" Lauwers shot back.

"You could get a lot of consideration for yourself," Schreider said in a quiet voice, "and save your friend's life if you would agree to continue your radio work as if nothing had happened."

He heard Lauwers say, "All right." Schreider tried to climb into the skull of this young Dutchman. Was he on the level? Secret services prepare their radiomen for just such an eventuality. They provide them with a set of security checks, tricky code symbols within the basic code, and also with a number of apparently innocuous danger signals, which they can send out without being detected even when operating under duress.

Schreider hesitated to let Lauwers operate the *Englandspiel* but he had no German aide who could do it. And the next transmission was scheduled for March 12, 1942. Lauwers could not miss it, lest he alert the British by his silence.

So on March 12, Lauwers was sent to his place again, prepared by Schreider. London responded: "We are planning to send Arbor. Please make arrangements for his reception." Lauwers paled; he had given the danger signal, and London had not recognized it. A hapless British agent, a major named Bingham who headed the Dutch section of S.O.E. in London, had made a blunder that delivered his whole organization to the Gestapo.

On March 27, 1942, "Arbor" dropped by parachute into the waiting arms of the Gestapo. And the carillon sang out: "Arbor arrived safely at 11:23 p.m. [2323] as planned." The *Englandspiel* was bringing them in.

If in August, 1943, exactly a year and five months after the first transmission of the *Englandspiel*, Major Bingham had taken stock of his organization in the Netherlands, he must have been well satisfied with the way it was going. He had managed to get fifty-four agents across to Holland and he knew of only three casualties. He had eighteen senders going, sixteen of which were operating with gratifying regularity. A sabotage organization, organized by his agent George Jambroes in preparation for

D-Day, had one thousand and sixty-seven men and women. Substantial amounts of supplies had been flown in for them. An underground with at least one thousand one hundred men and women stood behind the Jambroes Group to aid it at Zero Hour.

Major Bingham seemed to have good reasons to be satisfied with this achievement, except for one thing. His organization existed only on paper. Of the fifty-four agents Bingham sent in, one was dead and the others were all in the hands of the Gestapo. Jambroes himself sat in a cell and his group didn't have a single man. The underground was but a figment of Inspector Schreider's imagination.

Then it seemed that the *Englandspiel* would come to an abrupt end. During the night of August 29, 1943, two of Schreider's prisoners, Johan Bernard Ubbink and Piet Dourlein, broke out of jail and made their way to Switzerland, where they reported to General van Tricht of Dutch Military Intelligence. But Schreider still did not despair. He used one of his eighteen radios to smear the two heroes. "Ubbink and Dourlein escaped with German aid," he radioed to London, "to infiltrate the Dutch service. We urge appropriate measures against them." So when the two agents reached London, they were returned to jail and kept there for months, even though they had the true story of the carillon.

On November 23, 1943, in the pitch darkness of a stormy autumn, three more agents broke out of jail. They made their way to England and reported to their headquarters in Chester Square with the precious secret of Inspector Schreider.

There was nothing more Schreider could do but to send a last message to Messrs. Blunt, Bingham & Co., the Old Firm on Baker Street.

"We have known for some time," the message read, "that you have been doing business in the Netherlands without our help. Having been, as it were, your sole representative for quite some time, we regard this as a breach of confidence. Yet this will not prevent us, should you ever decide to visit us on a far greater scale, from receiving your emissaries with the same hospitality that we have shown your agents in the recent past."

After this message, the eighteen transmitters closed down for good. While it lasted, for two years and five months in all, this modern Lorelei lured more than fifty agents and saboteurs onto the rocks. It made arrangements for one hundred and ninety drops and actually received ninety-five of them. It received five hundred and seventy containers and one hundred and fifty parcels, with almost thirty thousand pounds of explosives, three thousand Sten guns, five thousand revolvers, three hundred Bren guns, two thousand hand grenades, seventy-five radio transmitters, one hundred special signal lamps, five hundred thousand cartridges, five hundred thousand Dutch guilders in cash and a substantial sum in other currencies.

It was the worst Allied defeat of the secret war.

20

On the Eve of D-Day

A stinging blow that Eisenhower suffered in North Africa in 1943 became partly responsible for the remarkably smooth invasion of France in 1944. It brought Kenneth Strong into his staff and assured superb efficiency in the intelligence preparations of *Overlord*.

In February, 1943, during the campaign for Tunisia, front line units sent back to Ike's headquarters reports about ominous stirrings of the enemy around Fandouk, Faïd, and Gafsa. They had all the characteristics of an imminent and massive counter-attack. The front-line observers expected the thrust to come from the direction of Faïd. However, Ike's own intelligence brass, after first dismissing the warnings as the pipedreams of green troops, finally decided that if and when a counter-attack came, it would come from the direction of Fandouk. The counter-attack came from Faïd. The Germans gained enormous headway before the Allied high command could properly comprehend what was hitting them. The Germans moved through the Kasserine Pass and pushed the Allies back some eighty miles at the point of the deepest German penetration on February 23.

"The G-2 error was serious," Eisenhower later wrote. "After the battle I replaced the head of my intelligence organization at AFHQ."

The replacement was Brigadier Kenneth William Dobson Strong of the Royal Scots Fusilliers. He was then forty-three years old, an ascetic-looking, wiry, intellectual soldier who had specialized in intelligence throughout his adult life. He was so utterly devoted to his specialty that he had not married, in the belief that only a bachelor, unencumbered by wife and children, could do justice to the all-absorbing demands of his chosen profession.

The oldest son of a professor, the brigadier was a product of British public schools and Sandhurst. Except for a brief spell when he commanded a battalion of Fusilliers, his career was confined entirely to intelligence. He had spent time in Germany, France, Italy and Spain, learning the habits and languages of those countries. His first overt intelligence assignment was in Berlin on the eve of the war. By 1943 his reputation as the British Army's outstanding expert on Germany was established.

The coming of Strong to Eisenhower's side was a dramatic illustration of the importance Ike attributed, and the part he assigned, to intelligence. Eisenhower was what one might call the thinking man's soldier. He felt really safe only when he was satisfied that the best possible intelligence was available to him, procured and prepared for his eyes by the best possible chief of intelligence.

On the eve of the invasion of North Africa, in the fall of 1942, it became necessary to establish surreptitious contact with pro-Allied French generals in Algeria and Morocco. Eisenhower toyed with the idea of personally going on that secret mission. "Since manifestly I could not go myself," he wrote, "I chose, from many volunteers, my deputy, General Mark W. Clark, to make the journey." Clark and his fellow "agents" sneaked to the rendezvous by submarine and experienced some of the perils of espionage. They were forced into hiding to escape detection by Vichy security forces whose suspicion had been aroused. This was the celebrated clandestine journey on which Clark lost his pants but gained invaluable information.

Later Eisenhower sponsored other such secret missions, one by Brigadier Strong and General Walter Bedell Smith, his own chief of staff, to negotiate the surrender of Italy with General Castellano at clandestine meetings in Lisbon in August, 1943; another by General Maxwell D. Taylor, who operated as his seeing-eye in Rome when the city was still held by the Germans.

Ike fully appreciated not only the importance, but also the thrills of such clandestine operations. In *Crusade in Europe,* he described them with the starry-eyed enthusiasm of an Eric Ambler fan. "Then began," he wrote, "a series of negotiations, secret communications, clandestine journeys by secret agents, and frequent meetings in hidden places that, if encountered in the fictional world, would have been scorned as incredible melodrama. Plots of various kinds were hatched only to be abandoned because of changing circumstances." He was especially impressed with Taylor's conspiratorial skill and daring in enemy-held Rome, "where his personal adventures and those of his companion added another adventurous chapter to the whole thrilling story." Ike added: "The risks he ran were greater than I asked any other agent or emissary to undertake during the war —he carried weighty responsibilities and discharged them with unerring judgment, and every minute was in imminent danger of discovery and death."

In England, between January and the end of May, 1944, Brigadier (later Major-General) Strong was responsible for a complex intelligence enterprise in preparation for D-Day. It consisted of three interrelated but essentially different manipulations. One was the collection of intelligence. The other was a negative effort to conceal the impending venture. The third was the development of elaborate deception measures to mislead the enemy as to the real Allied intentions, strength, and the direction of the attack.

This game of grand illusions began in January, 1944, as soon as Eisenhower arrived in England and assumed command of *Overlord.* At that time a nebulous smokescreen was put up, behind which the Germans were allowed to suspect feverish preparations for an imminent invasion of Western Europe. During those days and weeks, Ike's own movements were furtive and clandestine. The mystery was concocted to keep the Germans confused and to compel them to spread their forces all along an extensive front.

In March, a single, brand-new B-29 super-bomber was

flown to Bovingdon Airfield in England. Its arrival was leaked to the Spanish Military Attaché in London, from whose reports to Madrid the Germans were known to be getting considerable intelligence. In actual fact, the B-29s were intended for the Pacific, but the impression was created that they would be used against Germany. The deception resulted in much reshuffling of Germany's air defenses and in considerable wasteful exercise, when concentration on realistic defense measures was imperative.

In May, only weeks before D-Day, deception went into high gear. It was designed to exploit to the fullest Germany's major deficiency—the lack of a general reserve of troops. According to the estimate of the Allies' Joint Intelligence Committee, Hitler had a total of three hundred and thirty-six combat divisions, but only fifty-eight of them had been identified in France and the Low Countries. Almost two hundred of them were on the Eastern Front, locked in desperate battle with the Red Army. The rest were thinly spread from the Arctic Ocean to Italy, reflecting the plight into which Hitler had maneuvered himself when he bit off far more than he could digest.

In order to bolster their defenses in France, the Germans would have had to withdraw forces from elsewhere, and the Allied command resorted to deception to prevent this. Misleading information, supported by shadowy moves, was put out to convince the Germans that Ike intended to strike at Norway, where they had only twelve divisions. Strong was gratified when his agents in Norway reported the arrival of another German division there, when, if the Germans had known the truth, it was sorely needed in France.

On May 20, Commander Butcher recorded in his diary: "When we invade west of the Seine, we hope the Germans will believe that this is merely a minor operation and that they may expect the major thrust in Pas de Calais, thus keeping the Nazis from shifting troops from the latter place to the coast between the Seine and Cherbourg." During those days, Field Marshal Sir Bernard L. Montgomery was seen in the most unlikely and indiscreet places, indicating by his presence certain activities discernible to the trained intelligence analyst. This Montgomery was merely an actor resembling the real Field Marshal; the genuine article was preoccupied in places whose significance had to be quietly concealed from the enemy.

Elaborate efforts were thus made to permit the enemy to ascertain exactly what we wanted him to learn. The efforts to conceal from him the truth were even more elaborate.

The unprecedented magnitude of the impending operation, the ramifications of the preparations, and the very vastness of the Allied forces made it impossible to conceal everything from the enemy. A substantial portion of information had to be known to military attachés and other privileged persons in London known to be friendly to the Germans. Some preparations could not be concealed from the frantic reconnaissance efforts of the *Luftwaffe*. Many confidential communications had to be put on the air, and although they were encoded or enciphered, there was reason to believe that the *Luftwaffe's* so-called *Forschungsamt,"* a central cryptographic agency, was reading many of them.

Yet so efficient was the screening operation that the Germans had little hard intelligence in the end. They knew D-Day was coming, but they had little precise information from which to gauge our intentions, our timetable, our strength and the direction of our attack. While security was never taken for granted, today we know that it proved well nigh ironclad. In fact, aside from a harmless, bibulous indiscretion that threatened to reveal the date of D-Day, there was but a single major "leak" through which, it was feared, the Germans could acquire the sort of intelligence they so desperately and urgently needed.

In March, 1944, a package containing highly classified documents concerning *Overloard* was discovered in Chicago. Sent by the War Department's Ordinance Division through the mail, it was addressed to a private residence in a section of the city that was densely populated by people of German origin or descent. The package was improperly wrapped and the documents fell out. At least ten persons read them in the Chicago Post Office. It was then forwarded, not to the obviously improper address on the wrapper, but to the Army's 6th Service Command in Chicago. There, four more unauthorized persons had a chance to peruse the documents before agents of G-2 and the Counter Intelligence Corps got them.

General Clayton Bissell, new head of G-2 in Washington, entered the case personally, and directed the investigation. It developed that in the Ordnance Division, back in Washington, the package had been addressed by an American soldier of German extraction. The explanation he offered was anything but satisfactory. He claimed that his sister had been seriously ill in Chicago and he must have been preoccupied with her when he erred by addressing the package to her street address.

Was the soldier a spy? Was this clumsy handling of a sensitive package part of a greater espionage plot? The case was never solved to everybody's satisfaction. The persons who read the documents were placed under surveillance, as were the soldier and his family. Nothing derogatory was discovered about them. They were warned not to divulge anything they had read, but their discretion could not be guaranteed. Nevertheless, it appears that nothing ever leaked from them to the Germans— but for six weeks no one in the Allied High Command drew an easy breath.

An outstanding feat of D-Day screening was the concealment from the Germans of any knowledge of a couple of artificial ports. Called "Mulberries" and "Gooseberries," these were monstrous quays which were to be floated across the Channel and sunk in position to make improvised landing places for supply ships. This heavy flow of supplies would make it possible to concentrate the invasion on a single major landing. Special efforts were made to ascertain whether or not the Germans had any inkling of the piers. A week before the invasion, Strong was satisfied that the Germans still expected several landings, the first one to be diversionary. From this he deduced that they knew nothing of the Berries. When, only ten days later, the piers were in place, with merchantmen disgorging their supplies, the Germans simply refused to believe they were real and thought that the reconnaissance planes of the *Luftwaffe* had photographed some elaborate camouflage.

In the meantime, Intelligence was working feverishly, *collecting* information. The magnitude of the task cannot be adequately expressed. German units down to single platoons and squads had to be identified. Airports of the *Luftwaffe* had to be located and the *Luftwaffe's* strength established in number and quality of its planes, supplies and personnel. Detailed blueprints of the vaunted *Westwall*—the system of German fortifications all along the coast—had to be obtained. Specific information was needed about the coastal batteries, including some new ones, big naval guns removed from major warships and emplaced at strategic points. Rail traffic had to be monitored.

Intelligence had to find out about the condition of the landing beaches, minefields both on and off shore, and the intricate system of underwater obstacles. Those underwater obstacles represented a special problem that had to be solved at all costs. Among them Intelligence had identified gatelike structures of steel angles, called "Element O"; another, named "Tetrahedra," was a pyramid of steel angles about four feet, six inches each. Commonest were steel stakes consisting of I-beams or rails. If the ships were to get through to the beaches, these obstacles had to be destroyed, and they required hand-placed demolitions.

In the end, Strong and his special force succeeded in procuring virtually all the data needed, including samples of the mines and obstacles, enabling special demolition teams to practice on them in preparation for the real thing.

The nerve center of this fantastic activity was the War Room at Widewing, Eisenhower's invasion headquarters. There, all the pertinent data was spelled out and marked on huge maps. One map showed the beaches, also indicating the depth of water in which the troops were to wade ashore. Another map showed the location of gun emplacements, hedgehog defenses, barbed wire installations and minefields. Still another displayed all enemy airfields within striking distance of the invasion fleet.

Down on paper was the German Order of Battle, identifying all the commanding officers from Field Marshals von Runstedt and Rommel down to regimental leaders; and listing every unit with their combat characteristics. According to this Order of Battle, there were fifty-eight German divisions in the invasion area. Intelligence also identified some two hundred thousand dissident Russian troops deployed in France, former war prisoners recruited for this special force. The *Luftwaffe* was believed to have two thousand two hundred and fifty planes.

Where did all of this information come from?

The vast bulk of the data emerged from the routine sources of conventional Intelligence—from aerial reconnaissance and the painstaking study of aerial photographs; from monitoring the enemy's communications and intercepting his documents; and the other usual means of Intelligence collection. From time to time, special patrols were put ashore to bring back detailed information on certain obscure targets. Resident agents sent back additional information on specific installations, on last-minute changes in the Order of Battle and on certain objectives whose assessment required specialized knowledge.

It was a spectacular job, but it was performed with a minimum of melodrama and bravado. Whatever part the romantic variety of story-book espionage played in this intelligence effort, it was infinitesimal and insignificant compared with the routine, almost humdrum, teamwork of conventional Intelligence.

There was one area of friction and controversy that was sufficiently serious to cast a shadow over the operation. It was the role Frenchmen (or, for that matter, Frenchwomen) were to be permitted to play in this crucial effort aimed at their liberation.

Inside France, the army of resistance stood ready, but the role it was to play was still obscure. This was due mainly to Roosevelt's enduring annoyance with France (whose collapse in 1940 left him with a bitter taste) and his irrational hostility to de Gaulle, in whom he saw an egomaniacal troublemaker. Roosevelt refused to believe that de Gaulle had any influence

over men and events inside occupied France or, indeed, that
any real forces of resistance existed at all. His attitude was certainly not founded in fact. The evidence was available to the
President from Donovan's O.S.S., whose special teams, individual
agents and weapon instructors were plotting inside France in
close co-operation with the French underground. From 1943 on,
the O.S.S. was in London in force to support French resistance,
and in January, 1944, it developed a quasi-autonomous organization called Special Forces Headquarters (S.F.H.Q.), created
specifically for clandestine operations in connection with the
invasion. In that first month of S.F.H.Q., the Americans dropped
ninety-six containers of supplies for the French underground,
and this surreptitious support increased rapidly both in quality
and quantity until S.F.H.Q. was dropping five thousand containers in a single month.

   If the President had not wanted to take Donovan's word,
he could have gained all the evidence he needed from an objective and scholarly source, Commander Tracy D. Kittredge,
USNR. A distinguished educator in civilian life, Kittredge was
serving at U.S. Naval Headquarters in London as liaison officer
to de Gaulle and the French forces of resistance. Kittredge had
a most difficult and thankless task, for he had to wage his own
war within the war. He had to buck Roosevelt's prejudices as
well as a rather widespread and stubborn tendency within his own
command to take French patriotism with a grain of salt.

   As late as April 17, 1944, this attitude was reflected in an
entry in Butcher's diary. "The French railwaymen will not be
likely to help us," he wrote. "All of which makes me wonder if
we are hoping too much for French resistance." At the same
time, the Germans also distrusted those same French railwaymen,
on exactly opposite grounds. They decided to train their own
workers to run the railways after the invasion, convinced that
those Frenchmen would do them more harm than good. Events
proved the Germans right. During a three-week period, those
underrated French railwaymen's sabotage destroyed more rolling

stock than the Allied air forces succeeded in putting out of action in four months.

The British had an ambivalent attitude toward this clandestine force. On the highest political echelon, Churchill sought to humor Roosevelt by following his hands-off policy. At the same time, the Foreign Office under Anthony Eden maintained intimate relations with the Free French, humoring de Gaulle in turn.

Liaison was even closer between the French underground and the Special Operations Executive. The S.O.E. supplied many of the weapons and explosives the underground needed. Like O.S.S., it provided liaison personnel and weapons instructors. It also worked out plans for joint operations, mainly in espionage and sabotage. In the course of their French operations (between March 15, 1941, when the first mission was carried out, and the end of the campaign in 1944), the French section of S.O.E. trained and dropped three hundred and sixty-six agents, organized fifty resistance groups and carried out some four thousand supply missions.

In preparation for the invasion, French resistance was organized in two major groups. One, called the *"Grande Armée,"* operated somewhat loosely, under local leadership, executing haphazard, minor missions. Its major *raison d'être* was to form the reservoir from which the French Forces of the Interior, France's underground army, could be organized at the strategic moment. The *"Petite Armée"* was organized for direct action when needed, to carry out specific espionage missions and sabotage pinpointed installations. Members of the *"Petite Armée"* were chosen with extreme care. It was maintained as a more or less dormant force, its Sunday punch preserved for the invasion itself.

Unlike Roosevelt and some of his own colleagues, Eisenhower expected major contributions from the French. However, there was grave discrepancy between this noble expectation and the aid even he was prepared to give the French. On February 1,

1944, after considerable squabbling, the scattered underground groups were united in the French Forces of the Interior. In March, General Joseph-Pierre Koenig, one of de Gaulle's top-ranking and most gallant lieutenants, was named to command the FFI.

But not until April did the Allies agree to a plan for the utilization of the FFI in the invasion, and even then only on a humiliatingly limited scale. In the combat zone, members of the FFI were expected to supply only intelligence. Sabotage was to be conducted by them only in the rear areas. A number of plans were drafted, a "Plan Green" providing for the "complete para-lyzing" of the railways; a "Plan Blue" for the sabotage of public utilities; another plan for sabotaging fuel and ammunition dumps; still another for guerrilla harassment of the movement of enemy troops and material.

But, like some sort of reverse charity, sabotage in this case began at home. The Allies sabotaged those plans by withholding the promised arms and material support. Eisenhower sent only four specialists to establish radio contacts when a hundred times that many were needed. Instead of the agreed sixty tons of supplies to be smuggled into France by various clandestine means every day, the FFI received only twenty tons in a whole month.

On D-Day, only half of the FFI had the arms and supplies it needed for the execution of the plans. Even so, it was ordered into action and fought with such devotion and skill that Eisenhower later said the FFI had the effectiveness of fifteen divisions.

After the war, Eisenhower acknowledged the importance of this French contribution in glowing words: "Throughout France," he wrote, "the Free French had been of inestimable value in the campaign. They were particularly valuable in Brittany, but on every portion of the front we secured help from them in a multitude of ways. Without their great assistance the liberation of France and the defeat of the enemy in western Europe would have consumed a much longer time and meant greater losses to ourselves."

Those French clandestine forces whose very existence Roosevelt refused to acknowledge proved in yet another manner that they were not a phantom force. During four years of underground fighting the French resistance lost one hundred and five thousand of its members. Some thirty thousand of them were executed by the Germans; seventy-five thousand died in concentration camps.

"But perhaps the greatest achievement," Ronald Seth wrote, "was not in the injury which it inflicted on the enemy, but rather in the honor it restored to France."

21

The House On Herren Street

A day or two after D-Day, Eisenhower's headquarters issued a communiqué. It revealed the momentous military secret that the G.I.'s had been served ice cream in several delicious flavors all along the Normandy beachhead only some ten hours after the initial landing. This was meant to reassure the folks at home who still had a drugstore-counterview of the great war, but the invasion was more than the supreme efficiency test of a battalion of martial Good Humor men.

When, on D-Day, the first GI waded ashore in Normandy, he was one man against what historian Percy Ernst Schramm, keeper of the German High Command's official War Diary, described as "the maximum in available forces [the Germans] were capable of deploying in the West." It took some time for the Allies, pouring in from the Channel, to match the defenders man for man. Even a week after D-Day, when we had three hundred and twenty-six thousand men ashore, the Germans still outnumbered us about two to one. In the end it needed millions of Allied soldiers, and nearly eleven months, to defeat this stubborn and ingenious enemy, although he was engaged, as he chose to be, on several fronts.

Yet on June 6, 1944, when history's greatest amphibian operation was prayerfully mounted, there was a man, a single American, whose activities, had he been given proper scope and adequate support, might have assured victory without this fantastic effort.

The man was Allen Welsh Dulles, ex-diplomat and lawyer

in civilian life, now operating out of Switzerland in the invisible bowels of the great war. Long before D-Day, Dulles had been in touch with influential men inside the Third Reich who professed to be willing and appeared to be able to assure victory to the Allies without the prodigious undertaking of the invasion.

To say that Dulles might have won the war singlehanded may sound like a preposterous exaggeration, just as it may appear foolish and arrogant to pose the question: Was that historic trip across the English Channel really necessary?

The bold question appears justified in the light of the *total* picture that presented itself to the Allied leaders on the very eve of D-Day. Even from a strictly military point of view, the invasion was but the second half of a one-two punch, for the Allies were already on the Continent—in Italy. It would have been possible to conduct the crusade for Europe from this vast Italian foothold (where the Germans had twenty-three divisions), then fan out to the south of France and South East Europe (taking on thirty-one more enemy divisions) and fight our way up France and Eastern Europe to the vitals of Germany, without a cross-Channel invasion.

However, that is idle speculation. A far more important factor mitigating against the invasion from England was another situation, whose inherent opportunities, almost completely wasted, have received far too little attention in the histories of World War II.

On June 6, the *Wehrmacht* was no longer the monolithic force it had been. While the combat efficiency of the *Landser* was still extremely high, and the German army was still a formidable war machine, dissidence and despair had appeared like termites in the officers' corps and in various sectors of the home front. There was increasing determination among a growing number of Germans to terminate the war by a *coup,* even if it meant treachery, humiliation, and, indeed, defeat.

It is not simple to fix a time at which the distintegration began, but most probably it started in June, 1943. Early that month, a young lieutenant colonel of the German Army decided

that he had had enough. He was Claus Schenk Count von Stauffenberg, thirty-six years old when he decided to join the cabal of
anti-Nazi officers in the *Wehrmacht*. He was a scion of Swabian
nobility, and his extraordinary talents had attracted attention,
earning for him the nickname "young Schlieffen." He was in
North Africa with Rommel when he was severely wounded in
an air attack, losing one eye, his right, and two fingers of his left
hand. He was temporarily blinded even in his remaining eye. On
his bed in the field hospital in historic Carthage, when he feared
he had been utterly destroyed for any useful future, he made up
his mind to continue the fight, not against his country's foreign
enemies, but against the Nazis whom he had come to regard as
the greater foe. His wrath was concentrated on Hitler. It became
as obsession with him to kill the man he held responsible, not
merely for Germany's physical anguish, but even more for her
moral degradation.

Von Stauffenberg was a newcomer to an old plot. Hitler
had long been resented and detested by a group of high-ranking
officers of the Army. They firmly believed that his liquidation
would end the nightmare. They hoped at first to capture him
and hand him over to a court of German justice to be punished
for his deeds; then, when such a decorous approach seemed
impossible, they wanted to assassinate him.

Hitler's arrest was first contemplated in 1938, on the eve
of the Munich conference, by a group of generals led by Franz
Halder, the Army's new chief of staff (replacing General Ludwig
Beck, the spiritual leader of the dissidents) and Erwin von
Witzleben, commandant of the Berlin military district. Their
conspiracy was inspired and fired by Oster, the diligent plotter
inside the *Abwehr*, but Chamberlain's surrender in Munich took
the wind out of their sails. Then, on September 3, 1939, the
day of the outbreak of the war in the West, Colonel-General
von Hammerstein-Equord planned to use a visit of Hitler to
his headquarters to arrest the Fuehrer and overthrow his regime,
but Hitler did not show up.

The first assassination attempt was scheduled for early

November, 1939, stage-managed by Oster with Halder's help, but the latter, who was expected to back the plot and provide the military forces needed for its execution, lacked the courage of Oster's convictions. Aside from that, a nebulous attempt was then made on Hitler's life in a beer cellar in Munich. It brought in its wake such stringent security measures that Oster's assassin had no chance to get close to the Fuehrer.

Another attempt was planned for August 4, 1941. It was thwarted by a sudden tightening of security measures around Hitler, presumably because a hint had leaked to the Gestapo.

Von Witzleben returned to the picture in December. Everything was arranged for a showdown, when an emergency operation Witzleben had to undergo caused the plan to collapse.

Some of these plots had touches of what later became staples of television melodrama. One envisaged Hitler's assassination during a presentation of some new Army uniforms. A volunteer, modeling the new uniform, was to conceal a bomb on him. He was supposed to blow himself up and take Hitler into death with him by bumping into the Fuehrer with his fused infernal machine at the climax to this military fashion show.

Enticed by Oster, a small group of determined combat officers now assumed responsibility for direct action. Leader of this group was forty-two year old General Henning von Tresckow, chief of staff of Field Marshal von Kluge on the Eastern front. Von Tresckow was a man of superb gallantry and moral strength, his innate decency and patriotism concealed behind a perpetual sardonic smile on his handsome face. His chief aide in the venture at the front was Lt. Fabian von Schlabrendorff, the lawyer whose anti-Nazi hatred knew no bounds and whose courage blinded him to the perils of the undertaking. Back in Berlin, besides the omnipresent Oster, was General Helmut Stieff, chief of the Organizations Department of the General Staff, whose happy disposition hid an iron will, superb courage, and a deeply felt dissatisfaction with the Nazis.

In March, 1943, von Tresckow received word that Hitler would come to von Kluge's headquarters at Smolensk on an inspection trip. Tresckow promptly decided to kill the Fuehrer by blowing up his aircraft as it was returning. As soon as word reached Smolensk of this fatal mishap, the commander of a cavalry regiment, Baron von Boeselager by name, would stage a *coup de main* at Kluge's headquarters and take control of this army group. Insurrection was expected to snowball from there on. Stieff was to stage the *sequelae* in the Defense Ministry in Berlin. Oster and his aides were to handle the political phase of the rebellion.

The bomb was concealed in a harmless-looking package addressed to Stieff in Berlin. It was given to Colonel Brandt, one of Hitler's companions on the journey, who was told it contained two bottles of brandy. The plane with the lethal bottles and Hitler on board left on schedule—but the bomb was a dud! Far from having accomplished their mission, the plotters had to move fast to destroy the evidence in Brandt's hands before it could destroy them. Schlabrendorff flew to Berlin and retrieved the package before its true contents became known.

But the frustrated plotters would not give up. Von Stauffenberg, recovered but crippled, was attached to the General Staff to enable him to play a leading part in the conspiracy. The group—made up of conservatives as well as Social Democrats, clerics as well as atheists—had some of Germany's most prominent men slated to take key positions in a new government and ambitious plans to end the war and rehabilitate Germany. The caliber of these men and the quality of their plans held out the promise of success.

This, then, was the situation when Eisenhower arrived in London in January, 1944, to plunge into preparations for *Overlord*. If the potentialities of the German unrest made any impression on him, or if the historic opportunities of the situation were even perfunctorily recognized by the planners around Ike, it is not evident from either the documents of the era or from the post-war memoirs of the generals. As far as I can ascertain, no serious effort was made by Eisenhower to procure specific information about the fantastic ferment in the very core of the German High Command. He paid no attention to those lean and hungry-looking men, whose conspiratorial ardor Caesar once so justly feared, but concentrated on the strictly military aspects of the war he was expected to win by strictly military means.

Eisenhower resisted every attempt to draw him into this area. The possibility of a generals' revolt in Germany as a short-cut to the abrupt termination of the war was raised in his presence several times, the possibility only, not the probability, and not on the basis of any specific data. On January 27, 1944, Ambassador John G. Winant hinted at such a possibility, but was rebuffed by Bedell Smith, Ike's chief of staff. On April 14, Secretary of State Edward R. Stettinius, Jr. mentioned in passing that "if a proper mood [could be] created in the German General Staff, there might even be a German Badoglio," having in mind a German general who, like the Italian marshal, was willing to hand up his country on a silver platter. But Eisenhower expressed, not only doubt that such likelihood existed at all, but his disgust at dealing with German generals.

On the very highest level, President Roosevelt maintained his disdain of political warfare. He hampered rather than promoted it with his philosophy about the conduct of the war and its termination solely by unconditional surrender. Roosevelt was motivated by the revolting picture of Germany as it was remade by Hitler. He was also influenced by General George C. Marshall, a single-minded soldier with a somewhat narrow military outlook. To him war was but the clash of armies, and in his strict adherence to the best American tradition, he detested the political general. It was simply inconceivable to Marshall to make a deal with conspirators, even if it meant winning the war without further bloodshed. And, finally, there was a resolve deep in the President's soul never to make a deal with the "Junkers" of Germany, who, he thought, formed the core of Prussian militarism. He did not want even unconditional surrender as the result of a German conspiracy, but only one gained through the indisputable victory of Allied arms.

The pragmatic fact is that the President's unwillingness to use all means, including political means, to gain victory, substantially prolonged the war by withholding from the German rebels the essential outside aid and moral support for their own victory over Nazism.

His Majesty's Government under Churchill followed Roosevelt's lead, for yet another reason entirely its own. The bitter memory of the Venlo incident left its scars in Whitehall. Never again was His Majesty's government willing to listen to the siren songs of German patriots, for one could never know when they blossomed out as *agents provocateurs* or grinning double agents.

The German opposition tried frantically to establish surreptitious links to the Allies. As early as October, 1939, only a few weeks after the outbreak of hostilities, an envoy of the opposition, a prominent Catholic named Dr. Josef Mueller, offered to set up a working relationship with the British Government via the Vatican. From Vatican City, Mueller contacted London, in a venture that required substantial courage and almost ended fatally for him. An *Abwehr* spy planted in the Vatican alerted Berlin to Mueller's efforts, but fortunately for the clandestine envoy, the report wound up on Oster's desk and was promptly pigeonholed.

In February, 1942, the German diplomat Ulrich von Hassell (who was slated to become Foreign Minister in a post-Hitler cabinet) continued these efforts in Arosa in negotiations with a British envoy named J. Lonsdale Bryans. The Briton had to tell Hassell that he was unsuccessful in interesting the Foreign Office.

In November, 1941, the German opposition enlisted the aid of Louis P. Lochner, the AP correspondent in Berlin, to establish a tenuous contact with London via the United States; in April, 1942, a similar effort was made with the help of a Swedish financier named Wallenberg; and then, in May, the German Evangelical Church tried working, through the Bishop of

Chichester. Eden categorically told the Bishop the government was not interested.

Then, towards the end of 1942, an avenue suddenly seemed to open up and the hopes of the anti-Nazis were rekindled. In November, Allen W. Dulles arrived in Switzerland and set up shop in a house on Herren Street in Berne.

He was nominally a special assistant to the American Minister, Leland Harrison. In fact, Dulles was up to his neck in cloak and dagger; he headed the Swiss branch of the O.S.S., with *cognizance,* as it is called in the parlance of Washington, of Germany and South East Europe.

A native of Watertown, New York, where he was born in 1893, Allen Dulles was the younger son of a distinguished Presbyterian minister who had married the daughter of General Watson Foster, soldier, lawyer, editor, diplomatist, minister to Russia in 1880-1882, Secretary of State in 1892-1893.

From Princeton University (where he majored in history and philosophy and received a Phi Beta Kappa key), Dulles went to Allahabad in India to teach English in a missionary school. In 1916, he joined the Foreign Service, serving in Vienna and Berne. After World War I, Dulles headed the Near Eastern Division of the State Department by day and studied law by night. As soon as he had his law degree, he left the Foreign Service, kicking up a brief storm by complaining publicly about the inadequate salaries of American diplomats.

He practiced law in the firm headed by his elder brother, John Foster Dulles, and acquired a substantial German clientele. When an expert was needed to head the Berne branch of the O.S.S., with a pipeline to influential Germans, Donovan enlisted Dulles.

Dulles decided to bide his time before plunging into his actual mission. With all the frontiers closed, he was largely dependent on cable to send his reports to Washington, and he used this avenue shrewdly for a brilliant ruse. The code in which some of his cables were sent had been broken by the *Forschungsamt,* and in due course his dispatches were read in

Berlin. They attracted favorable impression for their objectivity, which was exactly what Dulles had planned. He hoped to attract Germans looking for an Allied agent willing to listen to them, and thus to organize a network of his own.

So he created a shiny new Allied trap to which a number of German mice quickly beat a path. Since much of the German dissidence was inside the Intelligence organizations, especially the *Abwehr;* and since Intelligence had easiest access to Dulles' intercepted bait, his earliest callers from that "other Germany" were some of his own opposite numbers. Among them was Hans Gisevius, a blond giant with impressive intellectual equipment, who was deeply enmeshed in various anti-Nazi conspiracies. Gisevius was a controversial figure inside the German opposition. He was a vice consul at the German Legation in Berne, under the *Abwehr's* jurisdiction, assigned to perform unspecified intelligence functions. From him, Dulles learned of the ripening plot against Hitler.

Early in February 1944, the plotters resolved to move at the earliest possible moment, before the Allies had a chance to land, in order to confront them with the reality of a new Germany that had rid herself of Hitler and was ready for peace. Elaborate arrangements were made: General Beck was to become chief of state and Dr. Goerdeler, the former Lord Mayor of Leipzig, was to be appointed Chancellor. Von Hassell was to receive the Foreign Ministry; von Witzleben was to become commander in chief of the *Wehrmacht,* the Defense portfolio going to Hoepner, an officer who had incurred Hitler's wrath and had been cashiered some time before. The indefatigable von Tresckow was to take charge of the police, while von Stauffenberg was to remain in the background as the gray eminence of the rebellion.

An assassination was scheduled for February 11, but was cancelled when one of the intended victims, Heinrich Himmler, did not show up at the meeting with Hitler, at which a bomb was to explode. On March 9, arrangements were made to kill Hitler with a revolver shot during one of his situation conferences, but it proved impossible to smuggle the assassin into the meeting. On May 15, the opposition received a tremendous boost through the appearance in its very center of two of Germany's outstanding soldiers, Field Marshal Erwin Rommel and General von Stuelpnagel, commandant of occupied Paris.

Dulles was kept posted of every move. It is presumed that he advised Eisenhower and Donovan. Whether Roosevelt was told of the conspiracy in the specific terms known to Dulles cannot be ascertained. It did not make any difference one way or another. The President had refused to sanction active American participation in the plot.

Dulles was torn between elation and frustration, between a burning desire to intervene in the *coup* and his orders to stay aloof. There he was, with his fingers on the feverish pulse of the German opposition, fully in a position to supply all the outside aid the plotters needed so desperately, and *thereby contribute decisively to the early termination of the war, making the invasion superfluous.* Yet his hands were tied. He lacked the authority to provide any support, not even a single fuse for a bomb, nor even any moral support. He had to sit back like a man dying of thirst, separated by an abyss he could not bridge, several feet from a spring of crystal clear water.

When the invasion came, the plotters were stunned and suspended action for the rest of June, except for Rommel, who started a campaign of his own, trying to persuade Hitler to throw in the sponge. Then, on the night of July 1, the decision was reached to set the plan into motion without any further delay. As the written record of that decision itself put it, "After the landing of the Allies, irreparable catastrophe can be avoided only by cutting short the war and stopping further bloodshed through the immediate formation of a new government— chosen from the leading members of the resistance movement— so constituted as to be acceptable to the Allies as a bargaining partner. *This presupposes the death of Hitler.*"

Von Stauffenberg was appointed Hitler's executioner. To assure access for him to Hitler's inner sanctum, he was made chief of staff to General Erich Fromm, commander in chief of the so-called *Ersatzheer,* the new last-ditch army scraped up from the bottom of Germany's manpower barrel. It was decided to carry out the act with a bomb consisting of two pounds of explosives to be detonated with a chemical-mechanical fuse of English make, set for thirty minutes delayed action. Stauffenberg was to carry that pancake bomb into Hitler's conference room in his leather briefcase. The bomb did not need to be of great power, since the contained concussion in Hitler's concrete map room would enormously increase its lethal effect.

On July 20, at 10:15 a.m., Stauffenberg flew into Rasenburg, accompanied by First Lieutenant von Haeften, his aide, and Stieff. He proceeded calmly to the officers' mess inside the *Wolfsschanze* where he had breakfast, waiting to be called to Gen. Buhle, with whom he had a business appointment. Then he accompanied Buhle to Field Marshal Keitel, at all times carrying his attaché case. At 12:20 p.m., he was ready for his fateful date with Hitler, but was shocked when he was told that the situation conference was to be held in the Tea House, a flimsy frame building, instead of the concrete bunker where it was usually held. The shift filled him with grave misgivings, but he decided to go through with the plan. Upon entering the Tea House, he appeared to lose his way, going into a sideroom instead of the conference room where Hitler was already waiting. He needed this moment of seclusion to activate the time-fuse.

When Stauffenberg entered the conference room—about thirty-seven and a half feet long by fifteen feet wide, with a huge table occupying its center—he found Hitler seated at the center near the entrance with his back turned to him. Keitel, seated at the Fuehrer's left, introduced von Stauffenberg to Hitler as an envoy of Fromm's. There was no seat reserved for Stauffenberg at the table, so he went to the far right corner where Brandt was seated, put the briefcase under the table and left, on the pretense of making a phone call to Berlin.

He was on his way out of Security Section A, riding with von Haeften to the airfield when he heard the explosion. He looked at his watch. It was exactly 12:50 p.m. He assumed that the Fuehrer had been killed. He arrived in Berlin, in the Defense Ministry on Bendler Street, in this firm belief, only to find the Ministry in an uproar. He was told that his bomb had failed to kill Hitler.

The rebellion was over before it could begin. A bloodbath of revenge followed, beginning with Stauffenberg's summary execution in the courtyard of the Ministry. Beck was present in the Bendler Strasse, his first visit since his resignation in 1938, returning in short-lived triumph to act as Germany's new chief of state for something like an hour. He alone was permitted the honor of committing suicide. Beck was nervous. He placed the gun at his temple, fired, but the bullet merely grazed his skin. Then he fired again and was mortally wounded, but somehow did not expire at once. Stauffenberg's scandalized boss, Fromm, told an aide rather casually to end the man's sufferings with a *coup de grâce*. This was the only act of mercy throughout the entire aftermath of the rebellion.

Eisenhower must have known that July 20 was the date set for the showdown in Germany, for Dulles had exact knowledge of the plot's timetable and had advised Washington of it. The O.S.S. had submitted the information to SHAEF Forward at Portsmouth where Ike was spending his last few days in England prior to moving his headquarters to France.

July 20 was a Thursday. Eisenhower was going on a cross-Channel flight to visit Montgomery and Bradley in France, then returning to SHAEF Main at Widewing. According to Butcher's diary entries, the General's major concern during those days was split between Monty's slow motion drive and the release of his dogs from quarantine. The plot was first mentioned in Butcher's diary under date of July 22 and the entry included the cryptic remark: "I'm excited about it, but Ike isn't." Otherwise Butcher's description of the event was full of inaccuracies, reflecting the widespread ignorance of these matters at Eisenhower's headquarters. After lunch on July 22, Ike agreed to see the press for some background chit-chat about the attempt on Hitler's life. The briefing consisted mainly of such platitudes as, "The *coup* against Hitler may have far-reaching effect, but just how cannot be guessed at the moment." The event was not deigned worthy of specific mention in Eisenhower's memoirs.

In Berne, Dulles was groping in the dark. Gisevius was back in Berlin. He had gone home in anticipation of the death of Hitler, hoping to carve for himself a niche in the new Reich. Gisevius survived the holocaust, as did a handful of the plotters, but hundreds, if not thousands, of patriots were destroyed. The bestial cruelty of the retribution could not be surpassed. It was not confined to savage gimmicks used in the executions to make the death agony of the victims as painful and prolonged as inhumanly possible. The torture was extended to the next of kin. The families were advised of the death of their loved ones in brief form letters that read, as in the case of General von Thuengen, one of the leaders of the rebellion:

"The former Lieutenant General Karl Baron von Thuengen was sentenced to death by the People's Tribunal of the Greater-German Reich, on charges of treason and sedition. The sentence was carried out on October 24, 1944. The publication of an obituary notice is forbidden."

Accompanying such letters was a bill. It contained the cost the family had to pay in marks and pfennigs for the last days of their loved one—300 marks for the death sentence, 1.84 mark for mailing charges, 81.60 marks for the cost of the defense, 44 marks for the cost of incarceration, 158.18 marks for the cost of the execution, and 12 pfennigs for the stamp on the envelope in which this macabre invoice reached the relatives.

The aftermath of July 20 was especially tragic in that it liquidated many of Germany's best men and women, depriving the country of a group that could have made the major contribution to the rehabilitation of their land in the post-war world. From the viewpoint of the Allies, an enormous opportunity was wasted to conclude the war in Europe but forty-four days after the invasion—nine months and eighteen days ahead of what eventually became V-E Day. That such an outcome was distinctly possible—that major military moves can be terminated through the proper exploitation of conspiracies in the enemy's camp—was proven by Dulles himself only a few month later when he had the authority to conduct an Intelligence operation on a historic scale, instead of being confined to the collection of information.

For the time being, though, Dulles was busy on Herren Street solely with the assembly of information and the collection of a network of spies and informants. Dulles was especially fortunate in having several spies in high echelons in the German diplomatic and intelligence hierarchy. They were, almost without exception, high-minded, highly-placed, unselfish German patriots, working without remuneration. The motive of these men was their anti-Nazi sentiment, but the Nazis called it treason and sedition. If it was treachery, the United States was not its sole beneficiary. As we have seen, the British refused to make any large-scale use of this source, but the Soviet Union made the most of these opportunities. Lucy (Rudolf Roessler) was working in Switzerland, too.

The quality of this espionage effort by Germans against the Third Reich was reflected in the caliber of the agents, the nature of the information, and the number of the documents supplied. Dulles once conceded that he had received the amazing total of two thousand and six hundred important documents from inside Germany, all of them photostats of originals. The number of documents Roessler received was also in the thousands.

Among these Germans were two men who had past associations with the United States and were emotionally committed to co-operation with this country. One was Otto Karl Kiep, a high-ranking career officer in the Foreign Ministry. He is still well remembered in New York, where he served as Consul General from 1930 to 1933. During the war years, when he represented the Foreign Office in the *Abwehr,* he became an important source of vital information. He managed to survive until January, 1944, when his clandestine group, the so-called Solf Circle, was penetrated by a Gestapo agent. Kiep was arrested, sentenced to death on July 1, 1944, and executed in Plötzensee prison on August 26.

The other was Adam von Trott zu Solz, a counselor of legation, member of a group of intellectual anti-Nazis called the Kreisau Circle. In the summer of 1939, Trott zu Solz established contact in Washington, D. C. with key Americans, and remained in touch with them throughout the war. Some of the most valuable intelligence Dulles received stemmed from Trott zu Solz. Deeply involved in the events of July 20, he was sentenced to death on August 15, 1944, and became a mere number in the *"Mordregister"*, as the Gestapo cynically called the roster of its victims—No. K-2063, dated August 26, 1944, the day of his execution.

Other diplomatists in this anti-Nazi group to which Dulles had access included Hans Berndt von Haeften, also a counselor-of-legation; Richard Kuenzer, a counselor-of-embassy; and Ambassador Friedrich Werner Count von der Schulenburg, who was the German envoy in Moscow at the time of the Stalin-Hitler pact in August, 1939.

Dulles never disclosed the specific sources of his intelligence, except to say that most of it had reached him through a mysterious go-between whom he identified only by his code name, George Wood. It is possible that Wood was a collective name for several informants.

Dulles managed to establish contact with an official in the Central Archives of the Berlin Foreign Ministry through whose hands passed the documents of the Ministry for filing. The usual procedure was to remove the documents after office hours and take them to Charité Hospital. The agent who arrived with the documents was actually wheeled into the operating room in the guise of a patient; the photographing was done in the operating room while apparently surgery was in progress. Then the originals were returned to the files before the office opened for business next morning, while the copies, on 35-mm Leica films, were smuggled to Dulles.

The value of the information he thus received was incalculable. At the time, German diplomats in neutral countries were sometimes secret agents, and the Foreign Ministry received intelligence from them that was not always confined to strictly diplomatic matters. Once the German Legation in Dublin radioed intelligence to Berlin about an Allied convoy that an agent had spotted assembling in New York. A copy of this signal wound up in Dulles' hands. The information that the convoy had been spotted was cabled to Washington, and the convoy was safely rerouted.

At one period during the war, an obscure Albanian who served as the valet of the British Ambassador to Turkey hit upon a lucrative sideline when he managed to pry open the little safe in his employer's bedroom where His Excellency kept his most highly classified papers. He delivered the loot to a Nazi agent at Ankara in exchange for a huge sum paid him in English pound notes. They turned out to be counterfeit, manufactured at a concentration camp by skilled inmates. The Germans came into possession of fantastic intelligence, including the alleged protocol of the Teheran Conference attended by Roosevelt, Churchill and Stalin. The leak was plugged when Dulles found out about it from his agents in the Foreign Ministry in Berlin. The British did not seem to be highly pleased when Dulles tipped them off to the indiscretion of one of their top-ranking ambassadors. From their conspicuous lack of gratitude, it was deduced that maybe the leak was deliberate and that Dulles had plugged a hole that his colleagues at British Intelligence were eager to keep open.

Melodrama was also frequent on Herren Street, partly because of the nature of the mission, partly because of Dulles' own innate fondness for the dramatic. A tall, tweedy, relaxed, professorial-looking, gregarious man, forever puffing on his pipe and laughing boisterously at even the hoariest joke, Dulles was more like a gifted amateur, an espionage buff, than the traditional spymaster. His quarters were in an apartment in a Fifteenth Century gray building, with a clanking front door leading into a medieval courtyard on the River Aar. The printed calling card on the apartment door identified its occupant as Allen W. Dulles, adding, "Special Assistant to the United States Minister."

Dulles preferred to conduct most of his business late at night when he was at his scintillating best and most relaxed, and when his visitors could come to him under the cover of darkness. Every night at midnight he called Washington on the trans-Atlantic telephone, conducting lengthy conversations in an ingenious oral code. This arrangement was not without its pitfalls and setbacks. At one time, the maid of the house turned out to be a German agent. At another time, the use of a compromised code led to a tragic mishap. Count Galeazzo Ciano, former Foreign Minister of Fascist Italy, was in touch with the Allies and this *rapprochement* was reported from Herren Street to Washington in an encoded cable. The code had been broken by a brilliant group of Hungarian cryptoanalysts, and the decoded cable was forwarded to Mussolini in Northern Italy, resulting in Ciano's execution.

Most of the time, Dulles handled in person only the most urgent and delicate matters. The actual management of the operation was in the hands of his aides, among whom probably most important was a young American of German origin, Gero von S. Gaevernitz, the son of Dr. Gerhart von Schultze-Gaevernitz, a prominent liberal politician in the Weimar Republic. Young Gero immigrated to the United States when the Nazis came into power and got himself a job in Wall Street. He had kept up a line to Germany where he had many friends, including several serving in the Foreign Ministry. Others in the Dulles menage included a brilliant young German-Jewish journalist, the nephew of Vicki Baum, author of *Grand Hotel*. Several Dulles aides were refugees from Nazi persecution, living precariously in Switzerland, whose immigration laws are exceptionally stringent. Since they could not very well concede that they were working for Dulles, but had no other visible means of income, the Swiss kept threatening them with deportation as undesirable aliens. The problem was solved by making arrangements with a "psychiatric

retreat" near Berne. The refugees were "committed" for the
duration, and were thus removed from the scrutiny of the Swiss
police, but could come and go as they pleased—a bunch of
"lunatics" very much at large.

In addition to its invaluable routine work, this team accomplished one exploit that established it as one of the outstanding organizations in all the history of espionage. It began in
January, 1945—at a time when two U.S. armies were pushing
the Germans out of the Ardennes bulge and an Allied offensive
penetrated into the Siegfried Line. In Italy, a huge German
army slowed the Allied advance there almost to a standstill. In
Northern Italy, Mussolini still held sway over a vindictive Fascist
Republic, harassed by intrepid partisans but protected and supervised by twenty-one German divisions.

The German military command was held by Field Marshal
Albert Kesselring, one of Goering's closest intimates. The political
command was in the hands of Dr. Rudolf Rahn, Hitler's personal
envoy to Mussolini. Somewhere between the two was a tall,
blond, hook-nosed, elegant ex-advertising man from Berlin, Karl
Wolff by name, a general of the fighting SS. A former aide of
Heinrich Himmler, he was delegated to watch over Kesselring
and Rahn. For all practical purposes, the blond Nazi was the
most important German in Northern Italy, living in a marble
palace at Fasano on Lake Garda amidst substantial pomp.

Yet it was an obscure, young SS lieutenant who emerged
from this chaotic setup as the real man of destiny. He was one
Guido Zimmer, and he was sick and tired of the war. He hoped
that the impending spring offensive of the Allies would force
the surrender of the Germans in Italy and permit him to go
home to his wife and children. He was shocked when, during a
visit of the Austrian *Gauleiter* to Wolff's palatial headquarters,
he overheard a plan to leave a scorched Italy to the Allies and
withdraw the army intact to an impregnable redoubt in the Alps
from where the Nazis could continue the war indefinitely.

This was not the only indiscreet thing Zimmer overheard.
From certain remarks of Colonel Eugene Dollmann, Wolff's

chief of staff, Zimmer assumed that Dollmann, too, had had his fill of the war. "If only we could get in touch with the Allies, we could stop this *verdammte* war once and for all," was the way Dollmann had put it.

Zimmer knew how to get in touch with the Allies! Among his acquaintances was a titled Italian playing it safe on both sides of the fence. He was Baron Luigi Parralli, a former representative in Europe of American automobile manufacturers. Parralli seemed to be a fascist, and was on friendly terms with Wolff and his Nazi ilk, but he also aided Italian Jews to escape and kept up friendships with certain liberals in Switzerland.

Zimmer told Parralli about Dollmann's remark, about widespread dissatisfaction among high-ranking SS officers, even going so far as to hint that Wolff shared it. Parralli agreed to carry the ball to the Allies, but got only as far as a schoolmaster named Max Husmann, widely known in Switzerland as a dedicated busybody with excellent connections. Husmann carried the tidings to a friend of his, Dr. Max Waibel, who happened to be a major in the Intelligence Division of the Swiss General Staff. This was how the vague idea of the embryonic plot eventually reached the Allies—from Zimmer to Parralli to Husmann to Waibel to Dulles.

Dulles was not entirely unprepared for this intelligence. His agents had reported to him distinct signs of dissatisfaction among the Germans in Italy. According to one such agent, a German staff officer, who was spending a day in Zurich, openly spoke of defeatism at his headquarters. According to another, the German consul in Lugano was shopping around for an Allied representative to whom he could talk peace.

Dulles decided to advise Washington and ask authority to open negotiations. Waibel was delegated as Swiss representative at the negotiations. In the meantime, Parralli carried young Zimmer's plot directly to Wolff and Dollmann and, as Zimmer had anticipated, obtained their agreement to negotiate. Wolff delegated Dollmann to represent him at the first meeting with the Americans, held at the Bianchi Restaurant in Lugano.

Such things take time, despite their desperate urgency. It was not until March 8 that Wolff himself actively entered the plot. He was met at Chiasso on the Swiss frontier by Husmann, who took him to Dulles in Zurich.

Wolff was ebullient, bearing gifts. Among them were two prominent Italian Partisan leaders he had picked from Gestapo jails in Verona and Milan as proof of his good faith. One of them, Professor Ferruccio Parri, happened to be an old friend of Dulles. He was destined to become Italy's first Prime Minister after the liberation.

Dulles listened silently to the garrulous Nazi as he promised to deliver Northern Italy, lock, stock and barrel. He appreciated Wolff's intentions, but realized that the Nazi lacked the power to make good. And it dawned upon Dulles that the deal was far too big, even for him. Never before had an intelligence operation been conducted on such an enormous scale for such high stakes. It had vast military implications, involving hundreds of thousands of soldiers and enormous stores. Even more important, it also had immense political implications. The Allies were committed to the Kremlin not to make a separate peace with the Germans, and this segment of the German Army that appeared ripe for the picking was big enough to warrant Soviet objections that might throw a monkey wrench into the deal.

To cover his own flank, Dulles asked Field Marshal Sir Harold Alexander at Allied Forces Headquarters in Caserta to send a couple of senior officers to participate in the negotiations. Alexander delegated Major General Lyman L. Lemnitzer of the U.S. Army, his chief of staff, and British Major General Terence S. Airey, his chief of Intelligence. A special O.S.S. team had to smuggle them into Switzerland. They lived with Dulles on Herren Street behind permanently drawn blinds, but there was a bit of incongruity in their carefully cultivated incognito. During the long wait, Airey acquired a companion, a dachshund named Fritzel. He sometimes threw all precautions to the wind and sneaked out of the old house to buy dog biscuits for Fritzel.

There were other complications, too. Wolff's job was to

persuade Kesselring to surrender. Just when the Field Marshal
appeared to agree, he was replaced by a timorous general named
Heinrich von Vietinghoff, who struck a Hamletian pose, when
confronted with the proposition. Then a new fly appeared in
the ointment. The Nazis, who had sent Wolff to spy on Kesselring, also sent an SS brigadier named Harster to spy on Wolff.
Harster, to whom Wolff in his innocence had confided the plot,
reported it to Himmler and the *Reichsfuehrer* instructed Kalten-
brunner to step in and abort it. By then, however, there was a
certain defiant autonomy in such matters among the regimented
Nazis, and, while Wolff made a tearful, abject promise to his
boss that he would drop the plot, he continued the negotiations
with increased vigor, urging Dulles to hurry up and consummate
the deal.

The Russians also got wind of the developments and put
such pressure on the Allies that, on April 23, Alexander instructed Dulles to discontinue the negotiations. They stayed
discontinued for only a few days, after which they were resumed
because the Allies decided this was too good a deal to abandon
on account of Russian objections.

Any maneuvers of this kind are crowded with unscheduled
mishaps and one such unexpected intervention almost thwarted
the deal. On one of his return trips from a meeting with Dulles
in Switzerland, Wolff's convoy was ambushed by Italian Partisans near a place called Cernobbio. Wolff tried the telephone
and put in a call to Waibel in Berne, asking for help. Waibel
alerted Gero Gaevernitz, who rushed to Chiasso where he met
a man named Donald (Scotti) Jones, an O.S.S. liaison officer
to the Italian Partisans. Gaevernitz instructed Jones to rescue
Wolff—and thus an American secret agent went to the aid of
a German general threatened by Italian resistance fighters! Jones
reached the villa where Wolff was hiding, extricated him and
took him through Partisan lines to safety, a feat he could accomplish only because *amico Scotti* was known and completely
trusted by the Partisans.

At last, on April 27, three months after Zimmer started the

ball rolling, two emissaries of the German High Command in Italy were flown to Alexander at Caserta and signed, on behalf of Vietinghoff and Wolff, the capitulation document. The Italian front was to cease to exist as of noon of May 2, 1945. The document was then flown to Bolzano where Vietinghoff and Wolff were waiting to ratify it. But they had an unexpected visitor, *Gauleiter* Franz Hofer of Austria, the man in charge of the mythical redoubt to which the German Army in Italy was to retreat for Hitler's last stand. Hofer telephoned Himmler and Kesselring, denouncing the plotters.

While Dulles in Berne and Alexander in Caserta were waiting for word that the war in Italy was over, fighting flared with new violence inside the German high command. Kesselring, peremptorily returned to supreme command in Italy, ordered that Vietinghoff and Wolff be arrested, but his orders were not carried out. Then he called Wolff on the phone, talking for more than two hours, trying to persuade him to cancel the surrender. Wolff refused to yield. At 10 p.m. on May 1, the cease fire orders went out to the German troops, effective at noon next day. At 11 p.m., the German radio suddenly announced that Hitler was dead, but Kesselring still refused to sanction the surrender in Italy. At 1:15 a.m. he was still obstructing the cease-fire order with the limited power at his command. He yielded at 4:30 a.m. when he finally realized that he was up against the united high command at Bolzano and, most important, against Karl Wolff, who proved a tower of strength in the crisis.

Seven and a half hours later the war was over in Italy. Instead of intransigent, last-ditch fighting, peace had been bought at an infinitesimal cost, in sweat rather than blood, by the big man in the rumpled tweed suit. Dulles proved that the secret service, so important in war, is capable of engineering peace out of the chaos and confusion of the conspiracy of men. This was the major lesson of the Dulles operation, a lesson we neglected to learn on July 20, 1944 in Germany, and then woefully disregarded in the summer of 1945, in Japan.

22

The Surrender of Japan

On the morning of May 8, 1945, President Harry S. Truman called reporters to his office in the White House to announce officially the surrender of Germany. When he completed the reading of his joyous proclamation in his flat Missouri voice, he personally distributed to the reporters a mimeographed "appeal to Japan," which was for immediate release.

The appeal read:

"Nazi Germany has been defeated.

"The Japanese people have felt the weight of our land, air and naval attacks. So long as their leaders and the armed forces continue the war, the striking power and intensity of our blows will steadily increase and will bring utter destruction to Japan's industrial production, to its shipping and to everything that supports its military activity.

"The longer the war lasts, the greater will be the suffering and hardships which the people of Japan will undergo—all in vain. Our blows will not cease until the Japanese military and naval forces lay down their arms in *unconditional surrender*.

"Just what does the unconditional surrender of the armed forces mean for the Japanese people?

"It means the end of the war!

"It means the termination of the influence of the military leaders who have brought Japan to the present brink of disaster.

"It means provision for the return of soldiers and sailors to their families, their farms, their jobs.

"It means not prolonging the present agony and suffering of the Japanese in the vain hope of victory.

"*Unconditional surrender does not mean the extermination or enslavement of the Japanese people.*"

Seated in front of a radio in my office in a Restricted building, I listened to the reading of this appeal with a lump in my throat, for I had written the statement the President had just released. It was the opening salvo in the Second World War's last major intelligence operation, the product of three years of groping and inching toward this goal.

In the Office of Naval Intelligence in Washington, D. C., I was part of a small group with a big objective—to bring about Japan's surrender by non-military means, or, as our basic directive, *Operation Order 1-45,* spelled it out: "To make unnecessary an opposed landing in the Japanese main islands, by weakening the will of the High Command, by effecting cessation of hostilities, and by bringing about unconditional surrender with the least possible loss of life to us consistent with early termination of the war."

This was a preposterous undertaking. Out in the vast Pacific, millions of men fought and bled toward victory. Yet here in Washington just ten of us tried to accomplish this same objective. This was Op-16-W, the Special Warfare Branch of O.N.I., a Secret operational intelligence agency preoccupied largely with psychological warfare and certain other special activities I still am not at liberty to disclose.

Op-16-W was formed in 1942, a few months after Pearl Harbor, the prodigal brainchild of one of the U.S. Navy's most extraordinary officers. He was Lieutenant Commander Cecil Henry Coggins, a naval surgeon specializing in obstetrics whenever he served in the Medical Corps. But most of the time he was off on special assignments, dabbling in all sorts of intelligence work. Dr. Coggins, a slight, crew-cut, narrow-eyed, humorless man of unbounded energy and enthusiasm, was, like Allen Dulles, an espionage buff.

BURN AFTER READING

Early in 1942, Dr. Coggins happened to read my book, *German Psychological Warfare,* and decided to become the Navy's pioneer psychological warrior. He envisaged the application of this kind of assault on the enemy navies, using persuasion instead of the compulsion of arms to paralyze the fingers, as he was wont to put it, that pulled the triggers.

I first met Coggins in August, 1942, when he called upon me in New York unannounced at the Committee for National Morale, where I then worked as director of research. He introduced himself, sat down at my desk and outlined to me in supercharged words an elaborate plan he had hatched to organize a psychological warfare branch inside Naval Intelligence. He invited me to join him as his chief of research and general idea man. I told him I could not very well hope to be accepted in O.N.I. because I was then still a citizen of Hungary and had been in this country less than five years. Moreover, little Hungary having seen fit to declare war on the United States, my status was that of an enemy alien.

"Never mind," Coggins said. "I'll fix that."

He gave me my instructions, as strange as this strange man was himself. This was in August, on a hot summer day, but Coggins told me: "Be in Washington on December 4. Go straight from the Union Station to the Fairfax Hotel. Don't register, but go directly to room 307 and enter without knocking. The door will be unlocked. Be there at 5 p.m. sharp. I am now going somewhere in the Pacific, but will see you in Washington."

More than three months later, at the exact time, I was on the third floor of the hotel, standing outside room 307, when the door opened. There was Coggins, and inside the parlor of the suite I found three more people. They were Captain Zacharias; Joseph Riheldaffer, an elderly commander; and a young lieutenant named Booth. Three hours later I was hired as a "secret agent," because my status as an enemy alien made any other entry into O.N.I. administratively impossible.

Coggins solved my draft status in a similarly melodramatic fashion. I was then classified 1-A, but Coggins called on my draft board in New York, identified himself as a physician and told them I had suffered a nervous breakdown and had to be committed to a "psychiatric institution." I was promptly reclassified 4-F and remained in that category until my thirty-eighth birthday, in September, 1944, when I ceased to be eligible for the draft and Coggins could take me out of the institution.

My office was in a restricted part of a makeshift frame building called "Temporary-L" near the Lincoln Memorial, an architectural survivor of the First World War. Op-16-W occupied three rooms flanked by Op-16-Z, headed by Riheldaffer, and a secret branch of the Bureau of Naval Communications.

Our neighbors at "Z" had one of the most fascinating jobs in war-time Washington: interrogating prisoners of war, exploiting captured documents, scanning censorship intercepts and doing odd jobs in cerebral espionage. They were, for the next four years, to supply the ammunition for our own operations.

My first job in 16-W was to devise a plan for a frontal psychological assault on the personnel of Doenitz's awesome U-boat arm. Up to one hundred and eighty enemy submarines were prowling all along the Atlantic Seaboard. We had hardly any defenses against them, and almost no offensive weapons.

Never before had a propagandist established within an American intelligence organization been given classified information and permitted to talk directly to the enemy. Now I suggested that we begin operations with a series of broadcasts to the U-boat men, based on this intelligence. The idea was promptly approved by Admiral Ernest J. King, Chief of Naval Operations.

I concocted a character who would act as the U.S. Navy's official spokesman to the officers and men of the *Kriegsmarine,* the German Navy. I created this personality at my typewriter out of thin air in a thirty-page legend like the cover story prepared for a spy. I gave the mythical person a name, *Robert Lee Norden,* because it sounded indigenously American with a slight touch of Confederate chauvinism, yet was easily understandable and pronounceable by the Germans. I gave him a rank—Commander, USN—sufficiently high to command respect, but not too high to alienate junior officers and enlisted men. I gave him a birthplace, parents, an education, a career, wife and children, hobbies and pets, until the character lived, at least in our own minds.

We breathed life into this figment of my imagination by placing the myth inside the body of a remarkable officer whom we found right next door at "Z." He was Ralph Gerhart Albrecht, a distinguished international lawyer in civilian life, a lieutenant commander in the Naval Reserve, doing delicate "special" jobs at "Z." Albrecht was tall, erect to the point of being ramrod stiff, his gray hair closely cropped, with a clipped mustache in the British style and a commanding presence and voice. He spoke German with absolute fluency and with only that slight touch of accent necessary to leave the listener in no doubt that the speaker was an American and not a renegade German.

To make him real, even in an administrative sense, we entered "Norden" in the Mail Room and applied for inclusion in the Naval Register. This was a wise precaution, for he was to receive bundles of fan mail from his audience, separated from him by an ocean and a war, yet finding means of writing to him. In the course of the war, Commander Norden delivered six hundred broadcasts to the German U-boat Arm. He became famous and respected by the U-boat men, except by Doenitz, who detested him.

In his broadcasts, Norden forever sided with the ordinary U-boat man, telling him that he was being sent deliberately into certain death by Hitler and Doenitz. Once, when my researches revealed that not a single non-com or enlisted man had ever received the coveted Knight's Cross of the Iron Cross, we wrote a script for Norden bemoaning this fact. The risks of operational cruises are identical for all ranks, he said. Then he asked, "Why this discrimination?"

A few days later we found an item on the ticker announcing the award of the Knight's Insignia to a couple of chief mates in the U-boat Arm, with the words: "The Fuehrer, upon recommendation of Grand Admiral Doenitz, was pleased to award the *Ritterkreuz* to," and so forth. Norden was on the air within hours, extending his congratulations to the decorated men from the lower deck, but adding, "There was only one error in the citation. The Fuehrer awarded the *Ritterkreuz,* not at the recommendation of Grand Admiral Doenitz, but at the recommendation of the United States Navy."

When we seized a disabled U-boat, we salvaged a copy of the German Naval Register and were appalled by the extraordinarily large number of flag officers in the German Navy. We added them up, and found that in a single month more captains were made admirals in Germany than U-boats were launched. We proceeded to point this out to the men, who habitually dislike admirals.

We realized that the fighting spirit of the U-boat men was high, and that any direct appeal to surrender would fall on deaf ears. Yet we wanted to plant the idea of this eventuality in their minds, so we decided to talk to them, not about surrendering, but about the best means of surrendering. We described an actual action during which a U-boat had been disabled. The men had nothing white on board with which to signal to the attacking U.S. destroyer to cease fire, since all the curtains and towels on the boat were green. We suggested that the men bring along something white for such an emergency. Sure enough, when the next boat signaled to an American warship that her crew was abandoning ship, it was done with a white cloth. Upon closer scrutiny it turned out to be the dress shirt of the executive officer, the only white object they dared to smuggle aboard in accordance with Norden's suggestion.

Captured documents had references to Norden and his "devastating influence on the morale of the men." If positive proof were needed, it was supplied by a U-boat skipper named Heinz-Eberhard Mueller, whose boat was sunk off the Virginia coast. Badly wounded, Captain Mueller was taken to the hospital at Fort Meade, Maryland, where his first request was to be introduced to Commander Norden. This request, flattering though it was, created a minor crisis, if only because "Norden" was a full commander while his voice was only a lieutenant commander. For the trip to Mueller's bedside Albrecht was given another stripe. Mueller received him with tears in his eyes and thanked him for his compassionate broadcasts, which, he claimed, made many a U-boat man more dependent on information from Norden than from the German radio.

The most dramatic Norden broadcast concerned a U-boat skipper named Werner Hanke, a fanatical Nazi and a strict taskmaster, respected but disliked by his men. When a British ship, the *Ceramic,* carrying dependents of soldiers to South Africa, was sunk in the South Atlantic, we established from secret intelligence reports that the U-boat that sank the ship was commanded by Hanke. We further knew that Hanke refused to give aid to survivors struggling in the water or to call for aid before he himself had escaped from the scene of the disaster.

Norden went on the air with a stern warning that Hanke would be made to account for his act, as a war criminal, after Allied victory. By a strange quirk of fate, a week after this broadcast, Hanke's U-boat was sunk by American planes and Hanke was found among the survivors. By a further coincidence, the admiral commanding the rescuing carrier happened to have read the English translation of the Norden script in which Hanke had been singled out. He ordered the prisoner of war to report to him at his quarters.

"You know," the admiral told him, "that the British are looking for you. I am now making for the Azores, where I am going to hand you over to them."

The U-boat commander crumbled under this threat. He admitted that he had heard the Norden broadcast and did his utmost to assure the admiral that Norden was wrong in his statements. The admiral was adamant. "You'll be handed over to the British," he said, "unless you co-operate with us."

"But how?" Hanke asked.

"You'll sign a paper signifying your agreement that you will co-operate with us wholeheartedly."

Hanke signed. He was then dismissed and was excluded from interrogation, but his men were shown the paper he had signed as an inducement for their co-operation. Hanke could never live down the shame. In the prison camp he committed suicide.

This was grim business, and it was working perfectly. According to Wallace Carroll, the distinguished *New York Times* correspondent who was an executive of the Office of War Information, the Norden broadcasts were "the single most effective propaganda weapon we had in the war."

In 16-W we also prepared leaflets, concocted rumors for distribution by agents among the U-boat men, and put together, among other things, a song book for German sailors in which every song prescribed another simple form of malingering.

Our most effective leaflet, for which Commander Coggins gave the branch a golden star, was initially as amusing as it was later effective. Officers from 16-Z found a peculiar little brochure on sailors captured from a German blockade runner. It was a guide to the brothels of Bordeaux, home base of the ship, with a map of the city indicating the houses of ill fame and identifying them by the names of their star inmates, such as Maison Fifi, Maison Mimi and so forth. The brochure also listed first aid stations in the city where the sailors could turn for prophylactic measures or treatment. There was a ration card attached to the brochure, indicating that each sailor was entitled to one daily visit to the ladies' establishments.

We reproduced five million copies of the brochure just as it was, even duplicating the bad paper on which it was printed, and dropped them over Germany. We added (in red) to only the last page. The addition read: "German women! Be grateful to the Fuehrer for taking such good care of your men!"

The Norden operation was of enormous *tactical* significance. In due course, Op-16-W was also given major strategic assignments, two in particular: to draft a critique of the meaning and morale implications of President Roosevelt's unconditional surrender formula; and to prepare a co-ordinated campaign

directed to the Japanese High Command, providing arguments
to be used inside Japan by advocates of surrender.

The unconditional surrender formula, proclaimed at the
Casablanca Conference in January, 1943, became a thorn in
our side. It became evident that it was stiffening enemy morale,
preventing our adversaries from even considering the idea of
surrender and prolonging the war. Eisenhower asked the Joint
Chiefs of Staff to do something about the formula, and in February, 1944, the Joint Chiefs commissioned Op-16-W to prepare
a brief on the subject with recommendations. "The questions,"
Zacharias wrote in *Secret Missions,* "which the experts of 16-W
were supposed to answer were, first, whether the unconditional
surrender formula was conducive to increasing or stiffening
resistance of the enemy; and, second, how we could alter the
formula without losing face or doing damage to our political
prestige."

When the formula was originally proclaimed, we in 16-W
regarded it as an outstanding psychological scoop because, as
Zacharias put it, "It revealed both our determination and confidence to carry the war to a victorious conclusion at a time when
the military situation did not seem to warrant such optimism and
confidence." However, by 1944, we had our doubts about the
wisdom and efficacy of the formula. Even before the assignment
reached us from the Joint Chiefs, I undertook research about
the historical origin and legal validity of the formula.

I established that it was based on a historical misapprehen-
sion, a distortion of the term Grant had used in the Civil War.
Moreover, I found that it was legally invalid and, as a matter of
fact, illegal under the Articles of War. In view of the provisions
of the Hague Convention, which clearly distinguishes between
the responsibilities of combatants and noncombatants in warfare,
the term could refer only to the manner in which hostilities are
terminated, and not to the future fate of a whole nation.

We nevertheless recommended to the Joint Chiefs that the
form of the formula be sustained for the sake of prestige with
the proviso that it "does not refer to conditions to prevail after

the war, which have to be made on the basis of explicit peace terms, and not under the blanket dictation implied in unconditional surrender." This preoccupation of 16-W with the unconditional surrender formula became of great importance later in connection with our assignment concerning Japan.

The Special Warfare Branch consisted of only a handful of people and its budget was less than the price of two torpedoes. We had an Italian desk, consisting of a single pretty WAVE lieutenant, Dorothy Sandler. We had a German desk manned by Professor Stefan T. Possony, now of Georgetown University, and Yeoman Ernst Erich Noth, now a professor at the University of Oklahoma. We had a Japanese desk, on which worked Professor John Paul Reed of the University of Miami; Dennis McEvoy, writer and linguist who could speak Japanese with amazing fluency; Professor Joseph Yoshioka, a noted Japanese psychologist; Francis Royal Eastlake and Clara Eastlake, children of the great American lexicographer who was author of a famed Japanese-American dictionary. Eastlake was an outstanding linguist, his sister a sociologist. Our naval adviser was Professor Bernard Brodie of Dartmouth College, author of *Seapower in the Machine Age,* a Mahanesque scholar and, to my mind, the outstanding and most lucid American expert on strategy in political scientific terms. I, in my lonely splendor, attended to research and special investigations, co-operating with each desk on the themes and composition of all their output, suggesting topics and themes for the Norden scripts, concocting rumors, writing leaflets and supplying arguments to our Officer-in-Charge to defend our own Branch in the face of snipings by diehard Naval fogies.

Coggins had left to serve as a guerrilla surgeon with Chinese partisans behind the Japanese lines in China. His place was taken by Commander William H. Cullinan, a radio news commentator from Boston, whose diplomatic tact was badly needed for our very survival.

Yet the most important member of the Branch was conspicuous by his absence. He was Zacharias. Nine months after

the establishment of the Branch, he was removed from O.N.I.
and sent to sea in command of the battleship *New Mexico*. This
was a heavy blow to us, as it was to the entire Naval Intelligence
establishment, for Zack was the most dynamic executive in O.N.I.
While he was still in O.N.I., Naval Intelligence virtually steamed
with activities. It was during his tenure that O.N.I. participated
in a secret mission that spirited an anti-Fascist admiral out of
Italy. He also co-operated closely with O.S.S. on several top
secret espionage projects and with the various branches of the
British Secret Service on ventures far beyond the narrow competence of Naval Intelligence. He left behind him an excellent
organization in every one of its branches, but especially in its
Japanese branch, headed by a Marine colonel named Boon and
a Navy captain named Egbert Watts.

The day before his departure, "Captain Zack" invited me
to his house and gave me a parting assignment. "Look," he told
me, "I am going to sea and will do what I can to contribute to
the military defeat of the Japs, but I am absolutely convinced
that we could better defeat them, and sooner at that, by non-
military means.

"I want you to make a comprehensive study of every
Japanese defeat situation in history and draw your conclusions.
Then think of arguments we could provide for those Japanese
in high places who dream of peace and need such ammunition."
This was in the late summer of 1943!

He was gone for two years, covering himself with glory.
During his absence, I partially retired to a cubbyhole in the
Library of Congress and, with the help of the Eastlakes and
Professor Yoshioka, carried out Zack's assignment.

My researches produced a fantastic conclusion. Although in
all their history the Japanese had engaged only in a few foreign
wars, they fought among themselves, clan versus clan, all the
time. We examined hundreds of such fratricidal battles and
found that rarely, if ever, was such a battle fought to the bitter
end. Contrary to popular legend, surrender was quite common

among the Samurai. The Japanese of the past rarely, if ever, committed suicide when defeated.

The findings of this research—an important part of the intelligence activity—answered the question, "Can it be hoped or expected that the Japanese will ever surrender?" in the affirmative. We had our data ready pending Zack's return, but he was transferred from his command at sea to shore duty as chief of staff of a Naval District on the West Coast. It was there, early in 1945, that Secretary of the Navy James V. Forrestal found him, nurturing a historic plan.

Zacharias was obsessed with the idea that he could persuade the Japanese high command to surrender, even unconditionally, provided certain assurances could be given, such as the assurance that the Emperor, symbol of the "Japanese spirit," would be permitted to remain on his throne. Zacharias outlined his idea to Forrestal and the Secretary decided to bring him back to Washington to carry it out. But even the civilian chief of the Navy proved powerless to overcome certain objections to Zack's second coming.

Forrestal was determined to give Zack his big chance, so he hit upon a compromise. He had Zacharias assigned to the Office of War Information, over which Zack's Naval enemies had no control, and then gave him a desk in his, Forrestal's, own office, reporting directly to the Secretary.

Zacharias arrived in Washington in February, 1944, and walked into 16-W out of the blue. He spent his first week in Washington going over all the intelligence reports, and his second week composing an estimate of the situation for the Secretary's eyes only.

I received him with a special "gift" that made him almost jump for joy. It was a single intelligence report, but of such monumental importance that he regarded it as the conclusive confirmation of his theory. This was how it came into our possession.

President Roosevelt had rewarded a good friend of his,

George Earle, former Governor of Pennsylvania, with an exciting appointment as assistant Naval Attaché to Sofia in Bulgaria, an excellent listening post. Earle had a lot of qualifications for the job, but discretion was not one of them. He was ingenious, imaginative, daring and intelligent, but he was also flamboyant and his temperamental boiling point was rather low. Earle performed so well that the Germans demanded the Bulgarian Government declare him *persona non grata*. Roosevelt had the Governor transferred to Turkey, where he made the friendship of a high official of the Foreign Ministry in Ankara and obtained through him copies of the reports of Turkish ambassadors in enemy capitals.

There was little of any importance we could cull from reports sent to Ankara from Germany or Hungary, but the reports of the Turkish ambassador in Tokyo proved of enormous value. We gave him the code name "Shark." Late on the afternoon before Christmas in 1944, I was alone in the office when an officer-messenger delivered a single five-page report. It was from Shark. It contained information of overwhelming importance.

Shark outlined in explicit detail the future course of Japan. He reported without equivocation that Koiso would soon resign as Premier, to be replaced by the venerable Admiral Suzuki, a confidant of the Emperor. More important, he told us that there existed a "peace party" on high echelons in Tokyo and that the Emperor himself had recently joined it. The major objective of the "peace party" was to obtain a clarification of our unconditional surrender formula and to explore the most favorable peace terms they could get. According to Shark, the Emperor was still on the periphery of the "peace party," chiefly because he was not sure whether he himself would be permitted to remain on the throne. If such an assurance could be given by the Allies, he would throw in his fate with the "peace party" and do everything he could to make it prevail.

Shark even outlined the course of events which would lead up to Japan's surrender. At the psychological moment, Suzuki, too, would resign to give way to an Imperial prince who reflected directly the Emperor's will and authority, and who would then arrange Japan's surrender, guaranteeing the "execution and observance of the surrender terms." As early as December, 1944, Shark even identified this Imperial prince as Prince Higashi Kuni, a cousin of the Emperor.

I was thrilled by this report and peddled it up and down in O.N.I., but found no takers. Even the experts of the Japanese Desk regarded it as a lot of moonshine. In O.N.I., within the Joint Chiefs and everywhere else in Washington, the possibility of Japan's surrender was viewed with an overdose of skepticism. Remembering my findings in the Library of Congress, I refused to share this pessimism.

Another one of my researches revealed that the much-vaunted Kwantung Army stationed in Manchuria was but a shell of its former self. Most of its elite regiments had been transferred to the fighting fronts in the Pacific and had been annihilated on Saipan and Palau. This was another report I peddled assiduously and for which I also found no takers.

When Zacharias walked into my office, I showed him the reports, and he took them to Forrestal, and then used them in his campaign to recruit supporters for his scheme in the White House and on Capitol Hill. Soon we had two enormously important sponsors, Admiral William L. Leahy, the President's chief of staff, and Senator Elbert Thomas of Utah, a former missionary in Japan who had the expert's appreciation of Zack's plan.

We did not know it then, and were not to find out until after it was too late, but a race was on between ourselves and scientists at Los Alamos and Oak Ridge who were working on the atomic bomb. It may seem lacking in a sense of proportion to mention these two projects in the same breath, and yet it is amply justified, because today we know that Op-16-W's scheme had an excellent chance to succeed. Its success would have obviated not only the invasion of Japan, but also the use of the A-bomb. Both projects had the same aim, to accelerate Japan's surrender without a bloody landing. Otherwise the two efforts were incomparably different. For one thing, Op-16-W had cost a grand total of ninety-seven thousand five hundred dollars to operate from the day of its inception to VJ-Day, while the Manhattan Project swallowed up two billion dollars to the time of the detonation of the first bomb. For another, the purpose of our project was to save lives, whereas the A-bomb was to claim thousands.

If there was a reasonably promising alternative, as I believe there was, to the use of the bomb on Japan, then it was folly to use that bomb before that alternative was given all its chances for success.

On March 19, Zacharias delivered into Forrestal's hands his proposed plan for a psychological warfare offensive. The draft spelled out the mission as follows: "The United States will conduct an intensive psychological campaign against the Japanese high command through an official spokesman of high rank in order to accelerate and effect the unconditional surrender of Japan without the necessity of an opposed landing on the Japanese main islands."

Forrestal approved the plan out of hand. Admiral King also approved it. The War Department had no objections. The Joint Chiefs hesitated for a few days, but then gave it their blessing. There remained only one approval to be collected, the final and decisive one—that of President Roosevelt. But Roosevelt was out of town and could not be disturbed. He was resting at Hyde Park after the tiresome and burdensome trip to Yalta.

Suddenly something happened whose tremendous significance was known only to us. On April 8, the cabinet of Koiso resigned and was replaced by one headed by Suzuki, exactly as had been predicted by Shark in December. This meant to us that the Emperor had definitely thrown in his lot with the peace party in Japan, and that Japanese efforts for an "honorable surrender" would henceforth be accelerated.

We redoubled our efforts, prepared the draft of a first broadcast to be delivered by the "Official Spokesman" and also drew up a statement to be issued by the President. It was envisaged as the first in a series of such presidential statements to spell out to the Japanese what we in Op-16-W called the "conditions of unconditional surrender."

The statement was on Roosevelt's desk in the White House, placed there by Elmer Davis, director of O.W.I., on the one day in April he spent in Washington on his way from Hyde Park to Warm Springs. He must have read and contemplated it because there were a few pale penciled changes in the draft when we got it back, but he left town without approving the project. A day later he was dead.

We felt this sounded the death knell for our project as well, because we thought it would take some time before Truman could be familiarized with the project, before we could "sell" the idea to him and gain his approval and co-operation. The world was preoccupied with the majestic events in Europe where Hitler's empire was collapsing like an overbaked soufflé.

Then Zacharias hunted up a middle-man who had a friend in the White House. The middle-man was Samuel R. Davenport; the friend, Matthew J. Connelly, who was Truman's appointment secretary. Davenport took the statement to Connelly, who placed it on top of the pile in the incoming basket on the President's desk. For several days, the statement made its way from the top to the bottom of the basket, as Connelly dutifully replaced it each morning. Then on May 8, in conjunction with his proclamation of VE-Day, Truman suddenly released it.

That same day, Zacharias went on the air, broadcasting in Japanese to the Tokyo high command, reading to them the President's statement. His words went out over powerful short-wave transmitters in San Francisco and Honolulu. Saipan put it on the air on the medium wave used by Radio Tokyo, enabling the five million Japanese who had sets to hear it, if they dared or cared. It was not aimed at them, although their eavesdropping was eagerly sought. It was explicitly and directly aimed at the

Emperor and his circle, at the members of the "peace party," and the Japanese high command, a select audience of perhaps five hundred listeners.

At this point a shadowy figure entered our plot, although he probably did not know we even existed. He was one Jiri Taguchi, a Japanese foreign correspondent who had been sent to Germany by Foreign Minister Togo to report to him privately and directly about the Third Reich's final agony. Our intelligence agents succeeded in obtaining a copy of his confidential message to Togo. It was a melancholy report, urging the Foreign Minister to do something so that Japan might escape Germany's fate. We put the correspondent's private message on the air, special delivery to the attention of Foreign Minister Togo, and anybody else who happened to listen in.

Agents' reports started accumulating, reporting Japanese reaction to the President's statement and the sudden appearance of an "official spokesman of the U.S. government" on the air. On May 20, we were informed by one agent that the statement and the Zacharias broadcasts had been discussed in a Cabinet meeting. On the nineteenth day of the campaign, we drew real blood. The first reply was given to Zacharias in a broadcast by an "official spokesman" of the Japanese government, Dr. Isamu Inouye.

"Japan," Inouye said, "would be ready to discuss peace terms provided there were certain changes in the unconditional surrender formula. We should like mutually to join hands in constructing an international machinery which strives toward world peace and the good of humanity."

Inouye indicated in so many words that he was not only answering the Zacharias appeal, but was expecting an answer from Zacharias.

"I should like to know," Inouye concluded his broadcast, "what Zacharias-*kun* thinks of these words from Japan." These words were significant, not merely for their direct recognition of the captain, but for the word *"kun"* attached to his name. Unlike *"taisa,"* which means "captain," and *"san"* which means

"Mr.," "*kun*" is a word used only between close friends, meaning something like "my good friend."

Agents reported that copies of Zacharias' broadcasts had been requested by the Imperial Palace. In Berne, Taguchi sought a secret meeting with the American minister, Leland Harrison. Although Taguchi had credentials signed by Togo, he was regarded as a free-lancing busybody and was not taken seriously. Another great opportunity was missed in a chain that could have led, piece by piece, to the surrender of Japan.

In April, the Emperor himself entered the picture. Using the Archbishop of Tokyo as his personal go-between, he secretly approached the Vatican to sound out the United States on what would be acceptable terms. The Pope assigned Pietro Cardinal Fumasoni-Biandi to handle the matter without committing the Vatican one way or another.

The aged Cardinal called in Harold Tittmann, an American diplomatic agent stationed in the Vatican, to transmit the Emperor's feelers to Washington. For some unexplained and inexplicable reason, this correspondence was not handled by the State Department, but by the Washington headquarters of the Office of Strategic Services. I remember distinctly that the reports were brought to us by the highest-ranking messenger ever to make the rounds in Washington, a brigadier general, one of Donovan's top-ranking aides. The Emperor's appearance in the plot filled us with great expectations, but we were instructed to forget it, on the ground that the feelers came to us via the Vatican. It was thought inadvisable to permit the Holy See to have anything to do with any short-cuts to Japanese surrender, for fear that public opinion in the United States might label and resent it as Papal intervention.

Every single move along these lines was recorded inside Op-16-W and, in the Washington of those days, it was the only seismograph to record these tremors. The State Department at that particular juncture was virtually paralyzed. Edward Stettinius was Secretary of State. He was a diplomat of rather limited scope, and, just at this stage, he happened to be too busy with preparations for the inauguration of the United Nations, scheduled to be held at San Francisco in June. The Acting Secretary in Stettinius' absence was Joseph Grew, long-time American Ambassador in Tokyo, ideally qualified to handle this intricate operation, but Grew had suffered a stroke and was not yet completely recovered. In addition, State was so confused by the several competing attitudes toward Japan and by the propaganda barrage of certain American factions arguing against the retention of the Emperor that it preferred to let sleeping dogs lie.

In June, a third peace feeler was made under rather sinister circumstances. In a highly-encoded communication, Togo told his Ambassador in Moscow, an experienced and wise diplomat named Sato, about the Zacharias broadcasts and asked him what he thought of them. Sato answered that they were interesting as far as they went, but Zacharias ought to be far more specific in spelling out the surrender terms. Several cables were exchanged by Togo and Sato, and then Togo suddenly instructed Sato in so many words to go to Stalin and ask him to mediate between Japan and the United States.

American cryptoanalysts, monitoring every outgoing and incoming broadcast in Japan, picked up and translated the dispatches. The translations were distributed to the few recipients eligible for them. They were given to Truman, of course, and also to Grew, but they were withheld from us.

The Japanese request for Stalin's intervention was explicit. Nobody who had access to those telegrams of Togo and Sato could question their sincerity or the urgency with which they hoped to pursue the matter. Stalin bluntly rejected the mediation request, and he also withheld any information about this most explicit peace feeler from us, his allies. In June, his Foreign Minister, the enigmatic Molotov, was in Washington in person, but he kept mum about the Japanese approach.

The situation was unique in diplomatic history. The United States Government knew that Japan was approaching the end and had asked Stalin to intervene, but it could not very well act upon this knowledge because the intelligence was obtained from the breaking of the Japanese diplomatic code.

The Swiss government knew about Taguchi's efforts on behalf of Togo but refused to recognize them as valid since they had been made by a non-official envoy.

The Vatican knew virtually directly from the Emperor that Japan was seeking frantically to find a *modus operandi* for surrender, but refused to handle the matter officially because it had no formal diplomatic relations with the United States.

Sweden knew that Japan was searching for a way out of the war because her own envoy in Tokyo had also been approached to use his good offices.

Zacharias was talking directly to the Japanese about the urgency and the possibilities of peace, and was being answered by government spokesmen from Tokyo, virtually begging him to give Japan the terms on which its surrender would be acceptable.

At this point I personally decided to take matters into my own hand and develop "terms" that Zacharias could then transmit to the Japanese in one of his broadcasts. The United States was so frozen to the unconditional surrender formula that it could not defrost itself without arousing public indignation, which Washington did not know how to guide or handle. The formula had been oversold to the American public. And the men in the State Department did not know how to get rid of it.

I collected all the various wartime declarations of Roosevelt, Churchill and Generalissimo Chiang Kai-shek that had some bearing on the surrender of Japan. I found five of them: the Atlantic Charter, the Cairo Declaration, Chiang Kai-shek's declaration of New Year's Day in 1944, the statement I wrote for President Truman, and Supreme Court Justice Robert Jackson's statement on war criminals.

I incorporated them in a letter to the editor of the *Washington Post*, firmly believing that it would quickly reach the Japanese. I decided to sign it merely *"An Observer,"* to create the impression that the letter was a U.S. Government-sponsored trial balloon. I not only expected that the Japanese would recognize them as the "terms" under our unconditional surrender formula, but also I hoped to commit my own government to them and thereby end this futile period of uncertainty.

I wrote the letter in my office, on Uncle Sam's time, on U.S. Government stationery, because this was not my property, my pride, my personal problem or my axe to grind. I did not even expect to get any credit for it. It was something I thought had to be said, shouted from the rooftops, so loud that it could be heard eleven thousand miles away in Tokyo.

The editor of the *Washington Post* was Herbert Elliston. He was my friend. I used to go to his small inner sanctum from time to time to "inspire" editorials about Japan. Now I went to him again and told him that I was up to my neck in this one-man "conspiracy" and wanted him to become my partner. I showed him the letter and asked him to publish it and support it in an editorial of his own. I also told him that I intended to remain in the background and pass the ball for the touchdown to Zacharias because, after all, he was the official spokesman. I asked Elliston to tell anybody who might inquire about the author of the letter that it was written by Captain Zack and that his views reflected U.S. Government policy.

Only then did I go back to the Navy Department and tell Zack about the letter, asking him to brace himself for fireworks, because I was determined to plug the letter in the National Press Club, and also to see to it that it would become a shot heard around the world.

Next morning Herb Elliston, bless his soul, ran the letter, a whole column long in the *Post,* and it was the talk of the town. It was a lavishly baited hook. For example, one passage said, "The Atlantic Charter and the Cairo Declaration clearly state that we seek no territorial aggrandizement. The Atlantic Charter, moreover, assures certain definite benefits to victors and vanquished alike."

Another passage was designed to reassure the Emperor.

"American military law," it read, "based upon historical precedents, as well as a decision of the United States Supreme Court, clearly specifies that conquest or occupation does not affect the sovereignty of a defeated nation, even though that nation may be under complete military control."

Then came the direct invitation: "If the Japanese desire to clarify whether or not unconditional surrender goes beyond the conditions contained in the five documents cited above, they have at their disposal the regular diplomatic channels, the secrecy of which precludes any public admission of weakness. They are aware that we know that Japan has lost the war. Such an inquiry could not possibly be misinterpreted, or display any weakness beyond that which now actually exists in Japan."

I did not have to go to the National Press Club to alert its members. The whole club was coming to Captain Zack, demanding to know whether he was the author of the letter and whether he spoke for the White House.

Typical of the press comments was a column our friend Duke Shoop of the *Kansas City Star* wrote: "A provocative open letter inviting the Japanese to open negotiations on unconditional surrender is being widely discussed here since it is believed that Captain E. M. Zacharias, the 'official American spokesman' of American radio broadcasts to the Japs, is the author. This provocative letter is like something out of a mystery thriller, but it is not at all out of the question that some such method might be taken to convey further to the Japanese what we mean by unconditional surrender."

Op-16-W was ablaze with excitement. We felt we were on the right path, moving steadily at a growing speed toward the climax of our effort. We somehow felt that the war in the Pacific was drawing to its close, despite the vicious nature of the fighting on Okinawa. We clearly distinguished between the stolid, automated Japanese combat soldier, clinging to caves and coves with obtuse bravado, with a sacrificial fighting spirit that was almost obscene because it had some mystic sexual undertones, and the suave and sophisticated, shrewdly-calculating statesmen in Tokyo who knew that the jig was up. Our targets were the statesmen, and our aim was to capture Tokyo with this verbal barrage.

The follow-up was very important. We could not afford to allow a moment's let-up in our dual campaign, aimed both at the Japanese and our own Government. What we were doing was clearly insubordination; still, we thought, if we were making policies, we were merely filling an abysmal vacuum.

Back at Op-16-W, my colleagues, Dr. Reed and Dr. Possony, aided by Dr. Yoshioka, were working on a haymaker of a broadcast for Zack, to reinforce the multiple themes of the letter to the *Post*. Its basic, dynamic message was reduced to four key sentences: "The leaders of Japan have been entrusted with the salvation, and not the *destruction*, of Japan. As I have said before, the Japanese leaders face two alternatives. One is the virtual destruction of Japan, followed by a dictated peace. The other is unconditional surrender with its attendant benefits as laid down by the Atlantic Charter."

By now unconditional surrender must have looked to the Japanese like the Biblical apple on the tree of wisdom. It was sinful, to be sure, but it also held out the promise of some consolations.

We released this broadcast to the press, and it appeared from coast to coast in prominent positions on the front pages of the dailies of July 21. *The New York Times* reprinted the whole broadcast. The *Washington Post* headlined: "U.S. Warns Japan To Quit Now, Escape Virtual Destruction."

The Japanese answered it on July 24. While the voice was that of Dr. Kiyoshi Inouye, we knew that the hand which drafted his answer was that of the Imperial Government. Inouye stated point blank: "Should the United States show any sincerity of putting into practice what she preaches, as for instance in the Atlantic Charter excepting its punitive clause, the Japanese nation, in fact the Japanese military, would automatically, if not willingly follow in the stopping of the conflict. Then, and then only, will sabers cease to rattle both in the East and the West."

However, our decisive broadcast, as Zacharias came to call it, unleashed a storm of another nature, right here in the United States. The broadcast hit the State Department like a bombshell. Our diplomatists suddenly realized that somebody was making foreign policy and pushing it into action. In their annoyance, they decided to destroy us by undermining our influence in the eyes of the Japanese. They mobilized their own spokesmen, journalists and radio commentators close to the Department, and told them to discredit Zacharias. Typical of their campaign was a commentary by Raymond Gram Swing on July 21, in which he denied "on excellent authority" (actually one Thomas Blake, a minor official in the State Department) that the Atlantic Charter was applicable to Japan and said that Zacharias' claim of being the "official spokesman of the U.S. Government" was "preposterous."

While this was going on in the United States, President Truman and James F. Byrnes, his new Secretary of State, were in Potsdam meeting Churchill and Stalin. Byrnes cabled the State Department for background about the broadcast, and the Department cabled back a reassuring despatch trying to show that "the Zacharias clique" was not making any headway.

It became essential to restore Zacharias' authority. As usual, Secretary Forrestal came to our aid. He called Washington's most influential correspondent, Arthur Krock of *The New York Times,* to his office and asked him to write a column which would tacitly reiterate that Zacharias was not a self-appointed apostle of peace, but an official spokesman, indeed, whose broadcast reflected the views and policies of the U.S. Government. Next morning Krock wrote: "Uneasiness has been expressed in this country over . . . the broadcast to Japan by Captain Zacharias . . . Captain Zacharias, though reiterating the requirement of unconditional surrender, told the Japanese people they can make 'peace with honor' at this juncture and that the benefits of the Atlantic Charter will go with it; and this has aroused fears it will persuade the Japanese we are weakening and that they can get even better terms if they hold out . . ."

Then followed the crucial portion of his column, inspired by Forrestal: "Captain Zacharias was working on a twofold problem this Government faces in the Pacific war, and the line he took in the broadcast is the high official attempt to deal with it directly. He sought (a) to persuade the Japanese people that their military leaders lie when they predict pillage, enslavement, dismemberment of the home islands, rapine and the overthrow of their sacred institutions as the inevitable consequences of unconditional surrender, the hope being that, if the Japanese masses can be brought to realize this, the war will be shortened and many American lives will be spared. He sought (b) to show the American people the effort that is being made to save those lives."

We were still apprehensive that Truman, who was maintaining ominous silence at Potsdam, might yet disavow us. Forrestal sought to prevent this. He asked Commodore Vardaman, the President's Naval Aide, to brief Truman on the issue. This intervention saved the day for us. While the President continued to refrain from taking a direct part in the controversy, he authorized Anthony Vaccaro, White House correspondent of the Associated Press covering him at Potsdam, to report that the President "tacitly approved the Zacharias broadcast."

Now we felt the time had come to invigorate the campaign by establishing direct, personal contact with the Japanese to discuss with them face to face the problems that had to be solved. One of the foremost Japanese militarists, General Oshima, had been captured in Germany, where he represented his country as ambassador to Hitler. We made arrangements to fly him to Washington and then, with him in tow, we prepared to go to an island in the Pacific to meet with emissaries of Tokyo.

As we saw it, Zacharias would go on this secret trip, accompanied by Dennis McEvoy and maybe Commander Douglas Fairbanks, Jr., attached to Admiral King's staff, who worked independently along lines similar to ours, trying to establish contact with personalities close to the Dowager Empress, who wielded great influence on the Emperor. We obtained permission to bring Oshima to Washington, and began making the arrangements for Zacharias' momentous trip, hoping to assure the participation of Japanese emissaries approximately on Zacharias' level. These were supposed to be preliminary talks, for the real negotiations would have to be conducted on a much higher level. But we expected that even these preliminary talks would produce vast areas of agreement, enabling subsequent negotiators to arrange the surrender without too much further delay.

We again enjoyed Forrestal's wholehearted support. The Secretary asked Zacharias to venture an opinion as to the date by which the surrender would become an accomplished fact. Zacharias answered without the slightest hesitation: "September 1." The date was exactly one month away, but we felt confident that we could deliver the goods.

On August 6, the atomic bomb was dropped on Hiroshima. It was followed by the dropping of a second bomb on Nagasaki on August 9. In between, the Red Army sneaked into the Far Eastern war by attacking the Japanese in Manchuria and scoring a few *pro forma* victories in great haste.

Zacharias was bitterly disappointed when his efforts blew up in the poisonous mushroom of two atomic bombs. "The stunning effect of the atomic bombs on world-wide popular imagination," he wrote in his autobiography, "caused an instant belief that the Japanese surrender was solely the result of atomic bombing. And that erroneous belief still persists very widely . . . Japan would have accepted our surrender terms even without the prodding which the two atomic bombs provided.

"Aside from its stunning and horrifying impact on human imagination and its production of a spectacular war climax," he wrote, "the atomic bombs' effect on the Japanese war was only to hasten, by a very short time, the Japanese expression of a decision already made."

Japan surrendered on August 14 and her capitulation was formalized on September 2 on board the battleship *Missouri*.

To save two weeks, the United States introduced history's most savage weapon into human conflict, and thus endowed war with an unprecedented horror. The United States did this at a time when a small band of dedicated men was ready to demonstrate that conflicts could be ended in an intellectual sphere by non-military means.

I shall be forever proud that I was privileged to belong to that small band of dedicated men.

BIBLIOGRAPHY

Bibliography

As it must be obvious to the reader, part of the material in this book is based on first hand sources—personal interrogations, unpublished eyewitness accounts, documents, as well as my own experiences—and part on published sources, the accounts of men and women who shared in this grand adventure or had a ringside seat at the secret war.

The following bibliography is prepared for those who seek information in greater detail on specific events cited above as well as on those operations not covered in this book.

The available literature is vast. The selection had to be confined to works which I thought were objectively the best or which appealed to me subjectively, for their intrinsic value or beauty. My gratitude goes out to their authors who have thus aided me in the preparation of this volume.

Abshagen, K. H., *Canaris, Patriot und Weltbuerger,* Stuttgart: Deutsche Verlags-Gesellschaft, 1949

Activities of Soviet Secret Service, Washington: Government Printing Office, 1954

Alsop, S. (with Braden, T.), *Sub Rosa. The OSS and American Espionage,* New York: Reynal & Hitchcock, 1946

Amé, C., *Guerra segreta in Italia, 1939–1943,* Roma: Casine, 1954

Bartz, K., *Die Tragoedie der deutschen Abwehr,* Salzburg: Pilgram, 1955

Bergier, J., *Agents secrets contre armes secrètes,* Paris: Arthaud, 1955

Best, S. P., *The Venlo Incident,* London: Hutchinson, 1951

Borchers, E., *Monsieur Jean,* Hannover: Sponholtz, 1951

Boveri, M., *Der Verrat im 20. Jahrhundert,* Hamburg: Rowohlt, 1956–57

Buckmaster, M. J., *Specially Employed. The Story of British Aid to French Patriots of the Resistance,* London: Batchworth Press, 1952

Buckmaster, M. J., *They Fought Alone. The Story of the British Agents in France,* London: Odhams Press, 1958

Busch, T. (pseudonym of Arthur Schuetz), *Entlarvter Geheimdienst,* Zuerich: Pegasus, 1946

Butcher, H. C., *My Three Years With Eisenhower,* New York: Simon and Schuster, 1946

Carroll, W., *Persuade or Perish,* Boston: Houghton Mifflin, 1948

Carré, M., *I Was the Cat,* London: Souvenir, 1960

Churchill, P., *Of Their Own Choice,* London: Hodder & Stoughton, 1952

Churchill, P., *Duel of Wits,* London: Hodder & Stoughton, 1953

Churchill, W. S., *The Second World War*, 6 vols., Boston: Houghton Mifflin, 1948–1952
Ciano Diaries, 1939–1943, New York: Doubleday, 1946
Collier, R., *Ten-thousand Eyes*, London: Collins, 1958
Colvin, I., *Chief of Intelligence*, London: Kimber, 1951
Colvin, I., *The Unknown Courier*, London: Kimber, 1953
Combined Operations, London: H. M. Stationery Office, 1943
Confidential Records of the French General Staff, Berlin, 1940
Cooper, D. A., *Operation Heartbreak*, New York: Viking, 1951
Dallin, D., *Soviet Espionage*, New Haven: Yale, 1956
Dalton, H., *The Fateful Years. Memoirs, 1931–1945*, London: Muller, 1957
Davidson, B., *Partisan Picture*, Bedford: 1946
Dedijer, V., *With Tito Through the War*, London: Hamilton, 1951
Derry, T. K., *The Campaign in Norway*, London: H. M. Stationery Office, 1952
Dixon, C. A. (with Heilbrunn, O.), *Communist Guerilla Warfare*, London: Allen & Unwin, 1954
Dourlein, P., *Inside North Pole*, London: Kimber, 1953
Downes, D., *The Scarlet Thread. Adventures in Wartime Espionage*, New York: British Book Centre, 1953
Duke, M., *Slipstream. The Story of Anthony Duke*, London: Evans, 1955
Duke, M., *No Passport. The Story of Jean Felix*, London: Evans, 1957
Dulles, A. W., *Germany's Underground*, New York: Macmillan, 1947
Eisenhower, D. D., *Crusade in Europe*, Garden City: Doubleday, 1949
Eppler, J. W., *Rommel ruft Kairo*, Guetersloh: Bertelsman, 1959
Farago, L. (ed.), *Axis Grand Strategy*, New York: Farrar & Rinehart, 1942
Farago, L., *War of Wits. The Anatomy of Espionage and Intelligence*, New York: Funk & Wagnalls, 1954
Feldt, E. A., *The Coast Watchers*, Melbourne: Cumberlege, 1946
Fernandez Artucio, H., *The Nazi Octopus in South America*, London: Hale, 1943
Firmin, S., *They Came to Spy*, London: Hutchinson, 1946
Fischer, G., *Soviet Opposition to Stalin*, Cambridge, Mass.: Harvard University Press, 1952
Flicke, W. F., *Spionagegruppe Rote Kapelle*, Kreuzlingen: Neptun, 1949
Flicke, W. F., *Agenten funken nach Moskau*, Kreuzlingen: Neptun, 1954
Foote, A., *Handbook for Spies*, Garden City: Doubleday, 1949
Ford, C. (with McBain, A.), *Cloak and Dagger. The Secret Story of the OSS*, New York: Random House, 1946
Fuller, J. O., *Madeleine. The Story of Noor Inayat Khan*, London: Gollancz, 1952
Fuller, J. O., *The Starr Affair*, London: Gollancz, 1953
Fuller, J. O., *Double Webs*, London: Putnam, 1958
Galang, R. C., *Secret Mission to the Philippines*, Manila: University Publications, 1948
Gauché, G., *Le Deuxième Bureau au travail (1935–1940)*, Paris: Amiot-Dumont, 1954
Gerson, L. D., *Schreider und die Spione*, Muenchen: Dom, 1950
Gestapo i Norge. Mennene, Midlene og Metodene, Oslo: Gyldendal, 1946
Gimpel, E., *Spion fuer Deutschland*, Muenchen: Suedd. Verl., 1956

Gisevius, H. B., *Bis zum bitteren Ende*, 2 vols., Zurich: Fretz & Wasmuth, 1954
Giskes, H. J., *London Calling North Pole*, London: Kimber, 1953
Goerlitz, W., *Der zweite Weltkrieg*, Stuttgart: Steingraeben, 1951
Goudsmit, S. A., *Alsos*, New York: H. Schuman, 1947
Guillaume, P., *La sologne au temps de l'heroism et de la trahison*, Orleans: Imp. Nouevelle, 1950
Haestrup, J., *Kontakt med England*, Copenhagen: Thuning & Appel, 1954
Hagen, W. (pseudonym of Wilhelm Hoettl), *Die geheime Front. Organisation, Personen und Aktionen des deutschen Geheimdienstes*, Zuerich: Europa, 1950
Hagen, W., *Unternehmen Bernhard. Ein historischer Tatsachenbericht ueber die groesste Geldfaelschungsaktion aller Zeiten*, Wels: Welsermuehl, 1955
Hassell, U.v., *Vom anderen Deutschland. Aus den nachgelassenen Tagebuechern, 1938–1944*, Zuerich: Atlantis, 1946
Haukelid, K., *Skis Against the Atom*, London: Kimber, 1954
Hawemann, W., *Achtung, Partisanen! Der Kampf hinter der Ostfront*, Hannover: Sponholtz, 1953
Hesse, F., *Das Spiel um Deutschland*, Muenchen: List, 1953
Hobatsch, W., *Die deutsche Besetzung von Daenemark und Norwegen, 1940*, Goettingen: Musterschmidt, 1952
Hofer, W., *Die Entfesselung des zweiten Weltkrieges*, Frankfurt: Fischer, 1960
Hollingworth, C., *The Three Weeks' War in Poland*, London: Dyckworth, 1940
Howarth, D., *The Shetland Bus*, London: Longmans, Green, 1953
Howarth, P. (ed.), *Special Operations*, London: Routledge & Paul, 1955
Hull, C., *Memoirs*, 2 vols., New York: Macmillan, 1948
Ignatov, P. K., *Partisans of Kuban*, London: Hutchinson, 1945
Ind, A., *Allied Intelligence Bureau. Our Secret Weapon in the War Against Japan*, New York: McKay, 1958
Jacobsen, H.-A., *Der zweite Weltkrieg in Chronik und Dokumenten*, Darmstadt: Wehr und Wissen, 1960
James, C., *I Was Monty's Double*, London: Rider, 1954
Jong, L. D., *Civil Resistance in the Netherlands*, Amsterdam: Rijksinstituut voor Oorlogsdocumentatie, 1950
Jong, L. D., *The German Fifth Column in the Second World War*, Chicago: Chicago University Press, 1956
Jowitt, Lord, *Some Were Spies*, London: Hodder & Stoughton, 1954
Kompani Linge, 2 vols., Oslo: Gyldendal, 1948
Koop, T. F., *Weapon of Silence*, Chicago: Chicago University Press, 1946
Kordt, E., *Wahn und Wirklichkeit*, Stuttgart: DVG, 1947
Kordt, E., *Nicht aus den Akten*, Stuttgart: DVG, 1950
Kovpak, S. A., *Our Partisan Course*, London: Hutchinson, 1947
Lampe, D., *The Savage Canary*, London: Cassell, 1957
Leverkuehn, P., *Der geheime Nachrichtendienst der deutschen Wehrmacht im Kriege*, Frankfurt: Bernard & Graefe, 1957
Lockhart, R. H. B., *Comes the Reckoning*, London: Putnam, 1948
Loeff, W., *Spionage. Aus den Papieren eines Abwehr-Offiziers*, Stuttgart: Rigler, 1950
Lonsdale Bryans, J., *Blind Victory*, London: Skeffington, 1951

MacDonald, E. P., *Undercover Girl*, New York: Macmillan, 1947
Maclean, F., *Eastern Approaches*, London: Cape, 1949
Marshall, B., *The White Rabbit*, London: Evans, 1952
Mashbir, S., *I Was an American Spy*, New York: Vantage Press, 1953
Maskelyne, J., *Magic—Top Secret*, London: Stanley Paul, 1949
Maugeri, F., *From the Ashes of Disgrace*, New York: Reynal & Hitchcock, 1948
Michel, H., *Histoire de la Résistance*, Paris: Comité d'Histoire de la Deuxième Guerre Mondiale, 1946
Miksche, F. O., *Secret Forces*, London: Faber & Faber, 1950
Montagu, E., *The Man Who Never Was*, London: Evans, 1953
Moorehead, A., *The Traitors*, New York: Scribner's, 1952
Morgan, W. J., *The OSS and I*, New York: Norton, 1957
Mosley, L. O., *The Cat and the Mice*, London: Barker, 1958
Moyzisch, L. C., *Der Fall Cicero*, Heidelberg: Palladium, 1950
Neuhaeusler, J., *Kreuz und Hakenkreuz*, Muenchen: Verlag der Katholischen Kirche Bayerns, 1946
O'Callaghan, S., *The Jackboot in Ireland*, London: Wingate, 1958
Passy, Colonel (pseudonym of André Dewawrin), *Souvenirs*, 2 vols., Paris: Raoul Solar, 1948
Pechel, R., *Deutscher Widerstand*, Erlenbach-Zuerich: Rentsch, 1947
Picker, H. (ed.), *Hitlers Tischgespraeche im Fuehrerhauptquartier, 1941–42*, Bonn: Athenaeum, 1951
Pinto, O., *Spy-Catcher*, New York: Harper, 1952
Pinto, O., *Friend or Foe?*, New York: Putnam, 1954
Pitt, R., *The Courage of Fear*, London: Jarrolds, 1957
Polish Ministry of Information, *The German Fifth Column in Poland*, London: Hutchinson, 1941
Ponomarenko, P. K., *Guerilla Warfare in the Occupied Parts of the Soviet Union*, Moscow, 1945
Psychoundakis, G., *The Cretan Runner*, London: Murray, 1955
Rachlis, E., *They Came to Kill. The True Story of Eight Nazi Saboteurs in America*, New York: Random House, 1961
Redelis, V., *Partisanenkrieg. Entstehung und Bekaempfung der Partisanen und Untergrundbewegung in Mittelabschnitt der Ostfront, 1941–43*, Heidelberg: Vowinckel, 1958
Renault-Roulier, G., *Profil d'un espion*, Paris: Plon, 1953
Rendel, A. M., *Appointment in Crete. The Story of a British Agent*, London: Wingate, 1953
Rothfels, H., *Die deutsche Opposition gegen Hitler*, Frankfurt: Fischer, 1958
Royce, H. (with Zimmermann, E., and Jacobsen, H.-A.), *20. Juli 1944*, Bonn: Berto-Verlag, 1960
Saunders, H. S. St. G., *The Green Beret*, London: Joseph, 1950
Schellenberg, W., *Memoiren*, Koeln: Verlag fuer Politik und Wirtschaft, 1959
Schlabrendorff, F. v., *Offiziere gegen Hitler*, Frankfurt: Fischer, 1959
Schreider, J., *Das war das Englandspiel*, Muenchen: Stutz, 1950
Schultze-Holthus, N., *Fruehrot in Iran. Abenteuer im deutschen Geheimdienst*, Esslingen: Bechtle, 1952
Schwarzwalder, J., *We Caught Spies*, New York: Duell, Sloan & Pearce, 1946

Seth, R., *The Undaunted. The Story of Resistance in Western Europe,* New York: Philosophical Library, 1956

Seth, R., *Secret Servants,* New York: Farrar, Straus & Cudahy, 1957

Sillitoe, Sir Percy, *Cloak Without Dagger,* New York: Abelard-Schuman, 1955

Sinevirskii, N., *Smersh,* New York: Holt, 1950

Smith, N. (with Blake Clark), *Into Siam, Underground Kingdom,* Indianapolis: Bobbs-Merrill, 1946

Sturani, L., *Antologia della resistenza,* Torino: Centro, 1951

Thorwald, J., *Wen sie verderben wollen,* Stuttgart: Steingrueben, 1952

Thorwald, J., *Die Ungeklarten Faelle,* Stuttgart: Steingrueben, 1950

Thorwald, J., *Der Fall Pastorius,* Stuttgart: Steingrueben, 1953

Tickell, J., *Odette. The Story of a British Agent,* London: Chapman & Hall, 1949

Tickell, J., *Moon Squadron,* London: Wingate, 1956

Trabucchi, A., *I vinto hanno sempre torto,* Torino: DeSilva, 1947

Vinogradskaya, Y. A., *A Woman Behind the German Lines,* London, 1944

Wehner, W., *Geheim. Ein Dokumentarbericht ueber die deutschen Geheimdienste,* Muenchen: Suddeutscher Verlag, 1960

Weisenborn, G., *Der lautlose Aufstand,* Hamburg: Rowohlt, 1953

West, R., *The Meaning of Treason,* New York: Viking, 1947

White, J. B., *The Big Lie,* London: Evans, 1956

White, L., *The Long Balkan Night,* New York: Scribner, 1944

Whitehead, D., *The FBI Story,* New York: Random House, 1956

Wighton, C. (with Peis, G.), *Hitler's Spies and Saboteurs.* Based on the German Secret Service Diary of General Lahousen, London: Odhams, 1958

Willoughby, C. A., *Shanghai Conspiracy,* New York: Dutton, 1952

Woodhouse, C. M., *Apple of Discord,* London: Hutchinson, 1948

Wucher, A., *Seit 5 Uhr 45 wird zurueckgeschossen. Ein Dokumentarbericht ueber den Beginn des zweiten Weltkrieges,* Muenchen: Suedd. Verlag, 1959

Yardley, H. O., *The American Black Chamber,* Indianapolis: Bobbs-Merrill, 1951

Zacharias, E. M., *Secret Missions,* New York: Putnam, 1946

Zacharias, E. M. (with Farago, L.), *Behind Closed Doors.* The Secret History of the Cold War, New York: Putnam, 1950

* * *

The documents consulted were far too numerous for individual listing, as were newspaper and magazine articles. Much material was found in the records of the various Pearl Harbor investigations; the transcripts and exhibits of the Nuremberg war crime trials; the findings and exhibits of the Canadian Royal Commission investigating Soviet espionage; transcripts and exhibits of U.S. Congressional hearings; publications of the Dutch Parliamentary Commission of Inquiry that investigated the tragic circumstances of the *Englandspiel;* the collections of Dr. de Jong's *Rijksinstituut voor Oorlogsdosumentatie,* the French *Comité d'Histoire de la Deuxième Guerre Mondiale,* and the *Office de la Résistance* in the Ministry of National Defense, in Brussels, Belgium.

I would like to list the following magazine articles with the acknowledgment of my debt of gratitude to their authors:

Abend, H., "So sorry for you," *Saturday Evening Post,* March 4, 1939, vol. 211, p. 7ff.

Chamberlain, J., "OSS demonstrated need for coordinated intelligence office," *Life,* November 19, 1945, vol. 19, pp. 118–120ff.

Davis, F., "The secret story of a surrender," *Saturday Evening Post,* September 22, 1945, pp. 9–11ff; September 29, 1945, pp. 17ff.

Donovan, W. J., "Intelligence: Key to defense," *Life,* September 30, 1946, vol. 21, pp. 108–110ff.

Gubbins, Sir Colin McV., "Resistance Movements," *Journal of the Royal United Service Institution,* May 1948, vol. 93, no. 570, pp. 210–223.

Hoover, J. E., "How the Nazi spy invasion was smashed," *American,* September 1944, vol. 138, pp. 20–21ff.

Hoover, J. E., "Hitler's spying sirens," *American,* December 1944, vol. 138, pp. 40–41ff.

Hoover, J. E., "Enemy's masterpiece of espionage," *Reader's Digest,* April 1946, vol. 48, pp. 1–6.

Hoover, J. E., "Spy who double-crossed Hitler," *American,* May 1946, vol. 141, pp. 23ff.

Nowinski, M. M., "Behind Poland's defeat," *American Mercury,* April 1940, vol. 49, pp. 400–404

Yoshikawa, T., with Stanford, N., "Top Secret Assignment," *U.S. Naval Institute Proceedings,* December 1960, vol. 86, no. 12, pp. 27–39

INDEX OF NAMES

Index of Names

Friedman, Col. W. F., 191
Froge, Captain Georges, 19
Fromm, General Erich, 264-265
Fuji, Ichiro, 182-185
Fuller, Jean Overton, 89
Fumasoni-Biandi, Pietro Cardinal, 293

Gaertner, Georg, 202
Gaevernitz, Gero von S., 270, 274
Gamelin, Gen. Maurice Gustave, 27-28
Gauché, Colonel G., 27-28
Gaulle, Gen. Charles de, 28, 233, 249-251
Gehlen, Major Reinhold, 120
Georges, Gen. Alphonse, 18
Gisevius, Hans Bernd, 262, 266
Giskes, Major H. J., 237-238
Godfrey, Admiral John Henry, 78
Goebbels, Dr. Paul Joseph, 2, 226
Goerdeler, Dr. Carl Friedrich, 40, 262
Goering, Marshal Hermann Wilhelm, 60, 74, 107-108, 109, 112
Goertz, Dr. Hermann, 94-95
Grew, Joseph C., 190-192, 294
Grieve, Constable, 102
Grosch, Lieutenant, 44-45
Grundherr, von, 62
Gubbins, Gen. Sir Colin McV., 84-85, 87-88, 222
Guderian, Gen. Heinz, 118
Guest, Winston, 219
Gustaf V, King of Sweden, 91

Haakon VII, King of Norway, 64-65, 76
Haeften, Hans Bernd von, 268
Haeften, Captain Werner von, 264
Hagelin, 59, 61
Halder, General Franz, 93, 106-107, 173, 256-257
Halifax, Lord, 36
Hall, Admiral Sir Reginald, 216
Hamel, Edmund, 135
Hamel, Olga, 136
Hammerstein-Equord, Gen. Kurt von, 256
Hamilton, Maxwell M., 190
Harnack, Arvid ("Caro"), 145-155
Harnack-Fish, Mildred, 145, 146-147

Harrison, Leland, 261, 293
Harster, 274
Hart, Captain Liddell, 89, 165-166
Hassell, Ulrich von, 40, 260, 262
Haushofer, Gen. Karl, 169
Heard, Captain William A., 190, 212
Henderson, Sir Nevile, 35
Henke, Commander Werner, 282-283
Heydrich, Bruno Richard, 15
Heydrich, Reinhard, 1-4, 12-16, 32, 37, 42, 47-48, 223-224
Himmler, Heinrich, 13, 224, 262, 275
Hirohito, Emperor of Japan, 287-288, 295, 300
Hitler, Adolf, 2, 4, 5, 8, 11-12, 18, 30, 36-37, 39, 41, 43-44, 57, 60-62, 63, 69, 71, 73, 74-76, 91, 93, 107, 113-114, 120-123, 125, 145, 147, 148, 165, 169-170, 211, 224, 245, 256-266, 271, 280-281, 300
Hocke, Lieutenant, 75
Hoenemanns, Major, 70-71
Hoeppner, General Erich, 262
Hoettl, Dr. Wilhelm, 16, 237
Hofer, Franz, 275
Hogarth, David George, 30
Holford, Lady, 81
Hoover, John Edgar, 191, 198-203
Horacek, Gen. Frantisek, 223
Horthy, Admiral Nicholas de, 236-237
Howe, Ronald, 54
Hull, Cordell, 122-123, 158, 199
Husmann, Prof. Max, 272-273
Hutchinson, R. E., 93

Inman, 46
Inouye, Dr. Isamu, 292
Inouye, Dr. Kiyoshi, 298
Ismay, Gen. Hastings Lionel, 82-83

Jackson, Robert Houghwout, 295
Jacob, Col. Edward Ian Claud, 79, 92
Jambroes, George, 239-240
Jodl, Gen. Alfred, 92, 94
Jones, Donald ("Scotti"), 274
Jones, Dr. Richard V., 111-112
Jordan, Mrs. Jessie, 50-51
Jowitt, Earl, 98, 102
Junge, Commander, 113

The Naval Institute Press is the book-publishing arm of the U.S. Naval Institute, a private, nonprofit, membership society for sea service professionals and others who share an interest in naval and maritime affairs. Established in 1873 at the U.S. Naval Academy in Annapolis, Maryland, where its offices remain today, the Naval Institute has members worldwide.

Members of the Naval Institute support the education programs of the society and receive the influential monthly magazine *Proceedings* and discounts on fine nautical prints and on ship and aircraft photos. They also have access to the transcripts of the Institute's Oral History Program and get discounted admission to any of the Institute-sponsored seminars offered around the country.

The Naval Institute also publishes *Naval History* magazine. This colorful bimonthly is filled with entertaining and thought-provoking articles, first-person reminiscences, and dramatic art and photography. Members receive a discount on *Naval History* subscriptions.

The Naval Institute's book-publishing program, begun in 1898 with basic guides to naval practices, has broadened its scope to include books of more general interest. Now the Naval Institute Press publishes about one hundred titles each year, ranging from how-to books on boating and navigation to battle histories, biographies, ship and aircraft guides, and novels. Institute members receive significant discounts on the Press's more than eight hundred books in print.

Full-time students are eligible for special half-price membership rates. Life memberships are also available.

For a free catalog describing Naval Institute Press books currently available, and for further information about subscribing to *Naval History* magazine or about joining the U.S. Naval Institute, please write to:

Membership Department
U.S. Naval Institute
291 Wood Road
Annapolis, MD 21402-5034
Telephone: (800) 233-8764
Fax: (410) 269-7940
Web address: www.navalinstitute.org